D1200803

85th Congress}
1st Session } JOINT COMMITTEE PRINT

SOVIET ECONOMIC GROWTH:
A COMPARISON WITH THE UNITED STATES

A STUDY

PREPARED FOR THE

SUBCOMMITTEE ON FOREIGN
ECONOMIC POLICY

OF THE

JOINT ECONOMIC COMMITTEE

BY

THE U.S. LIBRARY OF CONGRESS
LEGISLATIVE REFERENCE SERVICE

GREENWOOD PRESS, PUBLISHERS
NEW YORK 1968

Originally published in 1957 by the
UNITED STATES
GOVERNMENT PRINTING OFFICE

II

First Greenwood reprinting, 1968

LIBRARY OF CONGRESS catalogue card number: 69-10165

PRINTED IN THE UNITED STATES OF AMERICA

CONTENTS

III

Page

LETTERS OF TRANSMITTAL

JULY 5, 1957.

To Members of the Joint Economic Committee:

The enclosed material forwarded to you is explained by its opening letters.

WRIGHT PATMAN,
Chairman, Joint Economic Committee.

JUNE 28, 1957.

Hon. WRIGHT PATMAN,
Chairman, Joint Economic Committee,
United States House of Representatives,
Washington, D. C.

DEAR MR. PATMAN: In its report to the Congress of March 1, 1956 (S. Rept. 1606, 84th Cong., 2d sess.), the committee stated the Foreign Economic Policy Subcommittee "* * * during the coming year will continue its studies of: (1) Current economic trends behind the Iron and Bamboo Curtains, in the free world, and in the uncommitted regions of the world; * * *." Part of this work and the other directives to the subcommittee were met by public hearings in December 1956. The committee staff also was directed to undertake a study of economic trends in support of this program. This study is forwarded in compliance with that mandate.

I commend to your attention the enclosed material which throws light on the problems of comparative economic growth in the Soviet Union and the United States. It is understood, of course, that this study does not necessarily represent the views of the committee or any of its individual members. The cooperation of the Legislative Reference Service of the Library of Congress with this committee is greatly appreciated.

RICHARD BOLLING,
Chairman, Subcommittee on Foreign Economic Policy.

MAY 29, 1957.

Hon. RICHARD BOLLING,
Chairman, Subcommittee on Foreign Economic Policy,
United States House of Representatives,
Washington, D. C.

DEAR MR. BOLLING: More than 2 years ago the Joint Economic Committee sponsored a study conducted by the Legislative Reference Service of the Library of Congress entitled "Trends in Economic Growth: A Comparison of the Western Powers and the Soviet Bloc."

That study represented a notable assembly and analysis of the best available data for comparing both the status and the growth trends of the economies of the Soviet Union and its European captive countries on the one hand and of the United States and the associated states of Western Europe on the other hand.

With each month bringing startling new developments in the Soviet Union, the latest being the Khrushchev regionalization plan, it is important to have a current study to examine the economic setting in which these changes are occurring. Much has transpired since the time of the previous study to make important a fresh look at trends in economic growth, including both the apparent shifts in Soviet foreign economic policy and the new availability of data on the Soviet economy beginning in 1956. As to the first point, even though it remains a relatively closed system, the Soviet Union has offered technological aid and capital goods to quite a number of underdeveloped countries, and has bid for expanded trade with almost all nations that might be interested. Although a study such as this cannot read Soviet intentions to carry through such programs, it can explore the character of the economic support base on which the Russians might depend in such endeavors. The second point, relating to the new availability of data, is a recognition that quite recently the Soviet Government has become a little less secretive about economic data, and now has published for the first time in nearly two decades absolute data in a new statistical abstract on the Soviet economy entitled "Narodnoe Khoziaistvo SSSR." It has been followed by four other important volumes—those on Cultural Construction, Trade, Industry, and the Russian S. F. S. R. Within the limitations described in the first chapter of our new study, great advantage to economic analysts has accrued from the release of the several handbooks.

The present study is more selective than the previous report prepared for the Joint Economic Committee. It focuses its attention on key aspects of the Soviet economy, and uses the United States as a yardstick. This particular comparison was selected because these are the two industrial powers of the world whose relative development is most closely watched by all others. By keeping the exposition bilateral, the complexities of all comparisons at least are a little more manageable than would be one involving many nations. Political changes reduce the usefulness of any simple additions of economic strength into a Communist bloc and a free world bloc, or some lesser division of associated non-Communist states. This is true whether the purpose is trade potential or military potential. It would have been particularly interesting to go beyond the previous study made for the Joint Economic Committee to study the growth of Japan, India, and Red China, for example. But it seems premature to attempt a quantitative assessment of Red Chinese development when the Bamboo Curtain so effectively obscures any real check on the statistics provided by the regime which our Government does not recognize.

This study is limited in another respect. It has tried to concern itself with economic description of the sort persons in some third country might write about the two major economies. It is not a treatise on political organization, police-state terror, sociology, or psychological warfare. As Americans, we share a set of moral, social, and political values which make us abhor the particular route to economic development which the Soviet Government has pursued. The absence in this study of full discussion of the human suffering which has accompanied the growth of Communist power does not mean that it should be overlooked, but such discussion has not been the goal of this exposition. Our thesis, simply stated, is that on purely economic grounds the Soviet system has developed in a way which would be considered very unsatisfactory by our standards, and, we believe, unsatisfactory for the people of the Soviet Union as well as for the captive nations within the Communist orbit. At the same time it is important to recognize the dimensions of the Soviet threat as measured by their ability to produce military hardware and to produce industrial goods which might support their programs of trade penetration and technical assistance around the world, and this is more the concern of this study.

Any study made of an economy is faced with problems of balance in its presentation of facts. The problems are multiplied manyfold when two different economies must be compared, as is developed in this study. The first draft of this study was intended to be as close to the middle of the road in its judgments as was possible. On completion it was widely circulated among cognizant agencies of the executive branch of the Government and to leading private specialists in Soviet economic studies. As their comments flowed back in large volume, it was apparent that it is almost impossible to write a report which steers clear of interpretational controversies which rage among the best experts. This report, as revised, continues to try for a middle course, but now reflects either in text or footnotes ranges of opinion where qualified people disagree. It would be ideal if it were possible to give black and white contrasts of the two economies, but conceptual difficulties as well as inadequate data rule this out. Therefore, it must be understood that if one is to attempt a broad international comparison at all, the results can be regarded as only approximate. The study has attempted to state its assumptions, to qualify, to suggest further sources of information, and to discuss the problems of particular comparisons. Overall, the analysis appears to be sufficiently comprehensive and accurate in its implications to meet the purposes outlined in the beginning of the first chapter.

Because the availability of data keeps changing, construction of estimates based on indirect evidence is always improving, and the economies themselves are always evolving, these results should be considered provisional and partial. With additional time, staff, and facilities, a more comprehensive book could be prepared. This was designed deliberately to highlight major comparisons for general use, not to provide encyclopedic coverage with a great mass of supporting technical detail and calculation. Even so, the notes accompanying the tables tend to be lengthy because of the complexity of the data. Nor does the study involve much original research. It is a compilation and review of information obtained largely from published sources. But at the same time, the synthesis of these materials should answer many questions.

This study is but one part of the activities undertaken by the Joint Economic Committee on problems related to world economic growth and competition. Building on the foundation of the Report on Foreign Economic Policy issued on January 5, 1956, as Senate Report 1312, the Subcommittee on Foreign Economic Policy held hearings on Defense Essentiality and Foreign Economic Policy in June 1956. One part of that review explored the nature of modern war and its mobilization implications for national strategy, an important step supporting the analysis of this present study. Then in September and October 1956, I traveled to Bangkok, Thailand, as the United States delegate to the working party meeting of the Economic Commission for Asia and the Far East, to study the problems of economic development. On the way there, it was possible to travel by way of Moscow, Tashkent, Kabul, and New Delhi. This afforded some unusual opportunities to interview top Soviet economists on a range of economic policy concepts, and to meet with directors of India's economic-development projects. Finally, in December 1956, the Subcommittee on Foreign Economic Policy met again for 3 days of hearings on world economic growth and competition, at which time leading experts on United States and on foreign economic growth analysis were heard on comparisons of growth in the industrial nations, in the underdeveloped regions, and to explore the implications for United States policy. These hearings were helpful to firming the conclusions contained in this study. The printed record of the December meetings also contains on pages 170–175 a commentary on the trip to the Soviet Union referred to above. (A reprint of an article entitled "Kremlin Economists Disclose Red Plans," which appeared in Nations Business in January 1957, p. 25 and following.)

Throughout the past 2 years Dr. Charles S. Sheldon II, senior specialist of the Legislative Reference Service of the Library of Congress, has served as the staff economist for the Subcommittee on Foreign Economic Policy, and it is under his immediate direction and supervision that this study has been organized and carried out. The original work on this study was done by Mr. A. David Redding who was attached to the Legislative Reference Service specifically for this purpose.

In preparing this report Dr. Sheldon and Mr. Redding have had the benefit of detailed reviews and comments by individual specialists in the Departments of Agriculture, Commerce, Defense, Labor and State and the Library of Congress. Valuable comments have been received from reviewers in universities and in private research organizations. Altogether, over 40 authorities with special competence in one or more of the fields covered by this report gave generously of their time and talent at various phases in the development of the study. Some have chosen for institutional reasons that we not acknowledge their help specifically. In any event no outside reviewer can be held responsible for the use made of their suggestions in the final preparation of the study. We are deeply grateful for their assistance.

Among the persons consulted were: Gertrude Bancroft, coordinator for manpower statistics, Bureau of the Census; Abraham S. Becker, economist, Council for Economic and Industry Research, Inc.; Abram Bergson, professor of economics, Harvard University; George M. Cobren, National Income Division, Office of Business Economics, Department of Commerce; Nicholas DeWitt, associate, Russian Research Center, Harvard University; Warren

Eason, assistant professor of economics, Princeton University; Dimitri M. Gallik, economist, Council for Economic and Industry Research, Inc.; Milton Giffler, transportation economist, Department of Defense; Ernest S. Griffith, director of the Legislative Reference Service, Library of Congress; Gregory Grossman, department of economics, University of California; John P. Hardt, economist, Council for Economic and Industry Research, Inc.; L. M. Herman, Soviet area specialist, Bureau of Foreign Commerce, Department of Commerce; Holland Hunter, associate professor of economics, Haverford College; William A. Jaracz, Clearing House, National Science Foundation; Harold A. Kohnen, Legislative Reference Service, Library of Congress; Earl E. Miller, agricultural economics statistician, Agricultural Marketing Service, Department of Agriculture; Edmund Nash, international labor economist for the U. S. S. R., Bureau of Labor Statistics, Department of Labor; G. Warren Nutter, associate professor of economics, University of Virginia; Howard S. Piquet, senior specialist in international trade and economic geography, Legislative Reference Service, Library of Congress; Hilton E. Robison, agricultural statistician, Agriculture Division, Bureau of the Census; Michael K. Roof, senior social science analyst, Reference Department, Library of Congress; John Kerr Rose, senior specialist in natural resources and conservation, Legislative Reference Service, Library of Congress; Rose Marie Smith, statistician, United States Office of Education, Department of Health, Education, and Welfare; Timothy Sosnovy, consultant on Soviet housing and urban economy to the Library of Congress; Lazar Volin, special assistant, Foreign Agricultural Service, Department of Agriculture; Faith M. Williams, chief, Office of Labor Economics, Bureau of Labor Statistics, Department of Labor; Harold Wool, Department of Defense; Sergius Yakobson, senior specialist in Russian affairs, Legislative Reference Service, Library of Congress.

GROVER W. ENSLEY,
Executive Director, Joint Economic Committee.

SOVIET ECONOMIC GROWTH: A COMPARISON WITH THE UNITED STATES

CHAPTER I

INTRODUCTION

A. PURPOSE AND SCOPE OF REPORT

This report attempts to compare the economy of the U. S. S. R. with that of the United States from several points of view: (1) the volume of current production in various economic sectors; (2) the rate at which this production has been growing; (3) the relative emphasis placed on consumption, investment, and other uses; and (4) the likely rates and patterns of development of the two economies in the future. For this purpose, the report presents and interprets data on the major production sectors of the two economies (chs. II and III); on some of the resources devoted to production (chs. II through VI); and on the structure of the two economies, with particular attention to consumption and levels of living (chs. V and VI).

The question may arise as to the relationship of this report to the similar endeavor of over 2 years ago entitled "Trends in Economic Growth: A Comparison of the Western Powers and the Soviet Bloc." That study brought together for the first time on a comprehensive scale economic data on the Soviet Union, the United States, Western Europe, Canada, and the Soviet captive countries of Eastern Europe. It measured the differential effects of World War II on all these countries, and also made a preliminary postwar comparison, drawing some contrasts between the two major blocs of powers. The conclusions of that study are not inconsistent with the findings of this study, although there has been some improvement in availability of data, when one considers the changes in the time periods involved, and the limitation of this study to the two largest countries involved. (See appendixes (A) and (B) at the close of the present study.) Neither study should be interpreted as a worldwide assessment, or even a full bloc assessment of competitive economic positions.

The reasons for the change of approach are three: First, current interest focuses to a greater extent on postwar growth and upon a longer range assessment of the Soviet and United States economies, for the light which may be shed on future prospects. Second, staff and time limitations ruled out a comprehensive development of material on a larger number of countries; this in turn made possible selection of different time periods for study better suited to the narrower focus. Third, the earlier study coordinated the efforts of a larger team of researchers, which was necessary in so comprehensive an approach, and this combined effort carried out in a short time span led to some va-

riety of approaches in tables and data.   In the new study by restricting the scope, it has been easier to operate with a limited staff which
could integrate and relate all information in the report, while retaining a thorough review of component sections by outside specialists before going to final print.

In one sense, the objectives of this study are modest; it merely
marshals some of the essential economic elements that must be considered in any attempt to answer policy questions which are currently
engaging the attention of Congress and the American people.   It does
not attempt to answer the questions themselves.

In another sense, however, this objective is an ambitious one, in-
sofar as the study attempts to provide the kinds of economic facts
and interpretations that can legitimately be applied to many problems.   Multipurpose comparisons are notoriously difficult to devise,
and perhaps even more difficult to interpret.   They are ambiguous
because they lack focus; and they remain so until placed in
the context of clear-cut objectives and environment.   The observation
of different rates of economic growth in the two countries, for example,
is meaningless in itself; and no policy implications should be drawn
without first determining in what economic sectors the superior growth
has occurred, without then estimating the magnitudes of the current
and future claims against the output of each country (i. e., the uses
to which the output is put), and especially without at some point
taking account of the numerous noneconomic factors involved.

More specifically, this study does not pretend to answer such questions as the relative effectiveness with which the two economies
support their respective military strengths, their relative ability to
support foreign economic programs, and the political consequences of
maintenance of high rates of economic growth.   It does provide a considerable volume of interpreted economic material without which such
questions cannot be adequately answered.

Time, staff, and data limitations precluded comprehensive treatment
of the subject matter.   The presentation, therefore, has been highly
selective; only those trends within, and differences between the two
countries which were judged most important for present purposes
have been discussed.   Estimates have not been prepared or statements
qualified to meet every contingency;[1] and many points that might
be very important in other types of reports have necessarily been
omitted.   At the same time, it was often felt advisable to present provisional data and tentative interpretations on certain important
points where firm data or reliable estimates were not available.   The
alternative would have been the loss of certain insights which were
gained from making the study.

Time, staff, and data limitations also precluded adequate treatment
of the historical backgrounds of the two economies, the peculiar economic problems of each, the resources and geographical setting which
influence production, the foreign economic activities, and, perhaps
most important, the political and economic institutions and policies

---

[1] For example, levels of living in the Soviet Union could be perhaps one-third as high
as in the United States by certain standards of measurement and for particular purposes;
or the Soviet levels could be even lower than the 1 to 6 ratio indicated in ch. V.   In that
connection it should be stressed that the single-figure estimates used in most parts of this
report are intended to indicate only the general orders of magnitude involved.   They are
believed to fulfill adequately that objective, but they are not necessarily accurate enough
for other more specialized purposes.

in the two countries. Some of these aspects are, however, sketched briefly in this and succeeding chapters of the report.

The net result of the purposes and limitations is a highly selective report covering the major data on production and use of resources in the two countries. It is believed to be sufficiently comprehensive and accurate to sketch the most important economic outlines and magnitudes in the two countries. The need for information, compared to the public knowledge, is believed to be greatest with respect to the Soviet Union; therefore, that economy receives greater attention in this study.

B. HISTORICAL SECTION

1. The Soviet Union

Communist political control was established in the center of Russia in November 1917; but 3 additional years were required to expand this control over most of Russia and to overcome armed resistance to the regime. Communist control over the Russian economy was even slower in materializing. All the land and most of the larger factories were nationalized within the first year; but controls over agriculture were "limited" to requisitioning of agricultural products often by armed force. Bolshevik economic policies until the spring of 1921 could be considered effective only in that, in spite of civil war, the government did survive.

In the spring of 1921, a "new economic policy" was gradually instituted by the Bolshevik government. In an effort to harness private initiative to reconstruction tasks with which they were as yet unprepared to deal on a centralized, planned basis, Soviet authorities replaced the agricultural requisition method with a fixed percentage tax in kind on agricultural production; they allowed nationalized industries to buy and sell on the open market; they leased some small state factories to private individuals; and they allowed individuals to engage more freely in both service and production activities, especially in retail trade. All land, however, remained nationalized; direct control was maintained over the larger industrial enterprises, as well as over banking, transport, and foreign trade; and many restrictions on private economic activities were also maintained, and selectively increased during the twenties.

During the ensuing period, crisis followed on crisis; but by about 1926, both industrial and agricultural production had approximately regained the prewar levels. The needs for new capital equipment and plant were acute, however, as a result of intensive use, abuse, obsolescence, and war damage, coupled with inadequate replacement and maintenance. Some machinery for centralized planning was instituted in 1926, but its effects on the economy were limited, its importance being partly in the experience afforded Soviet planners prior to the start of formal planning several years later. The census of 1926 and other resource surveys provided information essential to a planned economy.

By 1928, the initial year studied in the U. S. S. R. for this report, Soviet industry had, on the whole, surpassed the pre-World War I production levels; but it was underdeveloped compared to any of the large Western Powers, especially in the production of machinery and chemicals. The state of technology was generally backward, and labor skilled in modern technology was scarce. Considerable production took place in factories; but home production and small shops still accounted for a substantial share of total industrial output, especially in the manufacture of consumer goods in the villages.

Agricultural output in 1928 had also reattained approximately the prewar levels. As in earlier years, Soviet agriculture was a low-yield, labor-intensive, relatively primitive operation, with principal attention devoted to grain; but unlike the prewar years, when agricultural products had been Russia's principal exports despite the low yields and the resultant low levels of living in both the countryside and the towns, such exports in 1928 were very low. The low efficiency of factory production in the area of consumers' goods gave the peasant little incentive to market his produce in the cities.

By 1928, the preparations of the Soviets for both political consolidation and industrialization had matured. Communist supremacy was assured by a systematic destruction of rural leadership, by the "dekulakization," regardless of costs and by the imposition of new controls in agriculture. State farms were established to guarantee essential supplies to the armed forces and the cities, while export needs were wrested from the peasantry at confiscatory prices. These moves simultaneously squeezed out a large labor supply from the farms and cottage industries for work in construction and industry. The speed of industrialization was substantially increased by technical borrowing from abroad. Nonetheless, many aspects of the plan failed, especially the attempt to gain extensive foreign credits. Despite these failures, the drive for industrialization continued ruthlessly. Heavy imports of machinery in the early years of industrialization were paid for by exporting grain even though it meant famine for millions of persons in Russia and the Ukraine in 1931; large-scale domestic production of capital equipment was paid for by depressing consumption generally from its already extremely low levels in 1928; and the costs in regimentation and repression were so enormous as to defy valuation.

The period after 1928 in the U. S. S. R. needs little further summary here. Industrial output increased rapidly up to World War II, although there was a slowing in the rate of increase after 1938 apparently because of conversion to military production, because of a decline in the availability of labor for industry, and also because of the effect of the purges on both management and labor. Some people believe the Soviet tendency to strangle initiative and to enforce iron discipline in that period was an added factor slowing growth. Agricultural output during the same period barely managed to recover from the ill effects of collectivization of agriculture and peasant resistance to it.

In 1939 and 1940 the Soviet Union annexed various territories on its western borders, chiefly Estonia, Latvia, and Lithuania, as well as substantial parts of Poland and Rumania, with consequent increases in total production, labor force, and population. In 1941 with the onset of war, production dropped precipitously, but it recovered quickly enough in the war-vital sectors so that with the aid of extensive lend-lease supplies from the United States, Canada, and Britain, the U. S. S. R. could continue functioning. By 1948 Soviet production generally, except in agriculture, had reattained the prewar levels. By 1950 reconstruction of war-damaged industrial facilities had been largely completed; both output and employment in Soviet industry were considerably above the peak prewar levels; both had been expanding at very high rates since the reconversion year of 1946; and they have continued to expand, though at lower rates, to the present. Soviet agriculture had recovered to a lesser extent than industry by 1950; but by 1955 agricultural production as a whole was significantly above the prewar levels, although this was still inadequate to meet the full needs of the Soviet population.   (See ch. III.)

2. The United States

Economic circumstances and goals in the United States have differed fundamentally from those in the Soviet Union.   Production levels in this country as early as 1900 were generally at about the same level as, or greater than, those in the U. S. S. R. in 1928. By 1928 the economy of the United States was much more advanced than that of the Soviet Union in the same year with respect to levels, variety, and quality of production; with respect to the structure of its labor force and population, which was concentrated much more in industrial and service occupations in urban areas; and with respect to its consumption and living levels, which were incomparably higher. Further, in contrast to Soviet moves in the direction of planning, centralized economic controls, and unprecedented emphasis on the production of heavy investment goods and plant, the United States has continued to rely heavily on consumer choice as to what products to produce, and on private decisions as to how fast and in what direction new investments should be made.   Such reliance, which is consistent with United States ideas of economic democracy and profit-loss incentives toward efficiency, has resulted in rapid increases in levels of living in the United States, and in continued emphasis on consumer goods production in abundance and in great variety, with a flow of benefits to all segments of the population.

By contrast to Soviet methods and aims, the United States places individual welfare first, even as it has undergone great changes in the economic role of government.   In some respects, ours has always been a mixed economy in which welfare considerations have played a part.   There have been homestead laws, railway land grants, protective tariffs, the Federal Reserve System, antitrust laws, and the progressive income-tax laws even in earlier days or before the period of this study.   In the period covered by this study, namely, 1928 to 1955, the role of government has expanded substantially. Public works programs, including power, river valley development, housing, highways, schools have been coupled with credit facilities for these and other purposes.   Federal responsibility has extended to fair employment practices, minimum wages, social security, and agriculture.   During World Wars I and II, vast amounts of Federal funds went into expanding our capacity to produce, including such industries as aircraft, shipbuilding, aluminum, steel, electronics, and synthetic rubber.   Because of its special characteristics, the atomic energy industry during the war and since has continued to be mostly public.   In 1946 Congress passed the Employment Act which recognized Federal responsibility for the growth and stability of the economy.   This Federal concern with so many economic matters makes all the more striking the difference in basic orientation and goals of the United States and the Soviet Union.   Government participation in economic affairs in the United States is aimed toward individual welfare or promoting the common defense; it is not directed toward an organized and relentless drive to push the growth of industry as a primary goal in itself and at the price of squeezing its people year after year, as has been the case in the U. S. S. R., where the aim seems to be to establish a base for world domination and world revolution.

3. Choice of periods for comparison

The year 1928 was chosen as the initial year to be studied in the U. S. S. R. for a variety of reasons: (1) It was the latest year prior to the inauguration of formal planning; [2] and the forced industrialization drive and the collectivization of agriculture had not yet taken place on a significant scale. (2) Production of Soviet industry and agriculture, though low compared to the United States, was not low compared to that in any previous year in the U. S. S. R.; and from many economic aspects, it was probably the best Soviet year experienced to that date. Agricultural production may not have been at quite the pre-Communist levels, but industrial production was on the whole higher than in 1913, the last prewar, pre-Communist year. Finally, (3) the year 1928 is also the initial year of the nonofficial, Western-computed index of industrial production relied on in this report.

In comparing rates of economic growth in the U. S. S. R. with those in the United States, choice, as a starting point, of any year after the Communist revolution of 1917 but prior to about 1926 or 1928, would present the Soviet Union in an unduly favorable light. That is, its rate of economic growth would be exaggerated both because of its abnormally low production in the years of post-World War I reconstruction coinciding with the first years of the Soviet regime in Russia and because of the fact that reconstruction is normally more rapid than the building of new capacity. Choice of any year prior to 1918 as the initial year of a period for comparison with the United States would place the base year in a period prior to Communist control; and if it were also a prewar year such as 1913, it would have the added handicap of ignoring the devastation of over 6 years of world and subsequent civil war.

The year 1950 was chosen as the initial year of the shorter period in which Soviet trends are compared to those of the United States, primarily because, as noted earlier, it was the first year after completion of reconstruction.

The terminal year of both periods, and of the study, is 1955, although data are presented in a few instances through 1956. The year 1955 was chosen as a cutoff point simply because it is the last full year for which extensive data are available. It was a normal year in that Soviet output increases were consistent with those of preceding years. Choice of 1954 or 1956 as the terminal year would not, it is believed, have changed the results appreciably.

The Soviet periods 1928–55 and 1950–55 seem, on balance, the best available for an international comparison, although there are unsatisfactory features to each which are discussed more fully in the chap-

---

[2] The first 5-year-plan period officially started on October 1, 1928; but its economic effects in 1928 were small. Previous planning efforts were relatively ineffective.

ters which follow. The longer period encompasses years of forced industrialization starting from a low base and with the very important advantage of being able to borrow advanced technology and technicians from the West, plus the advantage of a large surplus labor force in agriculture; but it also covers the war years in which the economy suffered tremendous damage, and it encompasses the years of heavy, probably nonrecurrent damage to Soviet agriculture as a result of collectivization and peasant resistance to it. The shorter Soviet period has the principal drawback of being too short.

The United States, as noted earlier, had a more advanced economy during both the long and short periods discussed above, and its economic structure and circumstances were different from those of the Soviet Union. Comparisons of economic trends in the two countries during the same periods are, therefore, satisfactory for only a few purposes. Moreover, for reasons which are discussed briefly in the following chapters, no period in United States history is entirely satisfactory even for the order of magnitude purposes of this study. Therefore, this report in some instances has had to fall back on data for some years in the United States as early as 1850; and comparisons are drawn between the two countries of the periods 1928–55 and 1950–55, as well as between the U. S. S. R. of 1928–55 and 1950–55 and the United States of earlier years.

C. PROBLEMS OF SOVIET-UNITED STATES COMPARISONS

1. Conceptual difficulties

Most of the conceptual problems of comparing the Soviet and United States economies arise from the differences in structure and maturity of the two economies. For example, a greater variety and higher quality of goods generally are produced in the United States than in the U. S. S. R.; and these goods are produced in different proportions in each country, with the proportions themselves varying from year to year. As a result, aggregation of all the different commodities into an index of production which is suitable even for a single purpose is difficult; and calculation of an index suitable for all, or probably even most purposes, is patently impossible. The problems of commodity composition of production and of value systems appropriate to use as weights are discussed in more detail in chapters II and VI.

There is a closely related conceptual problem of choosing representative and meaningful lists of commodities in making commodity-by-commodity comparisons of physical numbers of units produced in each country. That problem is discussed in chapter II, but it should be noted that a completely satisfactory solution is not possible owing to the above-mentioned differences in quality, variety, and importance of particular commodities in total production in the two countries. Further, rigorous adherence to comparability would have meant that few if any comparisons of physical units of output could be made. The compromise chosen was to compare a relatively large list of economically significant commodities for which data were available, after first having made every effort consistent with time and staff limitations to achieve comparability of coverage between the two countries. The coverage in most instances is believed to be sufficiently comparable for the present order-of-magnitude purposes, but, as noted below, information on coverage of the Soviet output, particularly, is often not readily available.

2. *Statistical difficulties*

For purposes of this study, United States data generally can be accepted with few reservations, although there are statistical deficiencies, some of which are discussed in the following chapter. The reliability of the Soviet data, on the other hand, has often been questioned. Because ultimate reliance of all Western studies on the Soviet economy, including this one, has been on statistics and information compiled and published in the Soviet Union—adequate data are unavailable from any other source—establishing the reliability of Soviet data is of crucial importance.

Soviet data have been criticized on a number of grounds, including the following: (1) Inadequate reporting and collating; (2) methodological and coverage noncomparabilities; and (3) outright falsification. Unquestionably, the distortion because of the first reason has been important, but still a considerable volume of data has been published, and Soviet statistics appear lately to have improved in this respect.

The methodological and coverage noncomparabilities have been even more serious. Regarding outright falsification in the sense of free invention or double bookkeeping, the majority of students of the Soviet economy have concluded that though Soviet statistics are often slanted, they are rarely falsified in toto.[3] Soviet statistics are often ambiguous as to both methodology and coverage, and sometimes intentionally misleading. In some instances (e. g., the value series on Soviet national income or gross production of Soviet industry), the methodological deficiencies have been very great, with the bias in a direction which shows the Russians in a favorable light. Improvements have been hampered by the Soviet attitude that statistics are an instrument which should serve the state; but, apparently because past deficiencies have hindered Soviet officials and professionals, some improvements appear to have been instituted during the past few years.

The consensus of Western experts is that Soviet data are usable if great care is taken. The reliability and accuracy of the statistics vary from series to series, but in general those data expressed in physical terms are apt to be better than those expressed in value terms. For that reason, this report relies almost exclusively on Soviet data expressed in physical terms.

The deficiencies and shortcomings of Soviet statistics discussed above were noted primarily in analysis of prewar Soviet data, and as noted, some improvements appear to have taken place, especially since about 1950. It is still too early to judge the reliability and quality of the large quantities of new statistics released in 1956 and

---

[3] Bergson, Abram. Soviet National Income and Product in 1937 (New York: Columbia University Press), 1953, p. 7. See also pp. 6–9, especially footnote 10, for a detailed discussion of this point.

1957,[4] primarily because detailed information on their coverage and mode of compilation and calculation has not been published to date. If, however, the old Soviet policy of withholding most economic data is actually in the process of being abandoned, the questions of reliability and quality will be more easily and definitively answerable in the future. At that time it would be possible to interpret the new data more accurately, hopefully through the availability of more Soviet notes on coverage, but in any event through the checks on internal consistency which more detailed data would facilitate.

Before leaving the question of statistical deficiencies and reliability of data, a note of caution should be sounded on the interpretation to be accorded the single-figure estimates and all Soviet data. All the figures shown are believed to be accurate enough for present purposes, although they are not necessarily correct to the extent indicated by rounding. They were preferred to ranges simply because of the insoluble problems involved in determining meaningful limits without giving the reader an unwarranted impression of reliability. Because of uncertainties regarding methodology and coverage, all single Soviet figures should normally be interpreted as if there were an "about" preceding them.

---

[4] The most important of the new publications to date are:

Tsentral'noe statisticheskoe upravlenie pri Sovete Ministrov, SSSR, Narodnoe khoziaistvo SSSR, Statisticheskii sbornik, Gosstatizdat, Moskva, 1956 (National Economy of the U. S. S. R., a statistical handbook), 263 pp.

Tsentral'noe statisticheskoe upravlenie pri Sovete Ministrov SSSR, Kul'turnoe stroitel'stvo SSSR, Statisticheskii sbornik, Gosstatizdat, Moskva, 1956 (Cultural Construction of the U. S. S. R., a statistical handbook), 332 pp.

Tsentral'noe statisticheskoe upravlenie pri Sovete Ministrov SSSR, Sovetskaia Torgovlia, Statisticheskii sbornik, Gosstatizdat, Moskva, 1956 (Soviet Trade, a statistical handbook), 352 pp.

Tsentral'noe statisticheskoe upravlenie pri Sovete Ministrov SSSR, Promyshlennost' SSSR, Statisticheskii sbornik, Gosstatizdat, Moskva, 1957 (Industry of the U. S. S. R., a statistical handbook), 448 pp.

Statisticheskoe upravlenie RSFSR, Narodnoe khoziaistvo RSFSR, statisticheskii sbornik, Gosstatizdat, Moskva, 1957 (National Economy of the R. S. F. S. R., a statistical handbook), 372 pp.

CHAPTER II

INDUSTRY AND TRANSPORTATION

INDUSTRY

A. INDUSTRY IN THE SOVIET UNION AND THE UNITED STATES IN 1955

1. Comparative levels of industrial production

Soviet industry (manufacturing, mining, and electric power) produced about one-third the quantity of goods as United States industry in 1955. This single-figure estimate is accepted by many Western scholars as being correct in general orders of magnitude, though—depending on the methods of estimating and aggregating—a range of, say, one-half to one-fourth or one-fifth could also have been obtained. In any event, the overall estimate conceals the widely disparate production ratios for individual commodities. As is partially illustrated in table 1 below, the Soviet/United States production ratios are generally higher in what is often referred to as heavy or producer goods industry, and lower in light or consumer goods industry; that is, Soviet industry is oriented largely to production of investment and producer goods,[1] whereas industry in the United States produces a much larger share of its output for direct personal consumption. Where the available statistics do not make this clear in a summary table, more detailed analysis shows the disproportionately high share of heavy industry in an economy of abysmally low consumer living levels.

For some purposes, therefore, the 1 to 3 output ratio for industry as a whole would be quite misleading, as, for that matter, would be any of the commodity ratios taken individually. For example, if the purpose of the comparisons were to measure production levels for personal consumption, the Soviet/United States output ratio would be very much below the 1 to 3 ratio for industry as a whole. But if the purpose were to measure economic strength in war-supporting industries, the picture would be more favorable to the Soviet Union than is indicated by the production ratio for industry as a whole. Further, Soviet personal consumption of such commodities is proportionately much less than in the United States. In 1955, for example, the U. S. S. R. produced about 43 percent as much steel as the United States—or, less than this country's production in 1917. In the Soviet Union, however, only an insignificant proportion of that steel goes into satisfying consumer needs for automobiles, washing machines, refrigerators, etc. The bulk of it—perhaps as much steel as in the United States—is available for production of military goods or for items conducive to further economic growth. The same

---

[1] Soviet calculations show "producer goods" as accounting for 70.6 percent of total industrial production in 1955, as contrasted with 39.5 percent in 1928. (See Tsentral'noe statisticheskoe upravlenie pri Sovete Ministrov SSSR, Narodnoe khoziaistvo SSSR, Statisticheskii sbornik, Gosstatizdat, Moskva, 1956, p. 52.)

kind of comparisons might be made for petroleum.   The relative absence of private automobiles leaves a very large share of petroleum for military purposes as well as heavy industry and agriculture.

TABLE. 1.—*Industrial production: Comparative levels in the U. S. S. R. and the United States in 1955*

Commodity and unit	U. S. S. R.	United States	U. S. S. R./ United States
EXTRACTIVE			
1. Lumber_____million cubic meters__	70.0	[1] 92.3	0.76
2. Fish_____million metric tons__	2.7	[1] 2.1	1.29
3. Salt_____do____	(6.2)	(18.9)	.33
4. Iron ore_____do____	71.9	[1] 94.7	.76
5. Manganese ore_____do____	(3.5)	(1.1)	3.18
6. Coal_____do____	310 (391.9)	[1] 450.3	.69 (.87)
7. Peat_____do____	51.0	(.2)	255.00
8. Crude petroleum_____do____	70.8	334.9	.21
9. Natural gas_____billion cubic meters__	10.4	264.5	.04
10. Bauxite_____million metric tons__	(1.0)	[1] (1.6)	.63
11. Chromite_____do____	(.6)	.2	3.00
12. Asbestos_____do____	(.2)	(.1)	2.00
13. Sulfur_____do____	(2)	6.1	------------
SECONDARY			
1. Coke_____million metric tons__	43.6	72.2	.60
2. Pig iron_____do____	33.3	70.6	.47
3. Steel ingots and slabs_____do____	45.3	106.2	.43
4. Copper, primary refinery_____do____	(.4)	1.2	.33
5. Zinc, primary smelter_____do____	(.3)	.9	.33
6. Lead, refined from mined and secondary_____do____	.2	.9	.22
7. Aluminum_____do____	.4	[1] 1.4	.29
8. Cement_____do____	22.5	50.6	.44
9. Building bricks_____billions__	21.0	[1] 7.1	2.96
10. Paper_____million metric tons__	1.9	27.1	.07
11. Synthetic rubber_____do____	(2)	.9	------------
12. Sulfuric acid_____do____	3.8	15.6	.24
13. Ammonia_____do____	(2)	2.9	------------
14. Caustic soda_____do____	.6	3.5	.17
15. Soda ash_____do____	1.4	5.1	.27
16. Mineral fertilizers_____do____	9.6	[1] 18.5	.52
17. Electricity_____billion kilowatt-hours__	170.1	624.9	.27
of which hydroelectricity_____do____	23.1	116.0	.20
CAPITAL GOODS			
1. Turbines_____million kilowatts__	5.6	(2)	------------
2. Electric generators_____do____	4.5	(2)	------------
3. Electric motors_____do____	9.0	(2)	------------
4. Diesel engines_____million horsepower__	4.0	(2)	------------
5. Machine cutting tools_____thousands_	117.8 (75.0)	[1]110.0 (50.5)	------------
6. Presses and forges_____do____	15.9	[3] (19.8)	.80
7. Electronics_____thousand metric tons__	(2)	(2)	------------
8. Metallurgical equipment_____do____	172.1	(2)	------------
9. Petroleum equipment_____do____	48.3	(2)	------------
10. Bulldozers_____thousands__	7.5	[3] 19.6	.38
11. Tractors_____do____	163.4	[3] 377.1	.43
12. Combines_____do____	48.0	[3] (58.1)	.83
13. Trucks_____do____	329.0	1,245.6	.26
14. Locomotives_____number__	982	[3] (2,070)	.47
15. Freight cars_____thousands__	34.4	[3] 42.1	.82
16. Ships_____thousands, gross tons__	(2)	(3)	------------
17. Civil aircraft_____metric tons, airframe weight__	(2)	464.3	------------
CONSUMER GOODS			
1. Meat and lard_____million metric tons__	4.0	13.3	.30
2. Dairy products_____do____	29.8	(56.0)	.53
3. Vegetable oils_____do____	1.2	2.8	.43
4. Sugar_____do____	3.4	7.3	.47
5. Soap, 40 percent_____do ___	1.1	(2)	------------
6. Footwear_____million pairs__	274.5	634.1 ¶	.48
7. Cotton fabrics_____billion linear meters__	5.9	[3] 12.4 (9.2)	.48
8. Wool fabrics_____do____	.3	[3] .4 (.3)	.75
9. Silk fabrics_____do____	.5	------------	------------
10. Linen fabrics_____do____	.3	------------	------------
11. Artificial and synthetic fabrics_____do____	.1	2.5	.04
12. Clocks and watches_____millions__	19.7	(30.8 (46.2)	.64 (.43)
13. Cameras_____do____	1.0	(4.9)	.21
14. Radios_____do____	} 4.0	14.5	} .18
15. Television_____do____		8.0	
16. Refrigerators_____do____	.2	[3] 4.0	.05

See footnotes at end of table, p. 13.

TABLE 1.—*Industrial production: Comparative levels in the U. S. S. R. and the United States in 1955*—Continued

Commodity and unit	U. S. S. R.	United States	U. S. S. R./ United States
CONSUMER GOODS—continued			
17. Washing machines_____millions__	0.1	4.4	0.02
18. Sewing machines_____do____	1.6	[3] (.8)	2.00
19. Bicycles_____do____	2.9	[3] (1.7)	1.71
20. Automobiles_____do____	.1	7.9	.01
MILITARY GOODS			
1. Nuclear material_____metric tons__	[2]	[2]	----------
2. Aircraft_____do____	[2]	[2]	----------
3. Naval vessels_____thousand displacement tons__	[2]	[2]	----------
4. Artillery_____metric tons__	[2]	[2]	----------
5. Vehicles_____millions__	[2]	[2]	----------
6. Electronic gear_____metric tons__	[2]	[2]	----------

[1] Peak or other higher years in the United States: Lumber, 1907, 108.6; fish, 1941, 2.3; iron ore, 1953, 106.3; coal, 1947, 624.0; bauxite, 1943, 6.8; aluminum, 1953, 1.5; structural bricks, 1908, 9.8; mineral fertilizers, 1954; 18.7.

[2] Not available.

[3] Peak or other higher years in the United States: Machine cutting tools, 1942, 375.0; presses and forges were 20.0 in 1951 and may have been even higher in World War II, but comparable data are lacking; bulldozers, 1952, 23.2; tractors, 1951, 617.0; combines, 1950, 116.1; locomotives, 1947, 3,651; freight cars, 1947, 101.9 cotton fabric, 1946, 13.3 (10.7)· wool fabric, 1942, 0.9 (0.6); refrigerators, 1950, 6.2; sewing machines, 1927, 0.6, bicycles, 1950, 6.2.

NOTES ACCOMPANYING TABLE 1

Although this table has attempted to compare production of a range of commodities in the U. S. S. R. and the United States, it is most important to keep in mind that differences in definition and coverage make exact comparisons dangerous. These data at best will indicate the general order to magnitude of relationships. Most of the commodities reported require some qualifications for their interpretation.

Where possible, 1955 data have been presented. Additional Soviet data for 1956, where known, are shown in tables 4 and 5. If the only figure given is in parentheses, it refers to 1954 or 1953 data as the latest available. In almost all categories, 1955 represents a peak year up to that time for Soviet production which typically has more growing to do before it reaches United States levels. From the nature of the United States economy which adjusts production over the course of time to varying demands, even though 1955 was the best overall year in United States industrial history, individual commodities have had peaks in some other years. For reference, these other peaks, to the extent they could be traced, are shown at the end of the table.

Attention is also called to table 4 of this chapter which gives a time series for some of the data presented here. In some cases, the trends are of greater interest than the absolute comparison presented here.

It will be noted that there are a few items where neither country had figures which could be presented in comparable terms. These have been left in to suggest a few items which it might be wished could be compared. The final section labeled "military goods" is a teaser in a sense. Neither country presents figures on its military output. The titles, which are not comprehensive, but suggestive in character, are a reminder that the whole table is selective, and does not give a complete comparison of industry. United States data are often for shipments rather than production, but this is not particularly troublesome for the present order of magnitude purposes.

U. S. S. R. sources

All the following items in the table are drawn from the Soviet handbook, Tsentral'noe statisticheskoe upravlenie pri Sovete Ministrov SSSR, Narodnoe khoziaistvo SSSR, Statisticheskii sbornik, Gosstatizdat, Moskva, 1956: Lumber page 58; fish, page 59; iron ore, page 55; coal, page 55; peat, page 70; crude petroleum, page 55; natural gas, page 55; coke, page 55; pig iron, page 55; steel ingots and slabs, page 55; cement, page 58; structural bricks, page 58; paper, page 59; caustic soda, page 55; soda ash, page 55; mineral fertilizers, page

55; electricity, page 55; hydro-generated electricity, page 55; turbines, page 56; electric generators, page 56; electric motors, page 56; diesel engines, page 56; machine cutting tools, page 55; presses and forges, page 55; metallurgical equipment, page 56; petroleum equipment, page 56; bulldozers, page 58; tractors, page 57; combines, page 57; trucks, page 56; locomotives, page 56; freight cars, page 56; vegetable oils, page 59; sugar, page 59; soap, page 59; footwear, page 58; cotton fabric, page 58; wool fabric, page 58; silk fabric, page 58; linen fabric, page 58; artificial and synthetic fabrics, page 58; clocks and watches, page 59; cameras, page 59; radios and television, page 59; refrigerators, page 59; washing machines, page 59; sewing machines, page 59; bicycles, page 59; automobiles, page 56.

The following data were drawn from other sources as given: Salt—1953 in Minerals Yearbook, page 950; manganese ore—1953 in ibid., page 763; bauxite—1954 in Commodity Research Bureau, Commodity Yearbook (New York), 1956, page 52; chromite—1954, in ibid., page 86; asbestos—1953 in Minerals Yearbook, page 190; copper—1954 in Commodity Yearbook, page 111; zinc—1954 in ibid., page 382; lead—1955 in ibid., page 208; meat from table 2 in chapter III; dairy products from table 2 in chapter III; sulfuric acid—1955 from Department of Commerce.

United States sources

The following are from the Department of Commerce, Statistical Abstract of the United States, 1956:

1953 data: Salt, page 728; manganese ore, page 746; peat, page 727; bauxite, page 728; asbestos, page 727.

1955 data: Mineral fertilizers, page 646; synthetic rubber, page 822; sulfuric acid, page 823; soda ash, page 823; electricity, page 529; hydrogenerated electricity, page 529; bulldozers, page 835; cotton fabric, page 816; wool fabric, page 816; silk fabric, page 816; artificial and synthetic fabrics, page 816; footwear (leather), page 820; crude petroleum, page 740; steel ingots and slabs, page 829; automobiles, page 549; meat, pages 683, 688; fish, page 716; refrigerators, page 838; washing machines, page 838.

The following are from the Department of Commerce, Survey of Current Business (July 1956), all 1955 data: Lumber, page S31; iron ore, page S32; sulfur, page S25; coke, page S35; pig iron, page S32; copper, page S33; aluminum, page S33; bricks, page S38; ammonia, page S24; caustic soda, page S24; freight cars, page S40; civil aircraft, page S40; vegetable oils, page S25; radios, page S34; television sets, page S34; cement, page S38; coal, pages S34, 35; trucks, page S40.

The following are from the Commodity Research Bureau, Commodity Yearbook (New York), 1956: Chromite—1955, page 86; zinc—1955, page 383; lead—1955, page 207; paper—1955, page 247; sugar—1955, page 329.

The following are for years and from sources as specified:

Natural gas—1955, American Gas Association, Gas Facts, 1955, page 26.

Tractors—1955, Department of Commerce, Facts for Industry, series M37B–125.

Combines—1954, Advance Census of Manufactures, 1954, series MC–35–1.6.

Locomotives—1954, ibid., series MC–37–3.1.

Bicycles—1954, ibid., series MC–37–3.

Sewing machines—1954, ibid., series MC–35–6.2.

Clocks and watches—1954, ibid., MC–38–2.1 (revised).

Cameras—1954, ibid., series MC–38–2.3.

Dairy products—1954, Agricultural Statistics, 1955, page 371.

Machine tools—1955, Statistical Abstract, 1956, page 836, and letter from National Machine Builders Association adjusted as explained in following commentary.

Presses and forges—1953, Department of Commerce, Annual Survey of Manufactures, page 201.

Specific commentary on comparisons

Table 4 of this chapter discusses comparisons among lumber, coal, crude petroleum, natural gas, electric power, steel, cement, paper, tractors, trucks, automobiles, cotton fabric, wool fabric, footwear, and meat. Those remarks apply in most cases equally to the material shown here. The coal comparison shows actual Soviet production in parentheses, a corrected figure for equivalent fuel values for ratio purposes. Adjustments are shown in fabrics as well, to reflect differences in width.

The following require additional commentary:

Fish: The Soviet figure includes the catch of whales and other sea animals as well as fish brought in from all over the world. Correspondingly, the United States fish catch includes that from Alaskan waters, but does not include whales and other sea animals.

Salt: The Soviet Government does not publish current figures of salt output, so a United States Government estimate had to be used.

Manganese: The Soviet Government does not publish current figures of manganese ore output. The United States figure includes manganese bearing ores of lower grade, so that the comparison tends to hide this country's heavy dependence upon imported manganese.

Peat: Peat is used extensively in the U. S. S. R.; it hardly counts in this country so far because other fuels are available in quantity.

Bauxite: Both countries import considerable amounts of bauxite, and this country at least uses alumina clays as an alternate source of aluminum. The Soviet Government does not report its current production, so a United States Government estimate was used.

Chromite: Soviet figures on chromite production are not currently published, so a United States Government estimate has been used.

Asbestos: Soviet figures on asbestos production are not currently published, so a United States Government estimate has been used.

Sulfur: No estimate is available for Soviet production of this important material.

Copper, zinc, lead, and aluminum: No Soviet figures are currently published on these strategic materials. It is important to note that in most years the United States imports some foreign ores for smelting or refining in this country of these metals. The Soviet Union has had some shortages if one is to judge from the efforts which have been made to purchase metals, particularly copper in Western countries.

Building bricks: It is not at all clear that the figures shown are comparable. The United States figures are only for standard bricks, and do not include all the building hollow tile commonly used in construction. It also should be noted that, although brick consumption is now rising in this country along with most other items, there was an earlier peak in use of brick in the United States before World War I. Since that time, concrete and steel, as well as hollow tile and cement blocks have played much more important roles in construction that used to be done in brick. The relationships between bricks and cement in the two countries reveal differences in current building habits, suggesting the Soviet Union uses methods common to an earlier period in the United States as well as not building concrete highways in like measure.

Ammonia, synthetic rubber: The Soviet Union does not publish data on these important products. Both countries habitually import considerable amounts of natural rubber, the United States leading in this respect.

Mineral fertilizers: This comparison is a very tentative one. The United States data are actually for consumption rather than production, and therefore reflect neither the very large exports made of phosphate rock and of ammonium nitrate, nor any imports which may occur. In addition, they do not reflect the consumption of phosphate rock in Florida or Illinois. Therefore this comparison, the only one which could be made readily, grossly understates the United States in comparison with the U. S. S. R.

Turbines, electric generators, electric motors: Soviet data are in millions of kilowatts of rated capacity. United States data could not be compared because such data are reported comprehensively only in value terms, and in numbers of units of various sizes. A crude estimation could be developed by statistical analysis of different capacity ranges, given time, but the comparison would be only approximate.

Diesel engines: A comparable United States figure was not located as there is a tendency in most tabulations to separate automotive diesels from other diesels, and not all data are translatable into the same terms.

Machine cutting tools: This is a most difficult, although important comparison to make; 1955 has been the highest Soviet year reported. Some reviewers have suggested the figure should be revised downward to eliminate inclusion of workshop tools, but home workshops of the type common in the United States are not a feature of Soviet life. This suggested lower figure, purely a guess, is shown in parentheses.

The United States figure was found by comparing the ratio of 1953 machine-tool shipments as reported by the Bureau of the Census with the smaller figure issued by the National Machine Tool Builders Association for that year. This ratio was then applied to 1955 data of the association to construct an approximate Census equivalent figure. The association figure is given in parentheses. All the United States figures are for shipments rather than production.

The difference between the Census and association figures is a question of inclusions. The Census figure is believed closer to the Soviet equivalent in including certain lighter tools not included in the association tabulation. The United States figures from both the association and Census, definitely exclude metal-cutting machine tools designed for home workshops, modelmakers, garages, and service shops. It is important to recognize that machine-tool building is an industry given to wide swings in production because even changes in continued upward growth of the economy can require both sharp rises and sharp drops in tool needs. The 1955 United States figure gives little indication, therefore, of machine-tool building capacity. For example, 1951 shipments were approximately 190,000, and 1942 shipments were approximately 375,000.

At best, any count of a mixture of types of machine tools of varying degrees of complexity and productivity is more a statistical exercise than a real comparison. The only conclusion which can be drawn is that machine tools which are of great strategic military and industrial importance are being manufactured in the Soviet Union in ever-increasing numbers, even though it is not possible to say in what year that production will be as great as in the United States.

Presses and forges: Both countries report figures, which are shown here, but there is no basis for comparing work capacity from simple numerical counts.

Electronics: The item is mentioned although neither country produces figures which can be compared. This is one of the most important growth industries in both countries, and the absence of data is a real gap in a comprehensive comparison.

Metallurgical equipment and petroleum equipment: Soviet statistics show rising outputs of such equipment. United States production of these items is large, but as with some other items given above, is not reported in terms which can be compared. The Soviet economy is beginning to show a new ability to turn on and off production of selected items as required, long the practice in the United States.

Bulldozers: Both countries report figures, but these do not measure the capacity of these machines. Further, there are many other types of specialized construction machines made in both countries. General indications are that the United States produces more special-use machines in this field so that the bulldozer production count would tend to understate the United States advantage in such machines.

Combines: Here again, there are figures to compare, but no real measure of work capacity, nor reflection of other specialized farm machines, of which the United States has both greater variety and greater numbers, attested to by the great difference in manpower employed in each of the two countries for agricultural work.

Trucks: These figures do not measure the work capacity of the trucks.

Locomotives: This is a very crude comparison because it lumps together all types and capacities of such motive power. Further, the comparison must be judged in the light of continued shortages of locomotives for the Soviet system where steam power still dominates and the United States situation where the conversion to modern diesels is virtually complete, and only replacements are being made.

Freight cars: Similar judgments apply to this comparison.

Dairy products: These are presented in terms of milk used, and are especially striking in light of the size of Soviet dairy herds which are larger than those in the United States. However, they tend to understate Soviet production because private production is not included.

Vegetable oils: These are both for nutritional and industrial purposes.

Sugar: This is given in both countries in terms of refined sugar production, and therefore differs from the raw-sugar figures given in chapter 3.

Soap: Although the United States issues soap-production figures, there are so many special kinds that they are not readily translated into quantities which can be compared.

Silk, linen, artificial, and synthetic fabrics: These comparisons are presented even though they are only approximate, as explained in table 4 where cotton and wool fabrics are discussed. Such linen as is used in the United States is imported. Silk as a general-use fabric in the United States has largely been replaced by other materials. The combined artificial and synthetic figure which the Soviet authorities report is mostly rayon and acetate. In the United States there is included a large segment of nylon, orlon, dacron, and other synthetics which do the work of either silk or wool.

Clocks and watches: The Soviet figures are growing rapidly and purport to include only timepieces. In the United States, despite many imports, there is large-scale production of many timing devices. Those for time-telling purposes, completely manufactured in the United States are reported as the smaller figure. The larger figure includes both other timing devices which contain clock or watch movements, plus some less than 5 million imported movements which were cased in this country. Still more complete watches and clocks are imported as well.

Cameras: Although figures are reported, they do not necessarily cover similar categories and qualities of cameras.

Radio and television sets: The Soviet figure is a combined one, and of course the figures do not measure qualities nor existing stocks. The United States has reached levels of availability discussed in chapter V which must be taken into account in comparing current production significance in the two countries. Larger screen television sets make up a bigger share of production here than in the Soviet Union.

Refrigerators, washing machines, and sewing machines: These also involve comparing a United States replacement market with the shortages in the Soviet Union. The United States produces larger sizes and special freezers for refrigeration, many automatic washers, and mostly electrically operated sewing machines; it also imports many additional sewing machines. Nor does the table reflect United States production of many newer products including air conditioners and special-purpose electric appliances.

Bicycles: This comparison must keep in mind that these machines have not been used seriously for transportation in the United States since the turn of the century, while they are still important in the Soviet Union as in a number of other parts of the world. The United States also currently imports many bicycles from abroad.

Military goods: These headings are listed with little expectation of presenting authorative and legitimate comparisons. Their purpose is largely a reminder that an important part of the industrial comparison is omitted.

2. Production shortages

News reports, both American and Soviet, frequently carry stories of shortages in the Soviet Union, as for example the statements by Khrushchev and Zademidko (the Minister of the U. S. S. R. Coal Industry) to the effect that the growth of coal output is lagging behind growth in consumption, especially in the European part of the U. S. S. R., and that there have been production shortages in recent years. Pervukhin made a speech in December 1956 concerned with the problems of shortages, and Khrushchev in his formal presentation of the decentralization "theses" on May 7, 1957, made reference to present and emerging production difficulties.

All of these reports clearly indicate that where there is so much smoke, there must be fire. These production difficulties are real, and the problem of a study such as this is to assess the degree to which they have affected the growth of the Soviet economy in the past, and what they may portend for the future. Neither this study nor any other, however, can answer with real certainty the size of difficulties in the future.

Every economy in some sense has shortages, and this is not surprising, for the very study of the subject implies that there is a problem in making best use of limited resources for satisfying competing demands. Under a market economy, there are more or less automatic forces which bring about these allocations with efficiency. It is a tribute to our free system that the United States is the most advanced, productive, and flexible economy both in aggregate and per capita terms of any in the world.

The Soviet system does not rely on market prices and costs to control the use of its limited resources as does the United States. In the interest of reaching certain planning goals, Soviet authorities will ignore some very high costs. It is inherent under such a system that such arbitrary decisions of planners may enable the rapid attainment of some goals, but at the price of reduction of total output and efficiency, and it suffers from the lack of built-in automatic corrective forces to care for imbalances which may arise. Soviet authorities are aware of these shortcomings in their economic mechanism, and are struggling to find ways of increasing their economic efficiency without abandoning fundamental doctrines of their controlled system; this is not easy.

Soviet shortages in production represent more than the normal imbalances which are always present as transient phenomena in any economy. This is not only because their reliance on detailed direction of the economy, which turns out in practice to have serious shortcomings—just as they scoff at market economies for their occasional anomalies. Soviet shortages are also very much a concommitant of an economy which is straining to the utmost to increase output in certain high priority sectors. Typically, with some exceptions, they have managed to reach plan goals in the highest priority areas, those related to heavy industry and to military strength; but this usually has meant serious shortfalls in lower priority areas, outstandingly civilian consumption. The United States is so far advanced that it has considerable reserve capacity in its economy so that most emerging shortages can be overcome rather rapidly. In contrast, the Soviet Union is pressing so hard on its existing plant and labor force that almost any needed increase can be overcome only by foregoing some other product or service. Some of these strains are cumulative, and events of the recent past in both the captive countries and the Soviet Union give a clue as to the formidable nature of problems which lie ahead. But shortages, even of an acute nature, are not a new development, and it is not possible to draw the inference from present difficulties that any fundamental change in Soviet trends is about to occur. Such changes may appear, but they are not predictable on the basis of experience to date.

More pertinent is the possibility that mistakes in planning and inefficient management are serious enough to make probable a slowing of the Soviet rate of industrial growth unless very valiant efforts are made in the years ahead. The 1957 Khrushchev plan for regionalization, even though aimed at elimination of these inefficiencies, is quite likely to have a retarding effect during the reorganization process. The rate of growth during the fifth 5-year plan, though high by world standards, was not as great as in the period 1928–37. Production in 1956 did not meet many important prorated shares of the sixth 5-year plan goals, further cut back in rates of increase from the previous plan. It would seem then, that shortages can be overcome only by a slackening of the pace, by a more economic price system which would be allowed to affect resource allocations, and to bring supply and demand into balance, and perhaps by according proportionately greater emphasis to the fulfillment of plans other than output (e. g., the profits or cost plans).[2]

Finally shortages may be viewed as long range in character associated with deficiencies in basic resource patterns. But even these are not fixed for all time because technology changes and requirements are altered. In overall balance, both the United States and the Soviet Union are more favorably situated than most countries in their basic natural resources simply because of their geographical size and varied climates. This study has not attempted a detailed geological treatment of the two countries. Prospecting is a continuing process, and some of the apparent though different shortages which each country has experienced are not necessarily permanent. There is a normal tendency in both countries to have used up the most obvious and accessible high grade deposits of minerals first, throwing a burden on lower grades, on more remote sites, or on imports. It is not yet clear that either country faces any insuperable barriers to continued economic growth caused by limitations of a mineral nature. Agricultural and human resources are discussed in greater detail in chapters III and IV, respectively. In the case of the Soviet Union, these are areas in which persistent shortcomings are likely to prevail, together with low levels of living including housing, discussed in chapter V.

3. Quality of production

There have been numerous complaints in the Soviet press during the period under review on the poor quality of Soviet-manufactured consumer goods. However, in the words of Allen W. Dulles, Director of the Central Intelligence Agency:

> Those who have assumed that we have superior technical skills, that we could produce atomic weapons, aircraft, and the like which are beyond the competence of the Soviets, have generally proved to be mistaken. * * * The Soviets have shown high competence in the field of nuclear development both for military and peaceful purposes. They have produced highly efficient aircraft, from heavy bombers to helicopters. They are highly competent in the field of electronics; their steel industry is efficient. * * *[3]

The two points of view on Soviet abilities may seem inconsistent; but in reality they simply illustrate again the lopsided or different character of the Soviet compared to the United States economy. By selected use of its resources of skilled manpower and best equipment, Soviet industry can produce high-quality output in any section which is given high priority by Soviet authorities. However, because such resources are scarcer in the Soviet Union than in the United States, Soviet industry could not at this stage attain the overall quality levels of industry in the United States. Therefore, they have concentrated their best

---

[2] The problem in the Soviet Union is considerably more complicated than the above discussion might suggest. For one thing, Soviet reliance on a price system as a major aid to, or substitute for, planning would be a major break with the past. For another, reliance on profit or cost plans in themselves might cause imbalances, as illustrated by the cartoon showing a Soviet clothing-plant manager puzzling as to what additional items of expensive fur or other adornments could be added to garments to increase their price and consequently plant profits. No concern was manifested by the manager for the low-priced but also low-profit items most in demand by consumers.

[3] Dulles, Allen, Russia's Growing Strength Could Be a Weakness, in U. S. News & World Report, May 11, 1956, p. 124.

efforts on heavy industry—machine building, armaments, etc.—while devoting the poorer resources to the consumer-goods sector.

B. PAST PRODUCTION TRENDS OF INDUSTRY AS A WHOLE

This report is concerned with past performance of Soviet and United States industry principally because past trends are one of the yardsticks by which the success of two competing systems can be measured, and because past performance may give some indication of future developments. Data on periods of comparable development probably shed most light on the relative ability of the 2 systems to expand production. Usually this requires comparing different sets of years in the 2 countries. Data on recent identical periods are most useful for making projections into the future.

International comparisons can provide varying indications or results. That is, by judicious choice of data, of methods of computing indexes of total industrial output, and of periods for the comparisons, the results could be changed significantly. A prerequisite for proper evaluation of the comparisons, therefore, is a determination of the reliability of the underlying data, of the appropriateness of the methodology employed in computing the indexes, and of the suitability for comparison of the particular periods chosen. The necessity for rectification of some Soviet data has already been mentioned.

1. Reliability of data and indexes

The data and indexes relied on for comparative purposes in this report (see table 2, column headed "JEC Staff" under U. S. S. R. and both columns under United States) are believed to be the most accurate and reliable available; further, they are judged to be adequate for the present "order of magnitude" purposes. However, since no single measure of industrial output is satisfactory for all or even most purposes involved in international comparisons, even if all possible care could be taken in its calculation, the indexes and rates may not be satisfactory for purposes other than intended here. Perhaps more important, even when it comes to establishing orders of magnitude, one cannot be certain that the calculations shown in table 2 would not be contradicted by equally reasonable but perhaps more comprehensive calculations as yet unmade.[4] The latter possibility is particularly troublesome with respect to the U. S. S. R. data, but also with the United States data shown for the late 1800's.

The deficiencies in the official Soviet industrial output index prior to 1950 are so great that, although it is shown for comparative purposes in table 2, it is not considered further in the text.[5] Rather, this study has relied on an industrial output index computed by a Western scholar from the more reliable Soviet data on output of individual industrial commodities. That index aggregated the individual series

---

[4] For example, the National Bureau of Economic Research is presently completing a 3-year study of Soviet economic growth which is apparently considerably more comprehensive than that of Professor Hodgman, whose study is the basis of the rates of Soviet industrial growth shown in this chapter. (See Hodgman, Donald R., Soviet Industrial Production, 1928–51 (Cambridge: Harvard University Press), 1954.) Preliminary indications are that the National Bureau study will show lower rates of growth than the Hodgman study; perhaps even lower than those adjusted from Hodgman's study for use in this report.

[5] As is noted elsewhere, the deficiencies in the official index of Soviet industrial production appear to be greater prior to 1950 than after that date, owing to adoption of new price weights for the Soviet index.

by means of weights which approach the value-added concept used in the United States; therefore, unlike the official Soviet series which refers to gross value of output, it contains little or no double-counting. A principal deficiency of the index is the exclusion of peasant household production as well as the output of small-scale industry. Adjustments have been made in an attempt to take account of this, and the index has also been extrapolated forward from 1953 to 1955.[6]

The United States data shown for the 1900's are probably as reliable as similar data anywhere in the world. Certainly they are more than adequate for present purposes. United States data for the 1800's, however, are much more questionable. Their coverage was limited to 12 manufactured commodities from 1867 to 1874, 21 from 1875 to 1899, and 30 from 1899 to 1907; and the statistical techniques and data in the 1800's are usually unsatisfactory for other reasons as well. The direction of bias resulting from the exclusion of all mining and electric power, as well as many manufactured products, cannot be judged without a detailed examination of the underlying data, their coverage, and the methods of combining the various series into a single index. Acceptance of the results based on the statistics for this early period must, therefore, be provisional.[7]

2. Suitability of the periods chosen for comparison (see table 2)

Later in this study there will be a discussion of the significance of rate of growth comparisons between nations. In anticipation of that discussion, it is necessary to state that comparisons are of interest for the light they may shed on future expectations, but that any effort to find really comparable periods to make a valid comparison is probably foredoomed to failure because exogenous factors never are equivalent. Secondly, because economies differ in structure, any rates which are developed are rates governing unlike things, and the tendency should be resisted to push significance of rates too far. This is separate and apart from the technical difficulties of constructing indexes discussed above in this study.

For reasons noted in chapter I, the year 1928 was chosen as the initial year of the longer Soviet period in which growth rates are compared with those in the United States. The year 1950 was chosen as the base year of the shorter period, because by that time Soviet industry had largely completed reconstructing its war-damaged in-

---

[6] The extent of the exclusion of small-scale industry cannot be definitively established at this writing. Professor Hodgman, who computed the index in question, noted in his monograph that it referred to large-scale industry. However, in response to reviews of his monograph, he has noted that in fact his index usually includes "the output of small-scale as well as large-scale industry. * * *" (Soviet Studies, July 1956, p. 35.)

The opinion of Prof. G. Warren Nutter, Director, Study of Soviet Economic Growth, National Bureau of Economic Research, Inc., as privately expressed to the committee staff, supports Hodgman's original view. Time and staff limitations preclude an independent review of the evidence. Therefore, the committee staff adjustment of the Hodgman index (col. 3 of table 2) should be considered as provisional, pending publication of the more comprehensive results of the National Bureau study.

Note also that other reviewers (e. g., Richard Moorsteen, in the American Slavic and East European Review, February 1956, pp. 119–124) have called attention to other deficiencies— as well as good points—of the index. Some of the deficiencies of the index, such as the omission of munitions and most machinery, give the index a deflationary bias, while others have the opposite effect.

Despite the uncertainties and deficiencies noted above, the committee staff holds to its opinion expressed earlier that the adjusted index is "the most accurate and reliable available" and that it is "adequate for present 'order-of-magnitude' purposes."

[7] The series referred to is given in Historical Statistics of the United States, 1789–1945, op cit., p. 179. The indexes calculated by Prof. Edwin Frickey in Production in the United States (Cambridge: Harvard Press), 1947, p. 54, cover a wider range of commodities but give an annual rate calculation practically identical with that in the former source, i. e., 5.3 percent instead of 5.2 percent for 1867–1907.

dustrial facilities. Both output and employment in Soviet industry were by 1950 considerably above the peak prewar levels;[8] and both had been expanding at very high rates since the reconversion year of 1946, and have continued to expand, though by smaller rates, to the present. The year 1955 was chosen, again for reasons noted in chapter I, as the terminal year of both periods.

With respect to circumstances extraneous to the Soviet system, the period as a whole was characterized by factors which were both favorable and unfavorable to rapid economic growth. The principal favorable factors consisted of a readily available advanced technology from the West, and a large "surplus" labor force in agriculture and, since the war, substantial economic advantages through control over their satellites; others which might be considered "mitigating" rather than "favorable" were lend-lease supplies and war booty. The principal unfavorable factors were the destruction during World War II and the disruption attendant upon industrial conversions both before and after that event. An unfavorable but not exogenous factor was the near catastrophe in agriculture as a result of the Soviet collectivization program. This might be considered along with the exogenous factors, however, since the collectivization process now has been completed. The Soviet periods 1928–55 and 1950–55 seem, on balance, the best available for an international comparison.[9] Neither of them appears to have been unduly favorable.

The United States periods 1928–55 and 1867–1907 were judged most satisfactory to compare with the Soviet period 1928–55. If a United States period more comparable to the Soviet years 1928–55 could have been found, the rate of growth of United States industrial output during that period might have been somewhat greater than that which actually occurred after 1928—principally because the United States in 1928 was at a much more advanced stage of industrialization than was the U. S. S. R.; that is, the United States, unlike the U. S. S. R., could not borrow advanced technology to apply to a relatively backward industry operating at relatively low levels. Other factors unfavorable to the United States, such as its severe depression lasting for one-third of the period,[10] tended to be offset by the plant expansion necessary to meet the logistics requirements of World War II in the United States economy.

The period 1867–1907 in the United States also seems moderately suitable for the comparison. The levels of industrial output as well as the percentage distribution of the labor force between agriculture and nonagriculture in the United States at the start of the period were similar to those in the U. S. S. R. in 1928. The United States may not have had as many advantages in advanced technology to borrow during the period, but this was probably offset in part by the greater availability of foreign capital, as well as skilled immigrant man-

---

[8] Living standards, however, were very low in that year—even using Soviet criteria.

[9] A proper balance is difficult—one could almost say, impossible—to achieve. Prof. Nutter argues that 1913 to 1955 is the best long-term period to choose. Others, such as Prof. Gregory Grossman and Mr. Norman Kaplan, argue that the period 1928 to 1955 is acceptable only if the war and early postwar years are first eliminated. The choice of this report happens to be a compromise, in this instance, between the two points of view, rather than concurrence with either. Professor Bergson suggests the addition to the comparisons used in this study, the period 1928–40. Dr. Shimkin would like 1940–55, too.

[10] By listing the depression of the thirties as an unfavorable factor, the assumption is made that such a severe depression is not an inherent part of our economic system.

power. On balance, therefore, the United States rate for the period seems suitable for the comparison,[11] although the exogenous factors might be considered as having been somewhat more favorable during these years in the United States than from 1928–55 in the U. S. S. R., primarily because industrial output in the United States was not burdened with fresh destructions of war in home industry during those years.

With respect to the shorter United States periods, two, 1950–55 and 1922–27, are reasonably comparable to the 1950–55 period in the U. S. S. R. In both countries the concurrent periods were not too influenced by exogenous events and both countries are industrially developed nations employing advanced technology in their industrial production. However, Soviet industrial output was only about a third that of ours during the period 1950–55; the economy employed more of its resources in agriculture in 1950, and in part for that reason was able to increase its nonagricultural labor force and industrial employment at a faster rate than was realized in the United States; its technological levels were generally lower than those in this country, so that although Soviet industry is relying more and more on native technological resources, it still borrowed extensively Western technological innovations; and it obtained some economic advantages from its controls over the satellite countries. Therefore it seems reasonable to conclude that the rate of increase of industrial output in a more comparable period in the United States would have been even greater than that actually realized in the United States since 1950.

The short period 1922–27 in the United States seems more suitable in most of the above respects. It was a postwar period, just as was 1950–55; United States industrial output in 1922–27 was roughly comparable in size to that of the U. S. S. R. during 1950–55; Soviet employment of its resources in agriculture, industry, etc., in 1950–55 was more similar to that of the United States in the earlier period than in 1950–55; and the overall levels of technology in the United States in 1922–27 more nearly approximated those of the U. S. S. R. in 1950–55 than did such levels in the United States for 1950–55. As will be discussed below, periods must be selected with care to avoid misleading conclusions related to stages of business cycles rather than to persistent trends. The years selected in this study avoid extreme contrasts between peaks and valleys in the terminal years, which would immediately invalidate the trends.

3. Comparison of production trends

Soviet industrial production appears to have increased at faster rates than United States industrial output in the periods chosen as most comparable for the best, though still limited, comparability. (See table 2.) The real extent of the disparity, however, is open to serious question. If trends in the two countries are compared during the same years, Soviet industry appears to have expanded at rates about double those in the United States: From 1928 to 1955, the data of table 2 show output of industry in the U. S. S. R. as having expanded by an average of 7.7 percent per annum, compared to 3.6 percent in the United States; and from 1950 to 1955 the annual average rate of increase appears to

---

[11] This study noted earlier that even the United States data, let alone the Soviet data, are of unknown reliability, and therefore comparisons must be considered provisional.

have been 9.9 percent for Soviet industry, compared to 4.4 percent for
the United States. Keeping in mind the limitations of such measures,
if the comparison is drawn between the U. S. S. R. in recent years and
the United States at a time when it was at more nearly the same stage of
industrial development, the United States rates for the longer period
are about 5 percent, compared to about 8 percent in the U. S. S. R.,
and for the shorter period are about between 5 and 6 percent, compared to about 10 percent in the U. S. S. R. Put succinctly, the
U. S. S. R. in the short-run present appears to be expanding its industrial output at a rate about twice as great as that in the United
States, while over a longer period the rate has been about 50 percent
greater than in this country.

TABLE 2.—*Indexes and annual average rates of growth of industrial production
in the U. S. R. R. and the United States for selected periods*

	Soviet Union						United States			
	Official		Hodgman		JEC Staff		1928	1955	1867	1907
	1928	1955	1928	1955	1928	1955				
Index of output_____	100	[1] 1,900	100	[2] 1,085	100	[3] 750	100	[4] 262	100	[5] 773
Annual average rate of growth in percents [6]_____	11.5		9.2		7.7		3.6		5.2	
	1950	1955	1950	1955	1950	1955	1950	1955	1922	1927
Index of output [6]_____	100	[7] 185	100	[2] 168	100	[8] 160	100	[4] 124	100	[4] 130
Annual average rate of growth in percents [6]_____	13.1		10.9		9.9		4.4		5.3	

[1] Index given as 2065 in Tsentral'noe statisticheskoe upravlenie pri Sovete Ministrov SSSR, Narodnoe
khoziaistvo SSSR, Statisticheskii sbornik, Gosstatizdat, Moskva, 1956, p. 46, and adjusted to 1896 (rounded
to 1900) to take account of territorial changes, on basis of information given in ibid. p. 45.

[2] Hodgman, Soviet Industrial Production, 1928-51 (Cambridge: Harvard University Press), 1954, pp.
89 and 134. Data were extrapolated from 1953 forward on the basis of relationships of Hodgman to official
Soviet data in the years 1950-53. Note that data refer to large-scale industry only, that base year is 1927-28
not 1928, and that no account is taken of territorial changes.

[3] Derived by staff on the basis of Hodgman data, estimates of share of small-scale industry and home
production in total industrial output in 1928 and 1955 (about 25 percent and 5 percent respectively), and
estimate of ratio of output in 1928 to output in 1927/28 (about 1.05). The formula (10.85) (1.05) divided by
(1.00) (1.05) (1.33) yielded a result of 11.39/1.40, or 8.16. The ratio of 8.16 was then adjusted downward to
7.49, to take account of territorial changes (see footnote 1, this table for basis); it is shown in index form
rounded to 750.

[4] FRB indexes covering manufacturing and mining, taken from Historical and Descriptive Supplement to
Economic Indicators, November 1955; and Economic Indicators, August 1956, Joint Economic Committee.

[5] Derived from data compiled by Warren M. Persons, in Forecasting Business Cycles (New York, Wiley,
1931), which are reproduced in United States Bureau of the Census, Historical Statistics of the United
States, 1789-1945, p. 179, series J-14. Data cover manufacturing only. Some additional details of coverage
are given in latter source, p. 176; see original source for further details. Alternatively, using data of Edwin
Frickey, [Production in the United States 1860-1914 (Cambridge, Harvard Press), 1947, p. 54], gives an
annual average rate of 5.3 percent.

[6] Derived from indexes.

[7] Narodnoe khoziaistvo SSSR, Statisticheskii sbornik, 1956, op. cit., p. 47.

[8] Derived by reducing Hodgman's index by 5 percent, in line with relationship of Soviet ratios of growth
of output by all and large-scale industry in same period (see Narodnoe khoziaistvo SSSR, Statisticheskii
sbornik, 1956, op. cit. p. 45).

Firm conclusions about rates comparisons are fraught with many
perils. Before interpreting the above results, it should be noted that
there have been other periods in United States history, including recent ones, during which our industry has expanded at rates substantially greater than those shown in table 2. For some purposes the

higher rates might be quite appropriate.[12] For present purposes, those rates might underestimate potential industrial competition from the U. S. S. R.   Several examples should clarify this point.   For the longer periods of 15 to 23 years, growth rates ranging from 6.5 to 8.0 percent per annum could be computed, and for the shorter periods of 5 to 7 years the range of annual average growth rates is from 8.9 to 21.5 percent.   (See table 3 below.)   In several cases, however, these rates compare years of peak industrial output with years of depressed output.   Thus, shifting the period 1938–55 back just 1 year so that the base year would be 1937, the best year of the thirties, and the terminal year would be 1954, a year of mild recession, would change the average rate of growth from 6.5 percent to 4.3 percent per annum— a reduction of one-third.   A more accurate rate, for present purposes, for the years of the late thirties to about the present, would be somewhere between the 4.3 and 6.5 percent figures cited.   Likewise, if the period 1921–26 were measured instead of 1922–27, the annual rate would rise to 10.5 percent instead of the 5.3 quoted.   This is because 1921 was a year when output was abnormally low for that period of United States economic history, and the choice of 1921–26 would have presented an indefensible picture for purposes of comparison. Because of the necessary qualifications attached to the rates shown in table 3, it seems realistic, therefore, to exclude them—unless special periods of extraordinarily high rates of Soviet industrial growth also are shown, such as for the period of post-World War II rehabilitation. It can be added parenthetically that Soviet production rates also correspond fairly closely to rates of increase in capacity.   If it were possible to measure growth of United States capacity, as contrasted with production, some of our rates might turn out to be higher.

TABLE 3.—*Annual average rates of growth of industrial output in the United States* [1]

[In percentages]

Longer periods:	Rates	Shorter periods:	Rates
1865–80	[2] 8.0	1938–43	21.5
1865–91	[2] 6.9	1865–72	[2 3] 11.6
1932–55	6.7	1921–26	10.5
1938–55	6.5	1937–44	10.8
		1876–83	[2] 8.9

[1] All the rates given are based on data in Historical Statistics of the United States, 1789–1945, pp. 179, 180, or Statistical Abstract of the United States, 1956, p. 792.
[2] Alternate rates derived from Edwin Frickey, Production in the United States, 1860–1914 (p. 54), are as follows: 1865–80—6.2 percent; 1865–91—5.8 percent; 1865–72—8.9 percent; 1876–83—8.7 percent; and an extra comparison, 1876–81—10.4 percent.
[3] The rate for 1865–72 is probably overstated, owing to the exclusion of mining products from the commodity coverage. See N. Kaplan in Bergson, Abram (editor), Soviet Economic Growth (Evanston: Row-Peterson), 1953, pp. 68 to 69.

4. Interpretation of the comparisons

The rates of growth shown in table 2 seem the most suitable and reliable of any presently available for a Soviet/United States com-

---

[12] The 1938–43 or even 1937–44 rates suggest, for example, that under emergency conditions, and given time, the United States could probably duplicate the high Soviet growth rates of recent years.   (See table 3, this chapter.)   Note, however, that in 1938 there were more than 10 million unemployed, that is, nearly 20 percent of the civilian labor force, as well as other unused resources.   That and other qualifications attached to the rates suggest that they are special-purpose rates which are of limited significance here.   But more to the point, it is very clear that the United States does not have to pay the price the Soviet Union has paid for its rapid industrial growth and our economy has no need for indiscriminate hothouse stimulation.

parison. They are subject, however, to several limitations or qualifications which should be noted again before the results are
interpreted: (1) The underlying Soviet data are subject to deficiencies
of reporting and collating, and the Western-computed index relied
upon in this report is not complete and has some uncertainties
which could be resolved or remedied only in part at this time.
Therefore, the results and interpretations should be treated as provisional, meaning the real gap in rates could be either somewhat greater or less. (2) A comparison of overall industrial growth in two
countries so different in stage of development, in composition of output, and in value standards, is not meaningful or adequate for all purposes. For example, the comparison by itself sheds little light on
economic strength—whether it is for economic competition in peace-
time, in cold war, in limited hot war, or in total war. (For such purposes, the data of table 4 will provide more insight.) Rather, the
comparisons shown in table 2 are intended principally to throw some
light on past events, so as to facilitate an understanding of the general orders of magnitude of present-day Soviet industry, as well as to
serve as background for the expected or likely future developments.
(3) The comparisons do not indicate which country's increment to
industrial production is larger in absolute terms. The size of the
production increase depends on both the rate of increase and the level
of production to which the rate is applied.

During the period under review, for example, the average annual
increment to industrial production was probably greater in absolute
terms in the United States than in the U. S. S. R. This suggests the
possibility of arranging the same data which show Soviet growth
rates higher than those of the United States in a seemingly contradictory table showing the Soviet Union apparently falling more and
more years behind this country, taking as the guide which past year of
United States production most nearly matched the level of Soviet
production for the years selected for showing. Such a table of lags
would not actually be contradictory, but it could be misleading. First
of all, it may imply that the Russians will never catch up, but will
indefinitely lag half a century or more behind the United States.
Second, it may imply that the number of years of lag reported is a
fair indication of how long the catching up process is going to take.
This study has concentrated its attention on rates because they bring
us one step closer to the calculation of where trends of production, if
continued, will bring the two countries in comparison. For a higher
rate of increased production maintained a number of years by the
smaller economy can reverse the trend to a bigger gap, and then allow,
in time, larger absolute increases than its rival accomplishes. But
rates can be misleading in isolation, too, until the starting base in each
case is known, as has been pointed out, and there has been a full
assessment of the probabilities that the prevailing rates can be maintained in the future. The really important fact which must not be
obscured by dissension over rate comparisons versus absolute gap comparisons is that the Soviet Union has created the essential industrial
base with sufficient versatility and technological backing to support
serious efforts in armaments production of an advanced order, to
expand the productive capacity of their economy still further, or to
engage in widespread international trading efforts of no small significance to the United States, if it so chooses.

Several conclusions seem to emerge from the comparisons presented and from an analysis of some of the factors which affected the rates of growth of industrial production in the two countries.

(*a*) *Apparent causal factors of more rapid Soviet growth.*—The factors which appear to be most responsible for the higher rates of growth of industrial production shown for the U. S. S. R. in table 2 are connected in varying degrees with the consistent drive by Soviet authorities toward rapid expansion of industry at all costs: namely,

(1) A higher rate of investment (share of gross national production to investment) in industry in the U. S. S. R. than in the United States, channeled in greater part into heavy industrial products for producing still more such goods. Owing to their totalitarian rule, Soviet authorities could invest a higher proportion of their total output—despite the high rate of military expenditures—simply by depressing or restricting consumption to levels below that possible under a system of free investment decisions made by business and consuming interests and ignoring the individual interests of the people.[13] Further, compared to the United States, they directed a disproportionately heavy share of capital investment into industry, and an even more disproportionate share into branches producing basic industrial materials and equipment where it would be most likely to lead to and sustain high rates of industrial growth.[14] Nevertheless, from present indications, the allocations were insufficient to provide for the extremely high planned growth rates desired by the top leadership.

(2) The subservience of all other economic goals to the major goal of rapid production growth in heavy industry. Rapid expansion of key industrial products is "the" major economic goal of Soviet planners and factory managers. Not only is there no concern in the U. S. S. R. about investing too much for fear of expanding industrial capacity beyond the point where products can be sold profitably, but there is a consistent drive to produce more and more heavy industrial goods regardless of the resulting economic imbalances, sometimes low quality of products, high costs, and low profits or even losses in particular enterprises or industries. The overall costs of this orientation have been very high, as is noted below, but the result on balance seems to have been a higher rate of growth of industrial output than would otherwise have occurred.

(3) The forced shift of labor from agriculture into industry and other nonagricultural sectors. The shift of labor from agriculture into industry would undoubtedly have occurred regardless of governmental actions. However, those actions speeded up and enlarged the shift in several ways: During the first few years of the period 1928–55, many peasants who showed signs of actual or potential resistance to collectivization, were shifted forcibly out of agriculture. Those considered most dangerous to the regime were sent to slave labor camps or were executed. From 1940 to 1955, the Soviet Government conscripted a sizable number of young people, principally from rural

---

[13] The references to gross investment in the Soviet economy are based on the data shown in table 1 of ch. VI.
[14] For comparative data on Soviet and United States investment, and for an interesting discussion of the relationship of investment to economic growth, with particular reference to the Soviet and United States economies, see Kaplan, Norman, Capital Formation and Allocation, in Bergson, Abram (editor), Soviet Economic Growth (Evanston: Row-Peterson), 1953, ch. 2.

areas, into training for Soviet industry, after completion of which they were required to work for a specified number of years in specified industries. Apart from this, by forcing collectivization of agriculture on an unwilling peasantry, and by initially depressing and later restricting real incomes on the farm, the government made even the low-paid urban work relatively more attractive than it would otherwise have been. As a result, millions of peasants were forced by economic pressure or by police order into nonagricultural work during the period 1928–55, 8 million of them in the first 4 years alone. By 1955 employment in both industry and nonagricultural work as a whole was between 4 and 5 times as large as in 1928.

(4) The borrowing on a large scale of technology from the more industrialized nations. Soviet authorities, especially in the formative prewar years, spared no efforts in borrowing the industrial technology developed in the West. They hired many Western technicians and imported the best equipment available. The results, when coupled with other Soviet efforts, including the heavy emphasis on training their own skilled manpower, were very substantial. Within a relatively few years, the backward production processes in many thousands of enterprises, particularly in the heavy industry sector, were modernized, even though by our standards there is considerable room for further improvement. And despite the difficulties involved in this transformation, the benefits to industrial growth in the U. S. S. R. were enormous. Even today, Soviet representatives visit patent offices of Western countries as a routine procedure to pirate the latest industrial concepts, so this process is a continuing one.

The innovator carries heavy costs that the follower does not experience in the same degree. For example, it would be interesting to have reliable data on speed of growth in the United States compared with Great Britain at a time when our industrialization was new and the British had already paved the way. Likewise, it would be interesting to compare the rates of growth attained by Japan at various times since 1870, and by Canada in the years since 1940. Such comparisons might offset Communist claims to superiority in speeding growth, even recognizing Soviet willingness to sacrifice present generations to future success.

(5) The lower quality and smaller variety of goods produced by Soviet industry, especially in the manufactured consumer goods sector. The quality was lower in considerable part because the best resources were diverted in larger quantities to heavy industry; the variety was smaller by intent. The two practices allowed a larger rate of growth to be registered than could otherwise have taken place. The fictitious nature of this element of growth will be more apparent if or when attempts are made to remedy the situation.

(b) *The economic costs of rapid growth to the Soviet Union.*—The economic costs of the all-out industrialization drive have been very high—exorbitant by United States standards, probably equally so by those of the Soviet peoples, but apparently not excessive by the standards of Soviet authorities. Those costs could be described as follows:

(1) Human costs: The principal economic costs, like the political and sociological costs which are beyond the scope of this report, could all be summarized under the category of "human costs." Certain of those costs, however, seem most appropriately described in this way.

Perhaps the most notorious and dramatic human costs were paid in the early thirties when widespread famine resulted from the government decision to export grain to finance its machinery-import program, despite the known lack of adequate food supplies especially in rural areas.   By doing little or nothing to relieve the famine which was worse in rural areas, Soviet authorities encouraged the shift of manpower to the cities.   The death toll was in the millions.

Equally notorious, and even more costly over the entire period, have been the forced-labor camps.   The relationship of these human costs to the forced industrialization program is less direct and more involved; and the camps might have existed regardless of the industrialization program.   But forced industrialization helped to set in motion and sustain the "need" for such a system of repression. The death toll directly attributable to the conditions under which forced labor has worked and lived undoubtedly has been in the millions.   The costs to those who survive physically cannot be measured.

Finally, among the human costs should be reckoned the daily costs paid by the Soviet people through low levels of living (see ch. V). Though less dramatic than the other costs listed above, they are both pervasive and persistent.

(2) Costs to production: The effects of the forced industrialization drive on rates of growth of industrial production were described earlier as favorable on balance, despite the high unit costs of production, the low profits, low quality, etc.   One additional cost, however, is more directly related to the holding down of production increases; that is, the inability to take full advantage of the benefits of specialization of production.   As a result of the economic imbalances brought on by the constant strain to increase industrial production rapidly, together with Soviet efforts to keep a high proportion of material and equipment working, supply lines in the Soviet Union are not dependable.   Consequently, each factory—to insure continuity of supplies and equipment for its own production plan—tends to produce some of its most essential supplies or equipment itself rather than depend on others.   Khrushchev, Bulganin, and other Soviet leaders have pointed out these deficiencies, but success in remedying them is likely to be slow unless there is some letup in the industrialization drive, accompanied by greater supplies of warehoused goods which can be moved quickly to correct imbalances, and increased emphasis on fulfillment of cost, profit, and composition of output, as well as of value of output plans.

The effects on agricultural production could not be accurately described as "favorable on balance," largely because of the connection between the forced industrialization drive and collectivization of Soviet agriculture.   (See ch. III.)   Soviet authorities saw in collectivization a means of assuring minimum supplies of foodstuffs and other agricultural products for the expected rapid expansion of urban needs.   In large part as a result of collectivization, however, production increases in Soviet agriculture barely kept pace with increases in the population.   The per capita production in Soviet agriculture which was at a very low level in 1928 compared to that in other Western countries, it is still very low today.

The effects on production of services not directly connected with industrial production could also be described as unfavorable, whether the services are passenger transportation, municipal facilities, or retail merchandising. With perhaps the major exception of education—and even here depending on the quality standard chosen—the results appear to have been a less rapid increase in such services than would have taken place in the absence of the forced industrialization drive.

(c) *Summary of interpretation.*—Two points of the interpretation of the data shown in table 2 seem worth summarizing. First, the apparent more rapid growth of Soviet industrial production seems largely but not completely connected with the forced industrialization drive, that is, with the priority Soviet authorities have accorded production of heavy industrial commodities. High rates of industrial growth could have been expected even in the absence of such a goal, owing to the technological backwardness of Soviet industry in 1928, the availability for borrowing of advanced Western technology and technicians, and the presence of a very large surplus of manpower in Soviet agriculture. Second, the costs of the apparently higher rate of growth of Soviet industrial production were excessive if judged by most non-Communist standards, and also by those of the bulk of the Soviet people.

C. PRODUCTION AND TRENDS IN SELECTED BRANCHES OF INDUSTRY

1. Problems of comparability

Data on production of selected industrial commodities in both the U. S. S. R. and United States are shown in table 4 below; and the rates of growth of production during selected periods are shown for most of these commodities in table 5. For the limited purposes of this report, the data are sufficiently comparable through time and between the U. S. S. R. and United States for the basic or producer goods shown, but less so for the consumer goods which are shown.

There are two basic problems with respect to the comparison of consumer goods production and trends that could be satisfactorily dealt with only in a lengthier study. The first is the marked difference in consumption and production patterns between the two countries. Manufactured consumer goods such as automobiles and washing machines, which are very important in United States production, account for an insignificant share of Soviet production (see table 1, this chapter); whereas some of the consumption goods which are very important in the U. S. S. R. are of relatively minor and diminishing significance in the United States. On the one hand, a comparison of percentage rates of growth of automobile production, for example, would show sizable rates for the United States, but fantastically high rates for the U. S. S. R., whose production of automobiles in 1955 was very small, but whose production in 1928 was insignificant. Such high rates of growth could easily be shown for United States production of automobiles during an earlier period, or for television receivers during the postwar period. On the other hand, a comparison of rates of growth of cotton textiles, for example, would show the United States in a misleading light, since its production in this branch has been much higher than that in the Soviet Union throughout the century, and there was consequently little reason for such production to expand in the United States, especially in view of the substitution of other textiles and use of imported fabrics.

The second problem relates to the comparability of Soviet data on consumer-goods production through time, owing to the exclusion in most instances of the output of small-scale producers, including home production and the output of self-employed artisans. Such production accounted for a very large share of consumer-goods output in 1928 compared to an insignificant share in 1955, so that use of unadjusted Soviet data would provide a very misleading picture of the rapidity of Soviet growth since 1928, as well as of the Soviet to United States production ratios in 1928 in many branches of consumer-goods manufacturing. The problem can, however, be ignored for the branches of heavy industry shown in table 4, as well as for cotton textiles, because the share of small-scale producers in that output in 1928 was insignificant for the purposes of this study; [15] the figures on meat production have been adjusted to take this exclusion into account: and the figures shown for shoe production up to 1937 have been placed in parentheses to draw attention to the fact that they are not comparable on this account to data for later years.

2. *Production in physical terms*

The Soviet data are shown in table 4 for selected years which usually denote the beginning or end of a period of some economic significance. The United States data are shown where available for the years 1900, 1920, 1928, 1940, 1948, 1950, and 1955, plus peak-year data if different from the foregoing, as well as for the first years in which United States output reached approximately the U. S. S. R. levels of 1928, 1950, and 1955. The latter years are starred (*) to enable a ready computation to be made of the number of years it took the United States to increase its output of the selected commodities from the Soviet output levels of 1928 and 1950 to the Soviet levels of 1955.

---

[15] Based on an unpublished manuscript by A. D. Redding, with original data taken from Soviet sources.

TABLE 4.—*Output of selected industrial products in the U. S. S. R. and the United States*

SOVIET UNION

Year	Lumber (million cubic meters)	Coal (million metric tons)	Crude petroleum (million metric tons)	Natural gas (billion cubic meters)	Electric power (billion kilowatt-hours)	Steel (million metric tons)	Cement (million metric tons)
1913	11.9	29.1	9.2	0.02	1.9	4.2	1.5
*1928	13.6	35.5	11.6	0.3	5.0	4.3	1.8
1932	24.4	64.4	21.4	1.1	13.5	5.9	3.5
1937	33.8	128.0	28.5	2.3	36.2	17.7	5.5
1940	34.8	165.9	31.1	3.4	48.3	18.3	5.7
1945	(1)	149.3	19.4	(1)	43.3	12.3	1.8
1948	(1)	208.2	29.2	(1)	66.3	18.6	6.5
*1950	49.5	261.1	37.9	6.2	91.2	27.3	10.2
*1955	70.0	391.0	70.8	10.4	170.1	45.3	22.5
1956	(1)	429.0	83.8	13.7	192.0	48.6	24.9

UNITED STATES

Year	Lumber Year	Lumber (million cubic meters)	Coal Year	Coal (million metric tons)	Crude petroleum Year	Crude petroleum (million metric tons)	Natural gas Year	Natural gas (billion cubic meters)	Electric power Year	Electric power (billion kilowatt-hours)	Steel Year	Steel (million metric tons)	Cement Year	Cement (million metric tons)
1900	*1859	18.9	*1871	42.5										
	*1879	42.8	*1901	244.7	*1902	8.6			*1902	(1)	*1890	4.3	*1897	1.9
	*1899	82.7	*1907	266.1		12.0				6.0		10.4		2.9
		(1)		435.8	*1915	37.9	*1906	(1)			*1910	26.5	*1909	11.4
	1907	108.6		597.2		59.7		11.0		56.6	*1917	45.8		16.6
1920		82.6		522.5	*1922	75.2		22.6	*1926	94.2	*1923	42.8	*1923	23.4
1928		86.7		464.8		121.5		44.4		108.1		52.4		30.4
1940		73.5	1947	624.0		182.4		75.3	(*)	179.9		60.8		22.7
1948		(1)		595.7		272.3		145.8		336.8		80.4		35.4
1950		89.7		508.4		266.1		177.9		388.7		87.8		39.6
1955		92.3		450.3		334.9		264.5		624.9		106.2		50.6

[1] Not available.

SOVIET UNION

Year	Paper (million metric tons)	Tractors (thousands)	Trucks (thousands)	Automobiles (millions)	Cotton fabrics (billion linear meters)	Wool fabrics (billion linear meters)	Footwear (million pairs)	Meat (million metric tons)
1913	0.2				2.6	0.1	60.0	(¹)
*1928	.3	1.3	0.7		2.7	.1	58.0	3.7
1932	.5	48.9	23.7		2.7	.1	86.9	2.1
1937	.8	51.0	180.3	0.02	3.4	.1	182.9	2.4
1940	.8	31.6	136.0	.01	4.0	.1	211.0	(¹)
1945	(¹)	7.7	(¹)	(¹)	1.6	.1	63.1	(¹)
1948	(¹)	56.9	(¹)	(¹)	3.2	.1	134.0	(¹)
*1950	1.2	108.1	294.4	.06	3.9	.2	203.4	3.1
1955	1.9	163.4	329.0	.11	5.9	.3	274.5	4.0
1956	2.0	184.0	358.0	.10	5.5	.3	314.0	(¹)

UNITED STATES

Band	Paper (million metric tons)	Tractors (thousands)	Trucks (thousands)	Automobiles (millions)	Cotton fabrics (billion linear meters)	Wool fabrics (billion linear meters)	Footwear (million pairs)	Meat (million metric tons)
1900	*1899 2.2; (¹)	(¹); *1909 2.0; *1918 132.7; *1919 164.6	(¹); *1904 0.7	*1908 .06; *1909 .12	1890 2.7; 4.1; 1909 5.7	1890 0.4; .4	*1870 80.6; *1899 218.0; 219.0; *1914 292.7; 1919 352.2	*1860 3.5; 6.6
1920	7.2	203.2	(**) 321.8	1.9	1921 (¹); 6.0	1919 (¹); 1921 .3	(¹)	7.8
1928	10.4	171.5	583.3	3.8	1929 7.5	1929 .3	1929 415.5	1928 8.5
1940	14.5	274.2	754.9	3.7	1939 7.6; 1942 10.7	1939 .4; 1946 .6	1939 463.5; (¹)	1940 9.7
1948	21.9	569.4	1,364.0	3.9	8.8	.5	1947 508.6	10.7
1950	24.4	542.4; 1951 617.1	1,332.3; 1951 1,417.4	6.7	9.1	.4	550.6	11.2
1955	27.1	377.1	1,245.6	7.9	9.2	.3	634.1	13.3

¹ Not available.

Starred (*) years on the United States tables represent the approximate points at which United States production had attained the levels later attained (if at all) by the U. S. S. R. in 1928, 1950, and 1955. In addition to certain years reported in common where available in both countries, the United States figures try to include data on a previous peak year if necessary, or on years close to a common year where common years were not reported.

Although this table has attempted to compare production trends in the two countries, it is most important to recall that differences in definition and coverage make very exact comparisons dangerous. These data at best will indicate the general order of magnitude of relationships. Most commodities reported require some qualification for their interpretation.

Lumber: United States data have been converted from board-feet to cubic meters. It is not known whether both countries are equally complete in reporting total production.

Coal: The Soviet Union produces more brown coal than the United States and the heat-producing quality of the Soviet tonnage, therefore, is enough lower that the 1955 total of 391 million metric tons was corrected in table 1 to 310 million tons. Corresponding changes would be needed in all earlier years if the measure were to be in heat equivalents to United States production.

Crude petroleum: United States data were converted from barrels at 7.418 barrels equals 1 metric ton.

Natural gas: The Soviet figure is given simply as "gas," and therefore may include manufactured gas. If the United States figures were to be increased to reflect manufactured gas, it would make a difference of less than 1 percent in the 1955 figure, but would have been a larger proportion in some earlier years when manufactured gas production was higher. The calculation was not pursued because of the commanding lead of this country, even without an adjustment.

Electric power: The basis for reporting and the coverage has changed in the United States, and may have in the Soviet Union as well. As in all cases, the detailed explanations of United States data are given in the principal sources used, and listed below. Soviet interpretative data are not as readily available.

Steel: Although the figures appear to be similar, there may be differences in the method of reporting output.

Cement: Soviet coverage may be broader, and the coverage may have been further broadened since 1928, exaggerating the trend. It is not clear that Soviet cement is equal in quality to that reported in this country. The United States figures cover hydraulic cement only. Figures in this country are converted from barrels at 376 pounds each, although over the years weights have not always been consistent.

Paper: The United States series combined paper and paperboard. The Soviet series may or may not have. But even if comparability required removing paperboard from the United States series, the total would be cut by only 50 percent, still manyfold the Soviet figures.

Tractors: In both cases the series cover farm tractors, exclusive of the garden type. A spot check of the United States data by tractor horsepower showed that the series presented would be modified very little in giving a Soviet table by horsepower, and adjusting United States data to match.

Trucks: The capacity and variety of types is not measured by the data shown.

Automobiles: In totals, the Soviet production is about where ours was in 1909; and these cars are largely for official use and for export.

Cotton fabrics: The comparison presented cannot be more than approximate, and needs interpretation to be read at all. Soviet data are presented in linear meters without adjustment. Over the course of time, average widths have varied, so no reliable conversion can be made to square meters. Linear meters may overstate square meters from 20 to over 40 percent depending upon the product mix of particular years.

The United States data are now reported in linear yards, although in earlier years, square yards were used. The Bureau of the Census has made approximate calculations on earlier years so that it is possible to present a series expressed in reasonably consistent linear terms. Widths in the United States are on the average greater, however, so that linear yards actually understate square yards by nearly 10 percent, at least in 1947 when calculations were made. Broad-woven fabrics only are included leading to a further slight understatement.

There are so many possible adjustments, each depending upon certain assumptions open to challenge that this table has merely made a simple conversion to linear meters. For 1955 only, the United States figure comparable to the Soviet may be close to 12.4 instead of the 9.2 shown. It must also be remembered that no adjustment to reconcile area figures can take into account thread counts, bleaching, printing, dyeing, sizing, shrinking, special weaving, and all the other qualitative differences which complicate sound comparison.

Wool fabrics: Many of the same complications attend any effort to compare woolen and worsted fabric in the two countries. Consequently, no adjustment has been made, except to convert the United States yardage in linear meters. As there are differences in average width, the United States figures are also comparatively understated, with 0.4 closer to comparability for the year 1955 instead of the 0.3 shown.

Footwear: Although the Soviet series is labeled leather shoes in the Soviet source, there is other evidence that the series may include all shoes, new and rebuilt, except for those made exclusively of felt or rubber. The data up to 1937 are probably greatly understated because of the apparent exclusion of shoes made by independent artisans. Likewise, the United States data are understated before 1919 by the absence of data on canvas shoes with rubber soles prior to that date.

Meat: It was not possible to use the official Soviet series on meat because of incompleteness in reporting. Therefore, figures which are explained in chapter 3, were brought forward to this table for purposes of the comparision. Trends on the production of other foods are covered in chapter III in moderate detail. The meat figures include lard, but exclude poultry and rabbits.

SOURCES

All Soviet data are from:

Tsentral'noe statisticheskoe upravlenie pri Sovete Ministrov SSSR, Narodnoe khoziaistvo SSSR, Statisticheskii sbornik, Gosstatizdat, Moskva, 1956, except for meat which is from table 2 of chapter 3.

The page references are as follows: Lumber, page 58; coal, pages 55 and 67; crude petroleum, pages 55 and 69; natural gas, page 55; electric power, pages 55 and 65; steel, pages 55 and 63, cement, pages 58 and 80; paper, page 59; tractors, pages 57 and 75; trucks, page 56; automobiles, page 56; cotton fabric, pages 58 and 83; wool fabric, pages 58 and 85; footwear, pages 58 and 87.

Supplementary figures for 1956 are taken by the U. S. Department of Commerce from Soviet sources.

United States data are mostly from the Department of Commerce Statistical Abstract of the United States, 1956, together with the Historical Statistics of the United States 1789–1945 and its 1952 Supplement. Some figures were drawn directly from appropriate volumes of the Census of Manufactures, and all 1955 data are preliminary, a number having been obtained from trade associations and Government departments as appropriate.

The detailed references are as follows:

Lumber: Historical Statistics, series F–109 through 1950; Survey of Current Business (July 1956), page S–31, for 1955.

Coal: Historical Statistics, series G–13 and G–16 through 1950; Survey of Current Business (July 1956), pages S–34, 35, for 1955.

Crude petroleum: Historical Statistics, series G–57 through 1950; Statistical Abstract, page 740, for 1955.

Natural gas: Historical Statistics, series G–59 through 1950; Gas Facts (American Gas Association), page 26, for 1955.

Electric power: Historical Statistics, series G–171 through 1950; 1955 from Statistical Abstract, page 529.

Steel: Historical Statistics, series J–165 through 1950; Statistical Abstract, page 829, for 1955.

Cement: Historical Statistics, series G–65 through 1950; Survey of Current Business (July 1956), page S–38, for 1955.

Paper: Historical Statistics, series F–134 through 1950; Commodity Yearbook, page 247, for 1955.

Tractors: Agricultural Statistics 1941, page 565 and 1955 page 435 through 1950; Facts for Industry, series M–37B–125, for 1955.

Automobiles: Historical Statistics, series K–225 through 1950; Statistical Abstract, page 549, for 1955.

Cotton fabrics: United States 12th Census 1900, volume IX, page 38 for 1890 and 1900; Abstract of Census of Manufactures 1914, page 60 for 1909; Facts for

Industry, series M–15A–02 for 1921 through 1950; Statistical Abstract 1956, page 816, for 1955.

Wool fabrics: United States 12th Census 1900, volume IX, page 98 for 1890 and 1900; Biennial Census of Manufactures 1921, page 305 for 1919; Facts for Industry, series M–15A–02 for 1921 through 1950; Statistical Abstract 1956, page 816, for 1955.

Meat: Letter from Agricultural Marketing Service for estimate of 1860; Agricultural Statistics 1941, page 407 and 1955, page 351 for other years through 1950, and Statistical Abstract 1956, pages 683 and 688, for 1955.

Footwear: United States 9th Census 1870, volume III, page 591 for 1870; United States 12th Census 1900, volume IX, page 751 for 1900; Abstract of Census of Manufactures 1914, page 148 for 1899; Biennial Census of Manufactures 1921, pages 564 and 1178 for 1919; Biennial Census for Manufactures 1929, pages 683 and 710 for 1929; Census of Manufactures 1947, pages 472 and 482 for part of 1939 and for 1947; Statistical Abstract 1956, page 820 for rest of 1939 and for part of 1950 and 1955; Leather and Shoes (October 20, 1956) page 30 for canvas shoes with rubber soles for 1950 and 1955.

Soviet output of the basic industrial products shown was, in 1928, at about the same level as United States output at or before the turn of the century. However, for the manufactured consumer goods shown, Soviet production in 1928 was much lower than production in the United States even in 1899 or 1900, the earliest years for which such data were generally available. The 1955 levels of Soviet production of the basic industrial products had been reached in the United States before 1899 for lumber; by 1906 for natural gas; in 1907 for coal; from 1917 to 1923 for steel, crude petroleum, and cement; and in 1940 for electric power. For the manufactured consumer goods, however, the United States had reached the 1955 Soviet output levels in about 1860 for meat, between 1899 and 1909 for cotton fabrics, between 1909 and 1914 for footwear, before 1899 for wool fabrics, and by 1909 for automobiles. Farm tractors of the 1955 Soviet level were produced here by 1919 and paper by about the turn of the century.

3. Rates of growth of production

Data on percentage rates of growth of selected industrial products in both countries are given in table 5 below. Several points are worth noting briefly.

(1) Soviet rates of growth during the period 1928–1955 have been greater for basic industrial products and producer goods than for most manufactured consumer goods. Rates were computed for only four of the latter, but the orientation of Soviet industry is also apparent from aggregate Soviet statistics which allege that output of producer goods was 38.91 times as great in 1955 as in 1928, compared to a ratio of 8.95 for output of consumer goods.[16] As noted in chapter I of this report, the magnitudes of the aggregate Soviet statistics cited above are grossly exaggerated, especially for years prior to 1950; but they serve for the limited purpose of indicating the orientation of Soviet industry.

For the period 1950–1955, some slight shift of priorities is indicated by the data of table 5. The shift apparently occurred because of the necessity for remedying the exceedingly low levels of living which prevailed at the end of World War II. (See chap. V.) The emphasis on basic and heavy industries, however, still existed during that period, though in lessened dimensions; and judged from aggregate

---

[16] Narodnoe khoziaistvo SSSR, Statisticheskii sbornik, 1956, op. cit., p. 46.

Soviet statistics, it is planned to continue during the next 5 years as well.[17]

Progress, in the single year 1956 has tended to lag behind both the rates of increase of the preceding 5 years and of the sixth 5-year plan as adopted by the XX party congress, with a few exceptions, notably fuels.

TABLE 5.—*Annual average rates of growth of production for selected industrial commodities in the U. S. S. R. and the United States*

[In percentages]

Commodity	U. S. S. R.				United States			
	1928–55	1950–55	1955–56	1955–60 plan	Various years		1928–55	1950–55
					Period	Rate		
Lumber	6.3	7.1	(1)	6.7	1859–79	4.2	0.2	0.6
Coal	9.3	8.4	10	8.7	1871–98	5.9	−.5	−3.8
Crude petroleum	6.9	13.3	18	13.8	1902–29	9.4	3.8	4.7
Natural gas	14.0	10.9	32	31.2	1906–30	6.9	6.8	8.3
Electric power	14.0	13.3	13	13.5	1902–29	11.6	6.7	10.0
Steel	9.1	10.7	7	8.6	1890–1917	9.1	2.7	3.9
Cement	9.8	17.2	11	19.6	1897–1924	10.0	1.9	5.1
Paper	7.1	9.6	7	7.9	1899–1926	5.7	3.6	2.1
Tractors	19.6	8.6	12	26.3	1909–29	26.6	3.0	−7.9
Trucks	25.6	2.3	9 }	7.9	{ 1904–29	32.3	2.9	−1.4
Automobiles		12.8	−9 }		{ 1900–1923	34.3	2.8	3.4
Machinery	(14.9)	16.8	(1)	12.8			5.5	6.4
Cotton fabrics	2.9	8.6	−8	4.2	1880–1905	4.1	1.2	.2
Wool fabrics	4.2	8.4	6	7.7		(1)	0	−5.9
Footwear	(5.9)	6.2	5	8.7	1870–99	3.5	1.6	2.8
Meat	.3	5.2	6	12.2	1860–1900	1.6	1.7	3.5

1 Not available.

Sources: All data were derived from table 4 except for the machinery entries. These rates were derived from the Tsentral'noe statisticheskoe upravlenie pri Sovete Ministrov SSSR, Narodnoe khoziaistvo SSSR, Statisticheskii sbornik, Gosstatizdat, Moskva, 1956, page 74 and from Pravda of January 15, 1956, page 2; this latter forward projection actually refers to all metalworking. The United States data are derived from the Federal Reserve Board index. The 1955–56 Soviet comparison was complied by the United States Department of Commerce from Soviet sources.

Coverage: See notes to table 4 for coverage of all categories except machinery. The machinery category in the United States covers all machinery except transportation equipment, whereas the Soviet category covers all machinery and equipment. Addition of transportation equipment to the United States category would add, according to a preliminary staff estimate, about 2 percentage points to the 1950–55 annual average rate, and less than 1 percentage point to the 1928–55 rate.

Unlike the rates shown for other branches of industry, which are based on physical output data, those for machinery are based on a value index. Hence there is more possibility of exaggerated rates of growth—as in fact occurred in substantial measure in the Soviet data especially prior to 1950. The 1929–55 rate in the U. S. S. R. covers metalworking other than machine building; the official rate for machine building alone would probably be still higher.

The United States column labeled "Various years" attempts to find an initial year either close to the 1928 Soviet level or the earliest year available and a

[17] The planned annual average rates are just over 11 percent for producer goods and nearly 10 percent for consumer goods, compared to rates of 13.8 percent and 12 percent realized per annum on the average during the period 1951–55. All rates were derived from official Soviet rates, and they are subject to the qualifications noted elsewhere as attached to Soviet aggregates. The rates for 1951–55 were derived from idem.; the planned rates for 1955–60 were derived from increases given in the directives of the sixth 5-year plan, Pravda, January 15, 1956. These planned increases, of course, may undergo some revision with the passage of time, but there had been no public announcement of a revised 1960 plan as late as May 1957.

terminal year 27 years later unless a higher level than that after 27 years appeared.   This is a very crude comparison with the 1928–55 Soviet data.

(2) Rates of growth of output of heavy industrial goods have been markedly faster in the U. S. S. R. than in the United States during both 1928 to 1955 and 1950 to 1955.   Further, it appears that starting from approximately the same output levels as in the U. S. S. R. in 1950, it took the United States more years in the branches of industry shown except for tractors, trucks, and automobiles to duplicate the increases in output realized in the U. S. S. R. in the 5 years from 1950 to 1955. (See the second and third years in the United States starred in table 4.) However, starting from approximately the same output levels as in the U. S. S. R. in 1928, which was usually about 1900 or earlier in the United States, the United States was able to best the 1928–55 Soviet output increase rates in about 7 industries, and to match it in 1, while taking longer to realize approximately the same output increase in another 6 industries (see table 5) and do even better where comparisons in years are available.   (See the first and third starred years in table 4.)   These comparisons are moderately consistent with the conclusions already presented of output trends for industry as a whole but strengthen a little more the contention that for comparable stages of development, the differences in rates of growth tend to diminish. The principal weakness of these comparisons is that only a few industries are shown, and a different group or a weighting system could swing the results the other way.   But they represent about the best illustrations available.

It should be noted that the official Soviet rates of growth shown for machinery output are unquestionably exaggerated for the period up to 1950, and there may be some exaggeration in the rates for the later years as well.[18]   It appears, however, that the Soviet rates since 1928 are significantly greater than the United States rates during most periods of this century; and there is little doubt but that current rates of growth of machinery output are significantly greater in the U. S. S. R. than in the United States.[19]

4. Atomic energy developments

Although comparable statistics are lacking, sufficient importance attaches to the question of atomic power to discuss major developments in the two countries.   It is difficult to make a complete assessment of relative progress in the United States and in the Soviet Union in the development of nuclear energy because military necessities have restricted the free flow of public information in considerable degree. Both countries have achieved the production of fission and thermonuclear weapons in a range of sizes, and apparently incorporate plans

---

[18] For the prewar period, see, for example, A. Gerschenkron, Soviet Heavy Industry: A Dollar Index of Output, 1927/28–37, Review of Economics and Statistics ,May 1955.   Regarding the post-1950 period, there shou'd be little or no upward bias in the official Soviet index of machinery output if the Soviet-reported changes in their methodology had been followed in practice.   There have been some indications that the new methodology in practice has not eliminated all of the upward bias, so use of the post-1950 rates must still be provisional.
[19] The indexes of machinery output, with 1940 equals 100, with data for the U. S. S. R. as follows: 1928—6; 1946—80; 1950—234; and 1955—571; and for the United States: 1928—78; 1948—204; 1950—224; and 1955—304.   The Soviet data were taken or derived from Narodnoe khoziaistvo SSSR, Statisticheskii sbornik, 1956, op. cit., p. 74; the 1928 figure covers all metalworking rather than machine building only.   The United States data are from the Federal Reserve Board index.   Note that contrary to Soviet practices, the United States data exclude transportation equipment.   Addition of data for this category would raise the 1955 to 1950 ratio of machinery output in the United States from 1.36 to 1.48, according to preliminary staff estimates.

for their potential use in certain military situations, which no one
wants to see arise. The questions of weapon stockpiles, nuclear strategy, effects of testing, and plans for international control lie outside
the scope of this study.

The United States has made large-scale commitments for the peaceful development of nuclear energy not only for research, medical, industrial and agricultural purposes with radioactive elements, but also
for the generation of electric power. The atoms-for-peace program
affords an opportunity for all friendly nations to share both in American technology and in supplies of enriched nuclear fuels. The United
States in exchange continues to have access to some supplementary
sources of nuclear raw materials, and the research experience of other
countries, as well as benefiting from improved prospects for a peaceful
and prosperous world.

The U. S. S. R. has made some overtures for nuclear aid to other
countries, but for the most part the recipients have been other countries within the Soviet bloc, although a few neutralist nations have
been offered some limited research assistance.

Undoubtedly the United States has the largest number of research
and prototype reactors operating. These are testing out a very large
variety of design concepts from which will be discovered leads to truly
economical power. Meanwhile the need for large-scale building of
primitive plants just to generate added kilowatts is not as compelling
in this country as it is in the United Kingdom, the Euratom countries,
or in Japan, to name a few. Supplies of conventional fuels and potential hydro developments postpone the day when nuclear energy is
needed, giving us time, if we pursue a program vigorously, to develop
more efficient reactors. There is a body of opinion, however, that this
country should embark on a larger program of early construction to
gain more experience with large plants, if only for the influence this
will have in helping the friendly countries of the world to develop
power as soon as they need it, which is almost immediately. Pending a
decision to embark on a new program of government construction of
large scale plants, and the receipt of private offers under the third
round of the demonstration program of the Atomic Energy Commission, the United States program is as follows for the years up to 1963:
Modest sized plants are testing generation of power with pressurized
water, and boiling-water systems, with organic moderated reactors,
with sodium-graphite reactors, with heavy-water reactors, with gas-
cooled reactors, with aqueous homogeneous reactors, with fast breed-
ers, and with liquid plutonium, to mention just the principal categories.
The locations and progress on these projects are reported periodically
by the Atomic Energy Commission. In addition, the first large-scale
plant designed solely to produce power will open in 1957 at Shippingport, Pa., generating 60,000 kilowatts of electricity with the first core,
and 100,000 kilowatts later with the second core. Following in the
next 3 to 4 years are large plants at Buchanan, N. Y., Rowe, Mass.,
Lagoona Beach, Mich., Dresden, Ill., and Beatrice, Nebr. Others of
smaller size will operate at Anchorage, Alaska, Piqua, Ohio, Hershey,
Mich., and Elk River, Minn. Others to be completed before 1965 include large plants in eastern Pennsylvania, in Florida, in Ohio, and
at least three other locations.

The Soviet Union is said to have an equivalent program which will
turn out even more kilowatts by 1960, but no building sites have been

opened for inspection, except for a small 5,000-kilowatt plant near Moscow established as early as 1954, which they claim to have been the first such plant in the world. Their announced program includes a range of some 10 experimental designs, roughly paralleling the extensive United States program of varied reactors. Additionally, they say they will soon have near Moscow a plant of the general size of that which the United States will open at Shippingport. Further, very large stations in the 400,000- to 600,000-kilowatt range are to be completed by 1960 near Moscow, near Leningrad, 2 more in the Urals, and others at points not yet announced. If these plants are built on schedule, the Soviet Union would win the first round of the "kilowatt race."

Future rounds will depend upon the effort made at basic research. The United States seems to have a good lead, but not one which can be viewed with complacency. Certainly in research on high energy physics, the Russians are making notable advances, and their experimental facilities have come in for high praise from Western scientific visitors. The Russians have also shown that they are aware of the general problems associated with harnessing thermonuclear energy for power-generation purposes, and must be assumed to have a research program going. It is too early to say whether the scientists of either country will be able to control such energy within the next decade or two.

The question of nuclear fuels deserves consideration in any assessment. The United States was originally dependent upon the Belgian Congo and Canada for uranium. More recently further prospecting has provided large-scale supplies particularly in the Colorado Plateau. Further research has shown ways ultimately to extract commercially useful amounts of uranium from a variety of sources, including granite, gold mine tailings, and phosphate rock. The United States could be independent of foreign sources of uranium for many years, but there is no particular reason to be when accessible sources are more quickly available in many places throughout the world.

There is no real information on the adequacy of uranium supplies in the U. S. S. R. Because the metal is relatively common, the long run outlook is that probably prospecting will turn up enough to take care of Soviet needs. The immediate postwar phenomenon has been for the Soviet Government to exploit under forced-draft conditions the mines of Czechoslovakia and East Germany. This suggests that either adequate Soviet sources had not then been discovered, or that the Soviet authorities were determined to get what they could from the captive countries while they were sure of it.

D. FUTURE TRENDS IN SOVIET AND UNITED STATES INDUSTRY

Past and present performance is the usual basis for any projection as to future performance, but it is far from a reliable one, even when combined with an analysis of all the factors influencing production. International events cannot be predicted sufficiently, nor could the effects of all the many factors at work be understood and evaluated quantitatively—even if the nature of forces outside of production could be predicted accurately. However, the problem can be reduced to a point where the order of magnitude of future trends in both

Soviet and United States industry could be projected with considerable confidence by assuming there will be no major war, no basic changes in economic systems, no major depressions, and no unusually startling technological developments in either country.

The principal factors affecting production, other than those mentioned above, are the volume and quality of the labor force, of capital equipment, and of raw materials, and also the quality of management. In addition, the factor of technology, which was excluded only to the extent of assuming no major new technological advances, deserves special attention. All of the above are discussed below in connection with the prospects for Soviet industry, the focus of this report.[20]

1. Technology

The Soviet Union started from a much lower technological base and has been able to adopt, directly or with modifications, technology developed in the West. The importance of this advantage has become less pronounced recently because of the narrowing of the technological gap between the U. S. S. R. and the most industrially advanced Western countries. Independent technological progress in the U. S. S. R. has been rapid and significant in recent years, particularly in areas of high interest to them such as military hardware and those industries closely associated with military production. The promise of future advances in technology by both Western and Soviet engineers and scientists remains bright (e. g., in further automation), so that, presumably, Soviet authorities would still be able to rely on significant technological improvements to boost their industrial output. It may be worth noting that some of the progress which lies ahead is not just one of introducing new technology, but of finding the right balance of techniques to yield lowest cost, not always easy for the Russians in the absence of good cost data and the market mechanism. Further, there are still many opportunities for applying existing technology in relatively backward activities of industry, for example, in auxiliary industrial processes and services as well as in some of the technologically starved consumer-goods branches of industry. Therefore, although a slowing up of technological improvements may be expected in Soviet industry, its inhibiting effects on growth of Soviet industrial output are not expected to be substantial. Likewise, no slowing up of United States growth as a result of technological lags need be anticipated either.

2. Labor force

(a) Volume of employment.—In sharp contrast to the earlier trends (see ch. IV), the total labor force in the U. S. S. R. is expected to increase substantially less during the next 5 years than during the preceding 5 years. This might incorrectly suggest that the industrial labor force also will remain virtually constant for some time to come. But because in 1955 Soviet industry employed only about 20 percent of the total labor force, increases in industrial employment could come

---

[20] Similar discussion of industrial prospects in the United States is available in such sources as: The Sustaining Economic Forces Ahead, materials prepared for the Joint Committee on the Economic Report by the committee staff, Joint Committee Print, 82d Cong., 2d sess., 1952; and Potential Economic Growth of the United States During the Next Decade, materials prepared for the Joint Committee on the Economic Report by the committee staff, Joint Committee Print, 83d Cong., 2d sss., 1954.

not only from new entrants into the labor force but also from shifts of presently employed workers out of other sectors into industry. The extent of the increase in industrial employment will, therefore, depend on a number of interrelated factors which render precise projection hazardous. Those factors are: (a) the success of the Soviet measures for raising both labor productivity and output in agriculture so as to release farm labor for nonagricultural work; or, alternatively, a Soviet decision to import more agricultural products to accomplish the same result; (b) the future availability of urban housing and other facilities; (c) the realization of increases in labor productivity in other sectors, such as services, government, commerce, and transportation, so as to reduce their needs for manpower; (d) the priority accorded to industrial output compared to output of other sectors; and (e) demobilization of military personnel. Judged in part from past Soviet experiences, including the fact that industrial employment has expanded at rates much faster than those for total employment, and from fragmentary evidence on continuing recruitment of manpower for industry,[21] it seems likely that industrial employment will continue to increase at significant rates during the next 5 years or so.[22] This is not to imply that such recruitment will be painless or automatic in character. Further, these rates are unlikely to be as great as the 5.8 and 4.2 percent annual average rates of increase for industrial employment realized during the periods 1928–55 and 1950–55.[23] The Soviet Government itself has projected lower rates for the future. Reasons to be developed in chapter IV include the relative slowing of new entrants into the labor force occasioned both by reduced birth rates during and after war and extended schooling.

(b) *Labor productivity.*—The quality of the Soviet labor force in industry has improved steadily, as education and training have become more widely available. Nonetheless the apparent (i. e., official) rate of increase of industrial output per worker has declined in recent years, except 1954 and 1955, perhaps because technological advances and increases in fixed capital per worker may have been less rapid than in the past. Such a decline normally has accompanied industrial maturation, and because the current rates are still high by the standards of most countries, some further decline in rates of growth of industrial labor productivity in the U. S. S. R. does not seem unreasonable. If it should occur, however, the Soviet rate of growth in the next 5 years at least probably will not decline to the United States level, for the following reasons: (1) Soviet investment is expected to continue at a high rate, and in a direction conducive to

[21] The statements of Khrushchev and other leaders that the needs of urban employers can be met largely through employment of present urban inhabitants, and the concurrent recruitment for agriculture in the new areas need not be inconsistent with the above evidence. The agricultural recruitment is limited and selective and does not represent a real reversal of the more general trends.

[22] This judgment is reinforced by discussion of certain aspects of some of the above factors throughout this report. In ch. III, the conclusion is reached that some shifts of labor from agriculture to nonagriculture will take place within the next few years and that the flow will be stepped up probably by about 1960. Industrial output is likely to continue to be emphasized in the future; and some increase in the allocation to urban housing is expected also—which will facilitate the rural-urban flow of manpower, but will divert some of it to construction activities. Finally, some increases in labor productivity in other economic sectors are expected, but whether they will be large enough to more than offset the expected increases in output of these sectors cannot be estimated at this time.

[23] Derived from data in Narodnoe khoziaistvo SSSR, Statisticheskii sbornik, 1956, op. cit., p. 190.

rapid economic growth; (2) opportunities for rapid productivity advances are still great, especially in auxiliary industrial processes and services, and in capital-starved consumer-goods industries; (3) less, rather than more, capital may be required per unit of output now that the Soviet Union has somewhat improved its technological and managerial base;[24] (4) training of the industrial labor force, including engineers, is planned to continue at a rapid pace; (5) gradual rectification of the "imbalance" between males and females in the industrial labor force also might contribute to greater labor productivity as more young people enter the labor force; and (6) the incentives of workers to produce more may be expected to increase concurrent with greater availability of consumer goods and the amelioration of some of the harshest features of Stalinism.

There are counterarguments, of course, which temper these judgments, but in net balance, relatively high Soviet rates, as suggested, seem likely. Some of the opposing elements to the previous points are considered in the following discussion on capital equipment, raw materials, and management.

3. Capital equipment

(a) *Availability of equipment.*—The absolute net increases in capital equipment available to Soviet industry undoubtedly will be greater than ever before, provided the basic assumptions stated at the outset of this section are realized. The percentage increases in net Soviet investment in industry, however, may fall to somewhat lower levels, for the following reasons:

(1) Change in the rate of overall investment:

The percentage rate of total investment may fall if, for political considerations, Soviet authorities conclude it is expedient to provide a sharply expanded volume of consumer or military goods quickly. Expansion of the military sector in particular would require new analysis, because such expansion could and probably would cut more heavily into investment than into consumption: in the short run it appears that military production can be increased more rapidly by such a diversion, and also the consumption levels in the U. S. S. R. are still so low that a new squeeze might be thought politically unwise. Regarding a possible decision to increase the relative production of consumer goods (to an unknown extent), it is entirely possible that some such decision has already taken place and it is allowed for in the analysis. That decision could be reflected initially in stable investment rates for both the entire economy and industry, or in a lower rate for one or both. Lower rates would suggest that consumer goods output was to be increased directly and immediately; stable rates, that there might be an intermediate stage during which investment would be directed to the manufacture of producer goods for later manufacture of consumer rather than more producer goods. Because of the above considerations, increases in capital investment for industry as a whole, and particularly for heavy industry, might well be at a significantly reduced rate, thus slowing up the rate of growth of industrial output in the future.

---

[24] On the last-named point, cf. the remarks by W. Leontief, in Soviet Economic Growth, op. cit., pp. 32–33.

On the other hand, if political and other consideration should dictate a reduction in the military sector, investment might well be the principal beneficiary because of the apparently greater ease of shifting to or from the investment and military sectors than to or from the consumption and military sector (both because of the nature of production processes and institutional factors). The effect of a sharp increase in the rate of investment to industry could boost the future rate of growth of Soviet industrial output very substantially. The likelihood of a sharp shift of effort of that nature, however, seems remote at this time.

(2) Diversion of investment to other sectors, principally agriculture and urban housing:

Most productive agricultural land in the Soviet Union already has been utilized (see ch. III); therefore, the imperative need for increased agricultural production can be met only by extensive working of marginal lands, whose very location in more remote areas will require heavy investments, or by more intensive efforts to improve yields of previously cultivated areas.[25] Both programs would involve heavy agricultural investments in machinery, fertilizers, irrigation, and even housing and transport, as well as increased consumer goods for agricultural workers. There is this to be said, however, for the problem of investment in agriculture. Much of the former effort was to replace either the losses in animal draft power that attended collectivization or the losses occasioned by war. Even maintaining the past rates of investment in agriculture therefore, in the absence of the former problem, should yield some tangible increases in agricultural output. Regarding the diversion of investment to overcome the acute shortages in urban housing and other facilities, no crash program to remedy these shortages is anticipated but some diversion of investment to this sector already has taken place, and further increases are not unlikely.

(3) Increased demand for replacement capital.

There is a new recognition on the part of Soviet authorities that high output may require attention not only to replacing wornout plant but writing off some high-cost plant as obsolescent when newer facilities can offer marked cost savings or much greater outputs. This has long been recognized in the United States, but some Communist writers previously contended that the problem of obsolescence was not important in a Socialist society. Now there is a greater recognition of the technological justification for classification of some facilities as obsolescent. However, so long as the rate of industrial investment remains high, and total output continues to increase rapidly—as is likely to happen—the absolute volume of new net investment in Soviet industry would keep pace with increases in existing capital stock, so that the effect of increased demand for replacement capital would be insufficient to depress new net investment substantially. It has been noted that increases in capital stock in Soviet industry might result in a higher ratio of capital stock to annual investment; and if so, a larger and larger share of new investment would be required simply to replace wornout or obsolete equipment, and the proportion of net to gross investment as well as the proportion of net investment to total capital stock would fall.

---

[25] Increased imports of agricultural products is an alternative; but it seems unlikely, for reasons discussed in ch. III, that imports would be increased to the extent necessary to avoid the need for greatly increased investments in agriculture.

(4) Capital windfalls:

Capital windfalls from World War II cannot be expected to recur, if the assumptions of this section are realized. War booty was acquired in both Europe and Manchuria, but those opportunities are now exhausted.

(5) Capital exports:

Capital exports to Red China in particular and to some of the captive countries or the uncommitted areas of the world may be important to the political aims of the Soviet Government. Event in Poland and Hungary almost certainly are forcing reversals of trade flows to the Soviet Union. These exports cannot help but reduce the availability of certain kinds of goods in the Soviet Union in the short run even if the return flow of materials relieves other strains on the Soviet economy.

(b) *Productivity of capital equipment.*—If Soviet authorities have allocated investments rationally, it could be assumed that they have supplied capital equipment first to those industries where capital would be most productive. However, although the assumption might be true with respect to the basic operations within heavy industry, it does not appear to be correct with respect to auxiliary versus basic work in heavy industry, or light versus heavy industry. Therefore, capital productivity probably could be increased by diverting investment from the basic operations to the auxiliary work within heavy industry, and in the short run, it could be increased also by allocating a larger share of industrial investment to consumer goods manufacturing industries—though success in the latter reallocation would depend to some extent on prior success in raising agricultural output.

4. Raw materials

Depletion of richer mineral reserves would increase costs by adding to the requirements for both labor and capital in mining, while depletion of the more accessible resources would result in higher transportation costs. The extra equipment and manpower needed here would, therefore, not be available for increasing output in other branches of industry. However, new reserves constantly are being discovered, and there are usually possibilities for substitution, in part owing to technological advances, so that although some depletion, especially the more accessible Soviet resources, has in fact occurred, this factor is believed to be of less importance, except perhaps for nonferrous metals, than would otherwise be indicated. But that depletion is a problem is undeniable from the size of the effort entailed in developing new sources in the East, with wage differentials to encourage workers to go there, and the investment in new railways and power sources.

5. Management and direction from higher Soviet authorities

Bungling, ineptness, and sometimes irrationality on the part of Soviet managers and planners seem widespread, judged from extensive reading of the Soviet press and industry journals. And indeed obstacles to innovation and innovators, and to honest, efficient operation in general are not only considerable, but they seem to be an inherent part of the Soviet economic system. One almost wonders how production increases could have been realized under those circumstances.

The true state of affairs is difficult if not impossible to ascertain, but a considered judgment is that despite the grave deficiencies, conceded by the Russians themselves, a managerial class which is capable of functioning reasonably effectively under Soviet conditions has arisen in the U. S. S. R. during the past several decades. There seems no reason to believe that this group will be any less adept in the future than in the past; and, in view of the announced greater decentralization of planning and controls in general, there is some reason to believe that it will function more rather than less effectively, since plant managers are increasingly men who have had considerable high-quality professional training, both academic and in actual production. But it is much too early to judge what the net effects of the Khrushchev decentralization plan will be. A planned society cannot stand too great a dispersion of authority, or the component parts will be working at cross purposes. Further, it should be noted that there has been no significant relaxation apparent in the Soviet drive on all levels toward higher output as the prime goal of the Soviet economy.[26] Increasing emphasis now may have been placed on qualitative improvements as well as on greater specialization of production by each factory;[27] and there appears to be some slight letup in the emphasis on producer versus consumer goods in response. But it is not clear whether this is due to a widespread impatience for realization now of some of the heralded fruits of communism[28] or whether it is primarily to give more incentive to workers to increase production of military and investment goods, as before. But so long as the primary incentives to managers and workers are based on fulfillment of increasingly high output plans, and so long as these are backed up by the highest Soviet authorities in investment, bonus, and other decisions, the stage is set for continued high increases in industrial output.

In balancing the differential effects of the expected changes in the above-discussed factors, it is important to recognize their interrelationship. For example, a diversion of investment from industry to urban housing and agriculture might lead to larger industrial employment and consequent increases in output, but the industrial output increases might be smaller than those which would have occurred if the original workers in industry had been provided with more or newer capital equipment, instead of diverting the investments to agriculture and housing. On the other hand, if the new housing were reserved as rewards for higher output, the net effect of the shift in resources might still be favorable to industrial production. Or, approaching the matter from another point of view, failure of Soviet authorities to provide more adequate housing might result in greater (or lower) industrial production losses than would take place as a result of diversion of

[26] The rates of increase of industrial production planned for the period 1955–60 are approximately the same as those originally planned for the period 1951–55.

[27] Regarding the emphasis on quality improvements, similar emphasis has been noted during other earlier periods. Without further evidence, therefore, it cannot be concluded that such an emphasis would conflict seriously with the main goal of increasing output. Regarding the emphasis on increasing specialization of production, similar comments seem to be in order. In any event, the effects of increased specialization would be mixed: increased output eventually would result from it, but in order to achieve significantly greater specialization, more reliable supply lines would have to be assured, and this would conflict with the all-out priority on increasing industrial output. Therefore, only slow progress will probably be made on the problem of increasing specialization.

[28] See discussion under point C3 (1), this chapter. Note also that diversion of capital and manpower from producer to consumer goods industries might even step up the Soviet rate of industrial growth in the short run, for reasons alluded to earlier in this section, even though the long-run effects would be the reverse.

investment from industry. If, however, the diversion of capital from industry to housing and agriculture is small,[29] the net inhibiting effects on the rate of growth of Soviet industrial output would be small.

The above examination of the factors influencing Soviet industrial output suggests that the rate of growth of Soviet industrial output during the next 5 to 10 years will slow down perceptibly, but it does not suggest that the slowdown will be sharp enough necessarily to cause the rate of increase to fall to the current level in the United States (near 4½ percent per annum) or even to a rate much below about 7 or 8 percent per annum on the average.[30]

TRANSPORTATION

A. A COMPARATIVE DESCRIPTION

1. Total volume of freight carried

Official statistics of total performance of the freight transportation systems of the two countries (see table 6) imply that by 1955, the Soviet Union was apparently at about two-thirds the level of the United States, leaving out of the comparison any questions of composition of the services rendered, or qualitative differences. If this were true, it would be striking because the Soviet economy has a total economic output about one-third that of the United States. Singling out railways, the chief means used, there appears to be little difference in the average length of haul (766 kilometers in the U. S. S. R. in 1955 compared to 695 in the United States in 1954). This would imply that much more freight or a heavier tonnage of freight is moved in proportion to the total output of the economy in the U. S. S. R., but it is hard to accept so great a difference. Perhaps widening the United States comparison to include other methods of transportation would pull down our average length of haul compared to that quoted for rail, so that the explanation of the Soviet disproportionately large ton-kilometer total would be a result of longer average hauls. Even so, the apparent high Soviet ton-kilometer figure is curious and may imply noncomparability with United States reporting procedures. Not all Westerners agree as to the causes for the Soviet high total.

One possible explanation for the size of the Soviet figure could lie in the reporting of ton-kilometers not in terms of freight actually moved, but according to rated weight-carrying capacities of cars with consequent overstatement of freight tonnage. On the other hand, the Soviet authorities claim to base their reports on waybill weights multiplied by official mileages, so that allowing for some circuitous routing, the actual Soviet ton-kilometer figure might run in 1955 about 65 billion higher than shown in the table.

There are other corrections which would have to be made to improve the comparison. Soviet practice in compiling motor truck ton-kilometers is definitely at variance with our practice on two counts.

[29] Actually the increases may come in large part as a result of those sectors receiving the same share of a larger total investment.
[30] The Sixth Five-Year Plan (Pravda, January 15. 1956, p. 1) called for an increase in gross output of 65 percent for the period 1955 to 1960, or 10.5 percent per annum on the average. Making some allowances for differences in concept of the measure and possible underfulfillment of plans, the range of 7 to 8 percent per annum is not impossible of attainment. But prediction is perilous and the changes of early 1957 suggest possible revision of the original plan and substituting a more modest proposal. However, no revision had been announced even as late as May 1957.

In the first place, they view the measure as one necessary to setting work standards rather than as a simple product. For this reason, local truck hauling is multiplied by a factor of eight before being added into the total including longer distance hauling. Secondly, because the Soviet figures attempt to measure all local hauling by truck, they are not comparable with United States intercity trucking data. Intercity trucking is still so small in the Soviet Union, it would almost be proper to eliminate the reported truck figure from the total for purposes of comparison. Still another adjustment that should be made in the interest of comparability would be to add to the United States figure that freight which is nonrevenue in character. The Soviet figure could be increased by an estimate for Caspian Sea traffic, and other coastwise traffic. In that case, United States coastwise traffic should be added, too.

These several adjustments have not been made in the tables of official data presented simply because they involve considerable estimating. If they were made, however, the Soviet ton-kilometer total compared with the United States would no longer be two thirds the level of the United States but might be closer to 60 percent, or even less. Partially offsetting this reduction, however, is the report that the Russians understate actual length of hauls, and that our average hauls are distinctly shorter than the rail-only average. We begin to come back to an explanation of their relatively high ton-kilometer figure as caused by longer hauls, a natural disadvantage in a country with economic activity scattered along the long belt from the Polish border to the Pacific.

Soviet projections of their traffic and some estimates on future United States traffic are presented for interest, but they would require extensive evaluation before they could be accepted seriously.

TABLE 6.—*Volume of freight traffic in the U. S. S. R. and the United States*

[In billions of metric ton-kilometers]

SOVIET UNION

Year	Rail-ways	Rivers and canals	Great Lakes	Motor-trucks	Pipe lines	Aircraft	Total
1913	76.4	28.9		0.1	0.4		105.8
1928	93.4	15.9		.2	.6		110.1
1940	415.0	35.9		8.9	3.9		463.7
1950	602.3	45.9		20.1	5.0		673.3
1955	970.9	67.4		42.5	14.0		1,094.8
1956	1,076.0	70.0		54.8			
1960 plan	1,378.7	121.3		85.0	84.0		1,669.0

UNITED STATES

Year	Rail-ways	Rivers and canals	Great Lakes	Motor-trucks	Pipe lines	Aircraft	Total
1890	111						
1913	440						
1928	637						
1930	569	13	(112)	30	41		765
1940	554	33	140	91	87		905
1944	1,090	46	173	85	194		1,588
1948	945	63	173	169	175		1,525
1950	871	75	163	248	189		1,546
1955	922	143	173	330	297	1	1,866
1960 (estimated)							2,327
1975 (estimated)	1,168	292	(226)	876	438	4	3,004

GENERAL NOTE.—Limitations in comparability are discussed in the accompanying text. Note also that coastwise water shipping as well as overseas shipping is not reported.

Soviet sources

Tsentral'noe statisicheskoe upravlenie pri Sovete Ministrov SSSR, Narodnoe khoziaistvo SSSR, Statisticheskii sbornik, Gosstatizdat, Moskva, 1956, with pages as follows: Railways, page 177; rivers and canals, page 181; motor trucks, page 183; pipelines, derived from percentages on page 174. Air freight is too small to affect the totals, and is not reported. Freight traffic on the Caspian and similar bodies of water which correspond to our Great Lakes is not available separately, and is not included. (1913 rail ton kilometers with 1939 borders was 65.7.) The 1956 data are taken by the United States Department of Commerce from Soviet sources.

United States sources

All data have been compiled by the Interstate Commerce Commission and are reported in its annual reports, in Transport Economics, and in various special bulletins: Some series undergo revision and are published with changing inclusions and exclusions. In the interest of simplicity, secondary sources have been used in compiling this table, with sufficient spot checking to original reports to insure best continuity possible.

Railways: 1890 to 1928 from Department of Commerce, Historical Statistics of the United States 1789–1945, series K–45, covers class I, II, III railways, revenue traffic, exclusive of mail and express. 1930–44 from Association of Western Railways, Railroad Facts (Chicago) 1954, page 5; 1948, Interstate Commerce Commission, 63d Annual Report, 1949, page 14; 1950, Interstate Commerce Commission, Transport Economics (October 1956), page 6. All data from 1930 on includes mail and express, and revenue traffic only.

Rivers and canals: 1930 from Association of Western Railways, Railroad Facts (Chicago) 1954, page 5; 1940–50 in Association of American Railroads, Railroad Transportation (Washington) 1954, page 38; 1955 in American Waterways Operators, New Dimensions in Transportation (Washington) 1956, page 35.

Great Lakes: United States domestic traffic only for 1930 given in Association of Western Railways, Railroad Facts (Chicago) 1954, page 5, and revised upward by committee staff to make comparable with figures for later years; 1940–48 in Mississippi Valley Association, Our Waterways (St. Louis), 1950, page 26; 1950 and 1955 in American Waterways Operators, New Dimensions in Transportation (Washington) 1956, page 35.

Motor Truck: 1930 in Association of Western Railways, Railroad Facts (Chicago) 1954, page 5; 1940–50 in Department of Commerce, Statistical Abstract of the United States, 1956, page 557; 1955 in Interstate Commerce Commission, Transport Economics (October 1956), page 6.

Pipeline: 1930 in Association of Western Railways, Railroad Facts (Chicago) 1954, page 5; 1940–50 in Department of Commerce, Statistical Abstract of the United States, 1956, page 557; 1955 in Interstate Commerce Comission, Transport Economics (October 1956), page 6.

Aircraft: Data are too low to be shown until 1955, which figure is from idem.

Figures in parentheses are estimated in part by committee staff.

1960 estimate of Charles Roos of the Econometric Institute reported in Railway Age, Centennial Issue, September 1956, page 159.

1975 estimate of Arthur Jansen of W. E. Burnett & Co., in Investment Digest for March 19, 1956.

All United States data converted from short-ton-miles to metric-ton-kilometers before totaling.

2. Division among different forms of transportation

In both countries, railways have the most important role in providing ton-kilometer freight service. In the Soviet Union, over 80 percent of freight ton-kilometers is carried by the railways, despite the intensive efforts to utilize the great rivers of that country. In the next 5 years, facilities for river, road, and especially pipeline transport are expected to undergo the greatest relative expansion, but railways will continue to play a little changed and still dominant role. In the United States, the position of railways has declined both relatively

and absolutely, particularly because of the expansion of both roads
and pipelines. The resulting contrast is marked: One of Soviet
extreme dependence on railways and one of better balance and alterna-
tives in the United States. It is interesting to observe that currently, the Soviet railway system claims to be providing just about
the same ton-kilometer service as are the railways of this country, but
this is still less than our peak in World War II. The water transport
figures are not really comparable, as the service on the Great Lakes
dominates our statistics, and no counterpart figures are available for
the Soviet Union. As explained above, there are not available reliable
figures for comparing the coastwise trade of the two countries. The
Caspian Sea trade, in a sense, is like our Great Lakes traffic but is primarily for the movement of oil; even if it could be measured it would
not match the freight ton-kilometers worked on our lakes. Perhaps
12 to 15 times as many ton-kilometers are moved by pipeline in this
country. The motortruck statistics show a ratio of sevenfold as many
ton-kilometers in the United States, but as explained above, this
vastly understates our lead, when one adjusts for intracity traffic and
for special Soviet weighting of their figures. Also, not all farm-to-
market traffic in the United States is tabulated, while the Soviet figures do include estimates for such traffic.

TABLE 7.—*The railway networks in the U. S. S. R. and the United States*

[In thousand kilometers of track]

Year	Soviet Union	United States
1870		85.1
1900		311.0
1913	[1] 71.7	401.9
1928	76.9	401.1
1940	106.1	376.0
1950	116.9	360.1
1955	120.7	[2] 355.6

[1] Soviet 1913 mileage in 1939 borders 58.5.
[2] Refers to 1954.

Soviet Union source

Tsentral'noe statisticheskoe upravlenie pri Sovete Ministrov SSSR, Narodnoe
khoziaistvo SSSR, Statisticheskii sbornik, Gosstatizdat, Moskva, 1956, p. 177.

United States source

Department of Commerce, Bureau of the Census, Historical Statistics of the
United States, 1789–1945, series K–1 for 1870, K–29 for 1900–40.
Department of Commerce, Bureau of the Census, Statistical Abstract of the
United States, 1956 edition, p. 559, for 1950–55.

3. Significance of railway network size

Because of the overriding importance of railways, it is worth examining the comparative size of the two railway systems. (See
table 7.) The Soviet Union geographically is almost three times
the size of this country. Their railway network is only one-third
the length of ours, or even smaller than our system in 1880. There is
little point in calculating length of line per square kilometer because
systems must be viewed in terms of need for service rather than in
terms of abstract averages. It is evident, nonetheless, that the United
States will have little occasion to build entirely new railway lines;
rather, this country has been tearing up track which is no longer

needed. In contrast, the Soviet Union has very clear needs for additional construction, and the principal question has been the relative priority of these construction projects compared with other needs of that country. Of course, the United States has continued to make substantial new investments in improved plant even though line mileage is falling.

According to the figures presented, the average volume of freight moved per kilometer of track in the Soviet system is about three times as high as that in the United States. This is partly because the Soviet Union has fewer alternate routes and fewer branch lines which in this country tend to have light traffic. Another part of the explanation lies in incomparable statistics, as discussed above.

In the period of railroad construction in the United States, it was common for railways to be built in anticipation of traffic, and our geographical growth was speeded thereby. In contrast, although the Soviet Union continues to project many future railway plans, in practice they seem barely to keep up with minimum needs, and other plans of the economy are given higher priorities for completion. Soviet authorities have long expressed as their goal adequate modernization of railways, but fulfillment has been lagging. If in fact they move anything like the tons per kilometer of line they claim, it is small wonder they are stressing new plans for double tracking, automatic train control, and electrification of many key routes, to accommodate this volume.

4. Qualitative comparisons between the two systems

By United States standards, the Russians have tended to mine their railways, practicing less than adequate maintenance. Not having undergone, as yet, the diesel revolution of this country, and only recently moving toward wider use of the automatic coupler and airbrake, and increased size of cars, the Soviet system is out of date. Many steam locomotives predate the 1917 revolution, and some of those that are newer were based on Czarist designs. Typically they lack automatic stokers, superheaters, and boosters. Not only is the inventory of freight cars smaller, but many are still 2-axle cars of low carrying capacity, and it will be years before 4-axle cars replace them. Roadbeds generally are below United States standards for anything like similar volumes of traffic, with lighter rails as well as less prompt tie renewal and ballast cleaning. Yards and stations also are generally below our standards, with few new automated yards being completed, either. There would be little point to installing such yards until modern couplers and brakes are universal. Signaling is on the whole not modernized, although a few trunk lines have improved equipment. Within the Soviet Union itself, the line clearance gage is generous, which allows easier movement of outsize industrial and military equipment as compared with almost all other countries, but this is of greater strategic significance than it is an economic asset. The present generally prevailing low quality level with its inefficiencies is reason enough for the Soviet Government to want to take vigorous steps to close part of the gap between the quality of their system and that of the United States. It remains to be seen, in light of past delays, whether they will complete on schedule their ambitious **plans to reballast and lay** heavier rails, to introduce electric **signaling** and train control, to electrify main line and suburban routes, and to replace obsolete steam power with new diesels or turbines elsewhere.

5. Passenger travel in the two countries

In total reported passenger kilometers, the United States supplies about six times the total travel, despite its smaller population. (See table 8.) Here again, though the figures are not really comparable, United States data cover intercity travel plus suburban commutation by rail. The Soviet data include more traffic which we would count as urban. The biggest difference between the two countries can be accounted for largely in terms of the United States use of the private automobile which is hardly a factor in the Soviet Union. The automobile in this country accounts for almost nine-tenths of passenger travel. In the Soviet Union, no effort is made to publish statistics on this means as they would be insignificant. Railway travel in contrast shows a different importance. The Russians today are providing almost as much railway service on their system of only one-third the trackage as the United States did at the peak of World War II. Our own memories of wartime crowding give a clue to what is the standard Soviet condition in lower-class cars. Soviet current volume is 2½ to 3 times that of the United States. Waterways in both countries play a small role, about equal in absolute terms. Bus travel in the Soviet Union is coming up rapidly to about half the volume of this country, in part accounted for by the statistical differences mentioned above, but it will have to wait on road construction in the Soviet Union if it is to be widely used. Soviet air travel is growing at a rate not quite as high as that of this country—in overall volume is less than one-tenth the United States amount. Most of the equipment and the volume of travel are similar to what was prevalent in the United States 15 years earlier. However, this may change, too, as new jets and turbo-props corresponding to the new planes being built in the United States come into service in quantity.

TABLE 8.—*Passenger traffic in the U. S. S. R. and the United States*

SOVIET UNION

[In billion passenger kilometers]

Year	Railways	Buses	River	Air	Total
1913	30.3		1.4		31.7
1928	24.5		2.1		26.6
1940	98.0	3.4	3.8	0.2	105.4
1950	88.0	5.2	2.7	1.2	97.1
1955	141.4	20.9	3.6	2.7	168.6

UNITED STATES

Year	Railways	Interurban	Buses	Inland waterways	Air	Private autos	Total
1900	26						
1913	56						
1929	50	(3)	11	2		248	314
1940	38	2	16	2	2	395	455
1944	154	3	44	4	4	243	452
1948	66	1	39	3	10	462	581
1950	51	1	42	2	16	648	760
1955	46	(1)	40	3	37	943	1,071
1965					64		
1975	64		(63)	(3)	129	1,448	1,707

GENERAL NOTE.—Limitations in comparability are discussed in the accompanying text. Coastwise water and overseas water and air travel are not included.

Soviet Union sources

Tsentral'noe statisticheskoe upravlenie pri Sovete Ministrov SSSR Narodnoe khoziaistvo SSSR, Statisticheskii sbornik, Gosstatizdat, Moskva, 1956, as follows: Railways, page 177; Buses, page 183; River, page 181; Air, Derived from percentages on page 175, by the formula:

$$\frac{\text{percent of air traffic}}{\text{percent of rail traffic}} \times \text{rail traffic}$$

Data are not available for intercity travel by private-type automobiles, but such travel is probably negligible.

No separate data are available for passenger traffic on the Caspian Sea and similar bodies of water which would correspond to the American Great Lakes.

1913 rail traffic shown is within present borders. Based on 1939 borders, the 1913 amount was 25.2.

United States sources

All data are reported by the Interstate Commerce Commission, usually in annual reports, and also in revised form or preliminary form in Transport Economics and various special bulletins.

In this instance, secondary sources have been used for convenience, and spot checked against original reports to insure consistency so far as possible.

Railways: in Department of Commerce, Historical Statistics of the United States, 1789–1945 and its 1952 supplement, Series K–41 for 1890 through 1950; Transport Economics (November 1956) page 5 for 1955.

Interurbans: 1940–50 in Association of American Railroads, Railroad Transportation (Washington) 1954, page 39.

Buses: 1929–55 in National Association of Motor Bus Operators, Bus Facts (Washington) 1956, page 8.

Inland waterways: Idem.

Air: Idem.

Private autos: Idem.

Projections are by Arthur Jansen of W. E. Burnett & Co., in Investment Digest (March 19, 1956).

Data in parentheses estimated by committee staff.

United States passenger-mile data converted before addition, to passenger-kilometers.

B. GENERAL ASSESSMENT OF THE PLACE OF TRANSPORTATION

1. *Overall assessment of transportation*

The statistics on transportation which have been presented are more useful for describing trends within each of the two countries concerned than they are for purposes of making absolute comparisons. This has been explained partly on methodological grounds, and partly in terms of qualitative differences. To move the assessment into more general terms, it seems logical to assume that Soviet transport services performed in the aggregate are probably roughly proportionate to the general level of Soviet industry and agriculture as compared with the United States. Thus, if the absolute overall comparison is about one-third as high production in the Soviet Union, transport, too, may be in the same range. This does involve balancing several imponderables. On the one hand, the great size of the Soviet Union, even with the attempts to decentralize industry involves some longer hauling, but specific statistical comparisons require some estimating. As to how a system, which is starved for adequate amounts of equipment can accomplish the movement of so many ton-kilometers, it is possible that some Soviet economies in transport which speed car turnaround and simplify freight handling would result from the nature of the Soviet economy. Emphasis on heavy industry and standardization should make for a greater percentage of bulk freight and routine standard packing and handling.

It is also possible that the performance record of Soviet transport is brought about in part by much more lavish use of labor, as well as intensive use of equipment. But the very fact that there is so much talk in the Soviet plans of need for modernization suggests that Soviet statistics which imply much greater efficiency in transport than that of the United States must be discounted.[31] Still, the Soviet Union is continuing in the sixth 5-year plan the postwar policy of relatively modest investments in transportation, compared with their needs.

Observation of actual practice in the Soviet Union shows that the transportation system is limited in its capacities and backward. For example, because of obsolete motive power, trains are much lighter than in this country. If the volume of freight traffic on lines really ran at three times the United States level, the number of trains might have to be six or more times as great. This would require double track or very advanced centralized train control, but in fact manual methods of signaling are typical on much of the system, and it is unlikely that traffic could be kept moving to attain the reported goals. Part of the answer undoubtedly lies in difficulties of average comparisons which are not appropriate, for traffic on many branch lines in the United States is so light that our main lines are not necessarily less busy than the overworked Soviet lines.

Even if car turnaround is shorter in the Soviet Union, to account for the high ton-kilometer volume produced with a limited number of smaller capacity cars on the average, it is improbable that car turn-around time is as short as reported. This would be so even with plentiful use of labor to replace scarce fork lift trucks, for freight yards are obsolete and train speeds are low.

At the same time that a healthy skepticism is shown regarding Soviet transport attainments reported in Soviet terms but viewed in United States concepts, the pendulum must not be swung too far. Years of making do with inadequate facilities have enabled Soviet transport organizations to continue in the face of adversity to render at least essential services. For example, severe winters cut seasonal rail capacity, but on occasion tracks over rivers are laid on ice to replace ferries. In World War II, railway tank cars were even pushed into water and towed like barges where enemy operations had cut regular rail routes.

2. Relation of Soviet transportation to the economy as a whole

The interest in Soviet transportation evidenced in this study relates of course to whether or not the system will inhibit the overall growth of the Soviet economy. Chapter III which follows will face a similar judgment on the place of agriculture, another retarded sector of the economy.

In summary, Soviet transport limitations to date have not prevented the attainment of the industrial progress described earlier in this chapter. It is a moot question whether a better allocation of capital resources would have included greater expenditure on transport, not

---

[31] Representative Thomas B. Curtis, in the Congressional Record of February 25, 1957, p. 2257, discussed in greater detail the shortcomings of Soviet transport.

only to modernize railways but particularly to improve roads. It is quite possible that the pattern of allocation which the Soviet authorities have followed is consistent with the attainment of the particular goals for heavy industry and military strength sought.

Again, it is also clear that the Russian consumer generally has not been favored with comfortable travel, but this was not an immediate Soviet ambition. Officials and other privileged people can ride on the few de luxe trains. The average citizen is restricted by income and in most previous years by the internal passport system from doing much general traveling about the country, other than on certain prescribed vacations for workers and in the shifting of people to new jobs. Ordinary trains are very crowded. Millions of unfortunates during the course of the Soviet period have been moved locked in boxcars, with no comforts at all.

For the future, the Soviet authorities speak of a modernized and extended railway system, of improved waterways, of better highways, more pipelines, and world-ranging turbine aircraft, not to mention the use of nuclear propulsion. Before any of these are realized on an extensive scale, the Soviet economy will have to set much higher priorities on their accomplishment than it has in the past.

Khrushchev on May 7, 1957, cited unreasonable and wasteful cross hauling and other transport uses as a reason for his plan of regionalization. This speech sharpens understanding of the critical relation between transport and industry. Transport can absorb great quantities of fuel, materials, and labor. If the new plans for regional responsibility are really effective in saving transport, the consequences would be important both for relieving pressure on other parts of the economy, and for making the present transport system more nearly adequate without heavy new expenditures.

CHAPTER III

AGRICULTURE

Agriculture has often been referred to as a retarded sector of the Soviet economy by Western specialists, and though in a different context, by Communist Party Secretary Khrushchev.[1] Both Western and Soviet observers also see agriculture as an inhibiting factor in future Soviet economic growth. There is little doubt about the accuracy of the first observation, and there is also little doubt that past Soviet failures in agriculture will inhibit overall economic growth in the future, as they have in the past, regardless of whether or not the correctible shortcomings are remedied. There is considerable disagreement, however, as to the extent of agriculture's inhibiting effect. In a speech at Leningrad on May 22, 1957, Khrushchev predicted early advances of vast proportions in Soviet agricultural output. The likelihoods are assessed in this chapter.

In evaluating past Soviet failures and successes and future prospects, as contrasted to trends and levels in United States agriculture, it is important (1) to establish the facts on agricultural production in both countries, and (2) to compare the resources now devoted to or potentially available for agriculture (namely, land, equipment, manpower, and a number of others grouped for convenience under management) and their utilization. Lest the evaluation be too narrowly based, however, it is important first to view Soviet agriculture and policies in the perspective of the general economic and political purposes of Soviet authorities facing the necessity for resolving agricultural and agriculture-related problems. As was described in chapter I, there is ample evidence that Soviet authorities faced a number of such problems in 1928, the beginning of the period under review. Some of the problems, together with the presumed Soviet purposes in each instance, and the results of Soviet policies by 1955 or earlier, are summarized below:

(1) To obtain regularly a sufficient volume of agricultural products to feed and clothe an urban population which was expected to grow rapidly (though not so rapidly as actually occurred).

The "regular" aspect of those needs required either some form of control over agriculture or the offering of favorable terms to the peasants. Soviet authorities chose the former policy, presumably, because they feared the individualistic tendencies of an independent peasantry, and also because they could not pay high prices in real terms for agricultural products without increasing production of consumer goods rapidly and, consequently, slowing down their rate of industrialization.

---

[1] See, for example, various books and articles on Soviet agriculture by Dr. Naum Jasny, including his Socialized Agriculture of the U. S. S. R. (Stanford University Press, 1949, 837 pages) ; the writings of Dr. Lazar Volin, including his A Survey of Soviet Russian Agriculture (U. S. Department of Agriculture Monograph No. 5, 1951, 194 pages).

The principal problem has been resolved by Soviet authorities at what might be termed a bare minimum level of success; that is, put negatively, the drive toward urbanization and increased military power was not thwarted by lack of basic necessities of agricultural origin.   Although supplies of animal products have been consistently inadequate measured by almost any standard, basic food grains have usually been available.   The periods of exception include 1930–33 when there was real famine in many areas, and during the war and early postwar years when near or actual starvation among civilians, especially in combat areas, was not uncommon.   Malnutrition also has often been a problem, especially among those incapable of working.

Soviet authorities were considerably more successful as judged by their own standards with the equally important side issues of control and social revolution.   Through forced collectivization (of two-thirds of the peasants by 1932 and over 90 percent by 1937) [2] they were able to obtain regularly at confiscatory prices "sufficient" food products for the urban population, avoiding the necessity of compensating the peasant for selling his agricultural products by providing manufactured consumer goods in exchange.   But equally important from the Soviet point of view, they gained control over the use of important resources, and the direction of production.   They also made a large and, for the Communist regime, potentially dangerous part of the Soviet population subject to state control.

The costs of Soviet policies for meeting the above problem were very high: mass starvation especially in rural areas in the early thirties, the resentful attitude of Soviet farmers toward the Soviet Government, and very meager increases in agricultural output during the 27-year period.   A direct expression of the peasant attitude was found in the livestock slaughter which was a major factor in the slow rate of agricultural progress and even retrogression which occurred.

(2) To obtain labor from agriculture so as to increase industrial output rapidly thereby reducing their dependence on non-Soviet countries and improving the country's military posture.

A precondition for a rapid increase was the withdrawal of labor from agriculture, as well as increased output of raw materials for certain branches of industry, and also, as noted above, the obtaining of sufficient food products and agricultural raw materials to supply the urban population.

Soviet policies were markedly successful in this respect: employment in factories and in nonagricultural pursuits more than quadrupled in the period 1928–55, and industrial output increased eightfold, mostly in the requisite heavy industries with most of the new entrants coming from agriculture.   These results were aided by the highly disruptive effects of Soviet collectivization policies in agriculture.   Political and economic conditions for Soviet agricultural workers became so bad that many, presumably mostly the younger and more vigorous, were forced to move to the new construction sites and factories.   And although urban living standards were low, they apparently managed to stay above those in agriculture,[3] so that the

[2] Tsentral'noe statisticheskoe upravlenie pri Sovete Ministrov SSSR, Narodnoe khoviaistvo SSSR, Statisticheskii sbornik, Gosstatizdat, Moskva, 1956, p. 99.
[3] The presumption that urban living standards, though low, were higher than those in agriculture through most of the period is widely held by Western experts.

net rural-urban flow continued at least until 1953. The explanation for the depressed rural living standards was the Communist agrarian policy and the system of compulsory deliveries of agricultural products at confiscatory prices, as well as low output in general, and destruction of livestock. The collective farmer was the residual claimant who received the short end of the stick—frequently inadequate distributions in kind and of cash for the purchase of manufactured consumer products, and also inadequate amounts of equipment with which to work. Because of his situation at the bottom of the economic structure, it has rightly been alleged that the rapid industrialization of the Soviet Union was primarily at peasant expense. Certainly, the peasant has received little but vague promises of future rewards. When farm mechanization was first started, Soviet officials may have hoped that agricultural problems would be overcome without great difficulty. Later they rationalized the continued failures in agricultural output as being due to industrialization.

(3) To increase agricultural output, to improve existing living levels generally, to pay for industrialization, and to obtain raw materials for certain industries.

Soviet agricultural policies have done very poorly in total, with their most marked failure the inability to provide proper supplies of food and clothing for the Soviet Union's people. The policies have been moderately successful in paying for industrialization and in providing industrial raw materials. Such an outcome, however, should not be surprising despite the early faith of Soviet leaders that more tractors would solve their food problems and raise levels of living, for when they realized that agricultural production would not automatically increase, they accorded a low priority to the goal of consumer welfare. In the early stages of industrialization, the export of foodstuffs to finance the importation of capital goods even in the face of starvation at home was a concrete manifestation of prevailing Soviet priorities.

It has also been a continuing goal of agricultural production to build up state food reserves to meet contingencies, both natural and military.

A. AGRICULTURAL PRODUCTION IN THE U. S. S. R. AND THE UNITED STATES

The above brief description and analysis of Soviet purposes and agricultural conditions should be juxtaposed to the results in Soviet agriculture as an aid to interpretation of the latter. Production is not equivalent to either production capacities or consumption, so in interpreting the comparisons of agricultural output in the United States and the U. S. S. R., account should also be taken of the much greater capacity of the United States to expand agricultural production quickly, as well as its more extensive international trade in agricultural products. Agricultural production data are given immediately below for both countries, and are followed by an analysis of the resources devoted to agriculture and future agricultural prospects.

United States agriculture also has posed complex problems for United States policymakers and farming interests, though the problems are generally different. Whereas the principal problem in Soviet agriculture has been to obtain sufficient production to feed the Soviet population, the principal problem in the United States has been how to market its abundant agricultural products, or how to help the individual farmer to adjust production to demand.

TABLE 1.—*Agricultural and food products: Ratios of production and livestock numbers*

	1955/1928		United States/U. S. S. R.	
	U. S. S. R.	United States	1928	1955
WEIGHTS—PRODUCTION				
1. Grain	1.36	1.19	1.69	1.48
Of which corn	4.09	1.21	20.52	5.92
2. Potatoes	1.44	.80	.31	.17
3. Vegetables	(1)	1.80	(1)	(1)
4. Fruit	(1)	1.26	(1)	(1)
5. Oil seeds	(1)	2.51	2.03	(1)
6. Raw sugar	2.64	1.64	1.79	1.11
7. Tobacco	(1)	1.67	3.00	5.00
8. Flax	(1)	----------	(1)	(1)
9. Cotton (unginned)	4.88	1.18	10.38	2.51
10. Wool	1.50	.75	1.00	.33
11. Meat and lard	1.08	1.58	2.27	3.33
12. Fish	3.13	1.50	1.75	.84
13. Milk	.99	1.29	1.45	1.88
14. Eggs	(1)	1.64	.42	(1)
NUMBERS—STOCKS				
15. Cattle	.89	1.69	.86	1.62
Of which dairy cows	.82	1.10	.67	.90
16. Hogs	1.13	.89	2.23	1.75
17. Sheep and goats	1.01	.68	.40	.30
18. Chickens	(1)	.94	2.39	(1)
19. Horses	(1)	.22	(1)	(1)
20. Oxen or mules	(1)	.25	(1)	(1)
PERCENTAGES				
21. Index of agricultural production	(1)	149	----------	----------
22. Index of agricultural production adjusted to a per capita basis	(1)	110	----------	----------

[1] Not available.

Sources : See table 2.

Coverage and special notes : Production, it should be emphasized, is not equivalent to consumption or to capacity, especially in the United States. For one example, the United States imports considerable quantities of Philippine and Cuban sugar, and exports agricultural surpluses.

The United States/U. S. S. R. ratios for livestock are probably understated, because this country's data refer to livestock on farms, and apparently exclude livestock on small garden-type plots as well as those in or en route to stockyards.

The 1955/1928 U. S. S. R. ratios for livestock refer to numbers in comparable boundaries; other U. S. S. R. ratios refer to output in territories within the U. S. S. R. in the years in question. The U. S. S. R. data have a combined sheep and goat figure for 1928, separate figures for 1955, the United States data cover only sheep. Therefore the 1928 United States/U. S. S. R. ratio understates the United States ratio to the Soviet figure.

A striking warning of qualitative differences not always readable in statistics is conveyed by these figures. They show that although the United States has 90 percent as many dairy cows as the Soviet Union, through better feeding and better breeding, total milk production is almost twice as great in this country (188 percent).

The gaps in the table represent cases where comparability problems of statistics were beyond easy correction.

The trends in agricultural production from 1928 to 1955 in both the U. S. S. R. and the United States are shown in table 1 (columns 1 and 2), and the levels of United States and U. S. S. R. agriculture in 1928 and 1955 are compared (again in ratio form) in columns 3 and 4 of the same table. Production data and numbers of livestock in physical terms are then shown in table 2 for 1928, 1955, and selected intervening years.

Certain difficulties of comparing the agricultural output of the two countries must be stressed. While the boundaries of the United States continental territory have not changed during the period of the comparisons, the Soviet Union has undergone a succession of changes. The 1913 Russian territories shrank as a result of World War I and civil war, but in 1939, the Baltic States were absorbed into the Soviet Union, and Poland was partitioned. By the end of World War II, there were further adjustments, all to the Soviet advantage. Unless these territorial changes are kept constantly in mind, there is serious danger of misinterpreting the apparent trends of production. It is also worth remembering the relative status of agricultural output in the two countries at the beginning of the period under discussion when comparing the growth of output in each. The United States has had surpluses in almost all of the period, and the principal change has been one of upgrading the quality of the diet, and adding to the value of retail foodstuffs through more advance preparation. American consumers also now enjoy a wide range of fresh foods or frozen foods, including fruits, vegetables, dairy and poultry products, and meats, on a year-round basis. In the Soviet Union, it has been a constant struggle from the beginning of the period to the present time to provide even a minimum per capita diet. The United States also has been more consistently and voluntarily engaged in foreign trade in agricultural products, even in the face of agricultural restrictions at home. Major imports of coffee, tea, sugar, rubber, and a host of other products are a routine part of our economic organization. Without domestic strain, large-scale exports of grains, soybeans, milk products, and other items have helped to feed friendly nations during World War II and form part of our aid programs, too. To overlook these differences in conditions would be very misleading in any statistical comparisons.

It seems clear that agricultural production as a whole in both 1928 and 1955, but particularly in the latter year, was greater in the United States than in the U. S. S. R. The extent of the lead would vary considerably, however, according to the method chosen for aggregating the various individual ratios shown in table 1. Total agricultural production increased between 1928 and 1955 by about 50 percent in the United States. It is much harder to estimate accurately the amount of increase in the same period in the Soviet Union because of incomplete information. Most Western observers believe that the Russian increases were less than those in the United States; some think they were greater. Just by examining the individual series shown, the Russian increases seem somewhat greater for the grains, other starches, and industrial crops, but smaller in meat and dairy products. Therefore the weighting system selected might influence the actual magnitudes of the index. Were it not for the annexed territories, it seems quite possible that on a per capita basis, the Soviet index would show little improvement in 1955 over 1928. It is easier to compare what has happened to individual crops than to generalize.

TABLE 2.—*Agricultural production and livestock numbers*

[Production in million metric tons; livestock in million head]

Commodity	U.S.S.R. prewar boundaries			U.S.S.R. postwar boundaries			United States				
	1928	1937	1940	1940	1950	1955	1928	1937	1940	1950	1955 (54)
OUTPUT											
1. Grain	73.3	96.0	------	96.0	85.0	100.0	123.8	118.9	115.8	141.9	147.8
Of which corn	3.3	3.1	------	(¹)	6.7	13.5	67.7	67.1	62.4	77.6	80.9
2. Potatoes	46.4	65.6	69.3	84.2	83.8	67.0	14.6	14.1	12.9	14.2	11.3
3. Vegetables	(¹)	(¹)	------	(¹)	(¹)	(¹)	9.3	11.8	12.5	15.8	(16.7)
4. Fruit	(¹)	(¹)	------	(¹)	(¹)	(¹)	12.1	13.3	13.0	15.0	(15.3)
5. Oil seeds	3.4	3.2	------	2.4	2.8	3.7	6.9	9.6	8.5	13.9	17.3
6. Raw sugar	1.4	2.7	------	.2	.2	.2	2.5	3.5	3.7	4.4	4.1
7. Tobacco	.2	.6	------	(¹)	(¹)	(¹)	.6	.7	.7	.9	1.0
8. Flax	.3	.6	------	.2	.2	.2	(¹)	(¹)	(¹)	(¹)	(¹)
9. Cotton (unginned)	.8	2.6	------	2.7	3.6	3.9	8.3	12.6	8.4	6.7	9.8
10. Wool	.2	.2	------	(¹)	.3	.3	.2	.2	.2	.1	.1
11. Meat and lard	3.7	2.4	------	(¹)	3.1	4.0	8.4	7.8	9.7	11.2	13.3
12. Fish	.8	1.6	------	1.4	1.6	2.5	1.4	2.0	1.8	2.2	2.1
13. Milk	30.1	26.1	------	30.0	25.0	29.8	43.5	46.8	49.6	52.9	56.0
14. Eggs	.6	.4	------	(¹)	(¹)	(¹)	2.5	2.3	2.5	3.7	(4.1)
STOCKS											
15. Cattle	60.1 (66.8)	47.5	39.6	48.4	58.1	59.7 (67.1)	57.3	66.8	68.3	78.0	96.6
Of which cows	29.3 (33.2)	20.9	17.3	22.8	24.6	27.2 (29.2)	22.2	25.0	24.9	23.9	24.4
16. Hogs	22.0 (27.7)	20.0	16.5	22.9	22.2	31.4 (52.2)	61.9	42.8	61.2	58.9	55.0
17. Sheep and goats	107.0 (114.6)	53.8	66.5	74.0	93.6	115.5 (142.6)	45.3	52.5	52.1	29.8	30.9
18. Chickens	199.0	150.0	(¹)	183.0	(¹)	(¹)	475.0	420.3	438.3	456.5	447.3
19. Horses	31.5	15.9	(¹)	17.8	(¹)	(¹)	14.8	11.4	10.4	5.5	3.1
20. Oxen [mules]	(¹)	(¹)	(¹)	(¹)	(¹)	(¹)	[5.7]	[4.6]	[4.0]	[2.2]	[1.4]
PERCENTAGES											
21. Index of agricultural output, 1928=100	100.0	(¹)	(¹)	(¹)	(¹)	(¹)	100	109	111	133	149

¹ Not available.

Notes on Soviet data

1. Grain: Data covers both grains and dry legumes, including at least wheat, corn, rye, millet, buckwheat, oats, and barley, and other grains including minor amounts of rice. The grain figures are adjusted to a barn yield basis, and therefore differ from all official Soviet releases. These are figures developed by Dr. Naum Jasny in the following sources: 1928 in The Socialized Agriculture of the U. S. S. R. (Stanford) 1949, p. 792; 1937, and 1940 in Soviet Grain Crops and Their Distribution, International Affairs, October 1952, pages 455, 456, and 459. 1950 and 1955 in More Soviet Grain Statistics, International Affairs, October 1956, page 465.

Corn: 1928 data from Sel'skoe Khoziaistvo SSSR 1935 (Moscow, 1936) page 316, 212–213 (errata slip) ; 1937 data from Planovoe Khoziaistvo No. 5, 1939, page 153; 1950 data from Planovoe Khoziaistvo February 3, 1955; 1955 data derived from the index given for 1950 through 1955 in Tsentral'noe statisticheskoe upravlenie pri Sovete Ministrov SSSR, Narodnoe khoziaistvo SSSR, Statisticheskii sbornik, Gosstatizdat, Moskva, 1956, page 101.

2. Potatoes: 1928 and 1937 given in Jasny, Naum, The Socialized Agriculture of the U. S. S. R. (Stanford) 1949, p. 792. 1940 prewar territories figure in Sotsialisticheskoe Sel'skoe Khoziaistvo No. 12, 1947, p. 28; 1940 postwar territories figure in Voprosy Ekonomiki No. 6, 1954, p. 33; 1950 in Izvestia April 17, 1951 given as 121 percent of 1940 prewar. 1955 in Sel'skoe Khoziaistvo April 25, 1956, given as 20 percent below 1950.

3. Vegetables are not included in the table both because of problems of comparability and because the Soviet authorities have not agreed on a consistent figure series. The only year for which there are published estimates appropriate to this table is 1928. Jasny, op. cit., on page 228 gives 15.1 million tons, and on page 595 gives 21.3 million tons, from alternate Soviet sources.

4. Fruits are not included in the table for lack of data, although the average for the period 1925–28 has been estimated at 2.2 million tons (ibid., p. 605).

5. Oil seeds: Sunflower seeds are the chief Soviet source; however all sources are combined here. Data for 1928 and 1937 are given in ibid., page 513.

6. Raw sugar: Data for 1928, 1940, and later from Narodnoe khoziaistvo SSSR, Statisticheskii sbornik, 1956, op. cit., page 91, adjusted upward by 10 percent to find raw sugar equivalents, the ratio which applied for the 1937 data in Volin, Lazar, A Survey of Soviet Russian Agriculture (Department of Agriculture Monograph No. 5, 1951), page 131.

7. Tobacco includes a coarse form called makhorka. Estimates from United States Department of Agriculture, Agricultural Statistics 1941, page 176 for years through 1940; and in 1955 edition, page 99, for later figures.

8. Flax: Data for 1928 and 1937 in Jasny op. cit., page 792.

9. Cotton is on an unginned basis, approximately 2.67 times as great as standard ginned cotton figures would be. Data for 1928 and 1937 are from Jasny, op. cit., page 795. The 1950 figure was the planned goal, on-the-root basis, and therefore quite possibly an overstatement. However, this same figure was quoted in Pravda on August 9, 1953, as the attained goal. The 1955 figure was obtained by applying the percentage increase over 1950 reported in Narodnoe khoziaistvo SSSR Statisticheskii sbornik, 1956, op. cit., page 101.

10. Wool: Unlike the United States figure which reports only domestic sheep wool, the Soviet figure includes wool from goats and camels. Both countries have to import wool. Data for 1928 and 1937 are given in Volin, op. cit., page 164; Pravda of March 21, 1954, reported 1953 production as 230,000 tons. The index in Narodnoe khoziaistvo SSSR Statisticheskii sbornik, 1956, op. cit., page 101, was applied to this figure to find 1955 production.

11. Meat and lard: On a carcass weight basis. As in the United States case, data exclude poultry and rabbits. Data for 1928 estimated from figures for 1927–28 and 1928–29 given in Jasny, op. cit., page 798. Data for 1937 from idem. Data for 1955 derived from Johnson, D. Gale, Observations on the Economy of the U. S. S. R., Journal of Political Economy, June 1956, page 188. Data for 1950 obtained by applying the 1955 percentage increase over 1950 reported in Narodnoe khoziaistvo SSSR, Statisticheskii sbornik, 1956, op. cit., page 101. In a speech at Leningrad on May 22, 1957, Khrushchev quoted per capita meat and milk comparisons for 1956 from which American students have derived corresponding 1955 totals. Although there is no further substantiation, Khrushchev implies a 1955 meat output of 6.5 million tons.

12. Fish: Data do not include whales and other marine animals. Figures are from ibid., page 89.

13. Milk: Data include milk both for fluid consumption and for secondary products. 1928 data estimated from the 1927–28 and 1928–29 figures given in Jasny, op. cit., page 798. Figures for 1937 and 1940 from idem. Figure for 1950 derived from milk yield per cow on collective farms only, given in Sovetskaia Kirgiziia July 18, 1952, 1955 figure was obtained by applying the percentage increase over 1950 reported in Narodnoe khoziaistvo SSSR, Statisticheskii sbornik, 1956, op. cit., page 101. As discussed under meat, Khrushchev implies an unsubstantiated milk production figure for 1955 of 42 million tons.

14. Eggs: Data for 1928 estimated from figures for 1927–28 and 1928–29 given in Jasny, op. cit. page 798. Data for 1937 from idem. Conversion from number to million metric tons made by multiplying by 5.67×10^{-11}.

15–17. Livestock data given in Narodnoe khoziaistvo SSSR, Statisticheskii sbornik, 1956, op. cit., page 118. Data for January 1 in the years stated. The larger figures in parentheses for 1928 represent data for territories within present boundaries of the U. S. S. R. Figures in parentheses for 1955 represent the only actual figures given for that year, but they are for October 1. Lacking any better correction, the 1953 ratios of January to October numbers have been applied to the 1955 data to make a more logical comparison over time. In the case of sheep and goats for which combined figures are shown, it is also possible to quote for 1955 separate figures, given in ibid., page 122. These are: Sheep, 102.2 (125.0) ; goats, 13.3 (17.6).

18. Chickens: Data for 1928 and 1940 from Jasny, op. cit., page 652. Data for 1937 from ibid., page 625.

19. Horses: Data given in this table are for all horses, rather than just those for farm work, and consequently the figures run higher than shown in table 4 in this chapter. The 1928 figure is estimated for January 1, based on a summer figure of 33.5 million given in Jasny, op. cit., page 786. The figures for 1937 and 1940 are January 1 counts in ibid., page 797.

20. Oxen: Figures on oxen are given in a later table to compare with work horses and with work mules in the United States. Oxen are included in the total for cattle given above in this same table.

21. Index of agricultural output: An index in real terms is not offered for the Soviet Union because there are not enough valid data available to make such a calculation meaningful. In addition to gaps in data, there is disagreement among experts as to the proper weighting system to be used. The text discusses the question further.

Notes on United States data

1. Grain: In order to match the Soviet category called grain, data have been combined for wheat, corn, barley, rice, oats, rye, buckwheat, and grain sorghum, plus the pulses, namely edible dry beans, dry field peas, cowpeas, velvet beans, mung beans, and garbanzos ; and two minor products, broomcorn and popcorn, are included. Such items as fresh peas and sweet corn are not included. Millet is not included because, unlike the Soviet Union, millet in this country is reported only as a forage crop.

Corn: This is shown separately to compare with the Soviet corn program. This is the total equivalent grain yield, about 10 percent over that harvested as grain.

2. Potatoes: The series includes both Irish and sweetpotatoes.

3. Vegetables: Only the commercial crop is included, and in principal producing States only, for the following 28 kinds: Artichokes, asparagus, lima beans, snap beans, beets, broccoli, brussels sprouts, cabbage, cantaloups, carrots, cauliflower, celery, sweet corn, cucumbers, eggplant, escarole, garlic, honeyball melons, honeydew melons, kale, lettuce, onions, green peas, green peppers, shallots, spinach, tomatoes, watermelons.

4. Fruit: This includes estimated commercial output of apples and strawberries, plus estimates of all peaches, pears, grapes, cherries, plums, prunes, apricots, figs, olives, avocados, oranges, tangerines, grapefruit, lemons, limes, and cranberries.

5. Oil seeds: This includes cottonseed, flaxseed, peanuts (picked and threshed), soybeans for oil, tung nuts, and sunflower. Unlike the Soviet Union, the amount of sunflower seeds is too small to be reflected in the figures.

6. Sugar: This is centrifugal raw sugar, produced both from beets and from cane, and represents the output of the continental United States and its Territories of Hawaii, Puerto Rico, and the Virgin Islands. It specifically excludes the output of the Philippines and of Cuba, although these are frequently added to United States totals because of trading and commercial relations.

7. Tobacco: This is total output. The United States does not grow makhorka.

8. Flax: Too little flax fiber is harvested in the United States to register in the table.

9. Cotton: In contrast to Soviet statistics, United States cotton data are normally given in ginned form. To make the figures more nearly comparable, it has been assumed that ginned weight is 34 percent of original weight, and the United States data have been converted accordingly.

10. Wool: This is on a greasy weight basis, from sheep only.

11. Meat and lard: This is on a slaughter-weight basis of beef, veal, pork, lamb, mutton, and lard.

12. Fish: This includes both fish taken by boats based in the continental United States and at interior points, plus the catch of Alaska, as much of this effort is based in Pacific Coast States.

13. Milk: This is total output, both for fresh fluid use, and for butter, cheese, dry milk, and other products.

14. Eggs: This is total output from chickens, converted from numbers to million metric tons by multiplying by $5.67 \times 10.^{-11}$

15–20. Livestock numbers are as of January 1 in the year noted. In the case of the United States, data are given on mules rather than oxen. Data on goats are not available. Only livestock on farms are included.

21. Index of agricultural production is that calculated by the United States Department of Agriculture, Agricultural Research Service, which uses 1947–49 as 100. This is the annual volume of farm production available for sale and for consumption on farms. (See Department of Agriculture, Agricultural Statistics 1955, p. 453, and 1941 p. 544.)

Sources of United States data

Information covering 1928 and 1937 was taken from the United States Department of Agriculture, Agricultural Statistics, 1941. Data for 1940 and 1950 were taken from the same volume for 1955. Data for 1955 are preliminary, and were taken from the United States Statistical Abstract 1956, first checking for consistency with the 1954 data in the 1955 Agricultural Statistics, to insure that comparable series were being used. In the very few instances where 1955 data were not available, 1954 data have been given but placed in parentheses.

Original data were given in a variety of measures including bushels, bales, bags, pounds, and tons. All were converted to metric measure using the conversion table to pounds given in the front of Agricultural Statistics, 1955, and then changing to kilograms.

Individual page references for data are as follows:

| | Agricultural Statistics | | | | | | | Statistical Abstract, 1956 |
| | 1941 edition | | | 1955 edition | | | | |
	1928	1937	1940	1940	1950	1954	1955	1955
Grain (and pulses):								
Wheat	9	9		1	1			658
Corn	49	49		27	27			658
Rye	36	36		14	14			658
Barley	80	80		40	40			659
Oats	67	67		35	35			658
Rice	101	101		19	19			659
Buckwheat		109–10		25	25			659
Grain sorghum	112	112		47	47			661
Dry edible beans	293	293		282	282			661
Dry field peas	328	328		290	290	290	(3)	
Cowpeas	306	306		294	294	294	(3)	
Mung beans					301	301	(3)	
Velvet beans	308	308		301	301	301	(3)	
Garbanzos						285	(3)	
Broomcorn	309	309		294	294	294	(3)	
Popcorn				300	300	300	(3)	
Potatoes, Irish	256	256		231	231			660
Potatoes, sweet	270	270		241	241			660
Vegetables	1 203	1 203		199	199	199		
Fruit	2 187	2 187		143	143	143		
Oilseeds:								
Cottonseed	145	145		111	111			660
Flaxseed	93	93		115	115			659
Peanuts	322	322		119	119			661
Soybeans	299	299		125	125			661
Tung nuts				131	131	131	(3)	
Sunflower		337	337					
Raw sugar	155	155		77	77			678
Tobacco	173	173		95	95			662
Flax			94		66			
Cotton	117	117		54	54			660
Wool	1 436	1 436		344	344			695
Meat and lard	407	407		351	351			683, 689
Fish		580		580	580			716
Milk	421	421		371	371			690
Eggs	472	472		423	423	423		
Cattle	339	339		302	302		302	
Dairy cows	416	416		364	364		364	
Hogs	360	360		318	318		318	
Sheep	383	383		330	330		330	
Chickens	457	457		398	398		398	
Horses	411	411		359	359		359	
Mules	411	411		359	359		359	

[1] 1954 edition.
[2] 1952 edition.
[3] Estimated from 1954.

The trends for the principal agricultural commodities in each country differ substantially: In the U. S. S. R. output of grain, potatoes, certain crops for industry (cotton and sugar beets), and the fish catch increased significantly during the period but there was little increase or even some decline in the numbers of cattle or the output of meat and dairy products (see column 1, table 1). As explained, the reasons for increases in items like grain lie both in territorial changes, and in the continued urgency to increase the supply of calories, easier done in the form of grain than through the extra step of feeding grain to livestock to obtain meat. Because of the meat shortage, however, the Soviet authorities are making strenuous efforts to increase feeds, including grasses. They have high hopes for the corn program to aid live-stock, although corn is not suited to Soviet soil and climate conditions to the degree it is in the United States and although this corn is taking some land away from proven crops. In the United States during the same period (see column 2, table 1), the largest increases were mainly in the commodities which have fared poorly in the U. S. S. R., namely, meat and dairy products, and numbers of cattle, to identify key ex-amples. These increases are results of improved consumer purchasing power in this country which has created a greater demand for better foods. United States cotton and corn production have not risen as much as has Soviet production of these items, but the United States has had the problem of surpluses, so there has been little incentive to ex-pand production, in contrast with the Soviet situation where shortages have been acute. United States production of grain, oil seeds, vege-tables, fruits, eggs, sugar, and tobacco all expanded, in some case pro-viding substantial surpluses for export, in other cases storage reserves, better consumption patterns, or even unwanted surpluses. The number of livestock other than cattle declined in the United States with no harm to the total meat supply. These declines in numbers are espe-cially striking when one considers the continued easy availability of meat in this country compared with the restrictions present in the So-viet Union.

As a consequence of the differential movements in production, the substantial United States leads in output of meat, dairy products, and tobacco in 1928 (see col. 3 of table 1) increased further by 1955 (see col. 4 of table 1); the United States lead in production of fish was ended; the size of the lead in grain, sugar, and cotton was de-creased; the Soviet lead in the production of potatoes continued enor-mous by our standards even though the United States has had potato surpluses, the Russians have experienced shortages.

B. RESOURCES DEVOTED TO AGRICULTURE

1. Land

Soviet agriculture in 1954 and 1955 sowed about 30 percent more land to crops than was sown in the United States (see table 3), whereas in 1928 the sown area in the United States was about 30 percent larger than that in the U. S. S. R. The reversal of positions reflects the 65-percent increase in sown area in the U. S. S. R. between 1928 and 1955 compared to a slight decline in the United States which has deliberately restricted the area under cultivation to prevent over-supply due to rising productivity.[4] Essentially the Soviet increase above the United States level came after 1950 with the breaking up of grasslands which may not be cultivated permanently. Territorial changes also influence the apparent Soviet growth.

---

[4] The data for 1928, taken from the sources cited for sown area in the notes to table 3, are 148.1 million hectares in the United States and 113 million in the U. S. S. R. Nearly 20 million hectares of the increase in Soviet cropland took place in 1955, and an increase of nearly 40 million hectares occurred between 1950 and 1955.

TABLE 3.—*Land utilization in the U. S. S. R. and the United States in 1954*

	Million hectares		Percentage	
	U. S. S. R.	United States	U. S. S. R.	United States
Agricultural land	648	518	29	67
In farms	486	421	22	55
Plowland	220	186	10	24
Sown area	186	135	8	17
Public land	161	96	7	12
Nonagricultural land	1,581	253	71	33
Total land area	2,229	771	100	100

The data for the U. S. S. R. and the United States are not rigorously comparable. They are adequate for purposes of this report, but not necessarily so for other purposes. See footnotes to this table and consult original sources for further details.

Sources

Tsentral'noe statisticheskoe upravlenie pri Sovete Ministrov SSSR, Narodnoe khoziaistvo SSSR, Statisticheskii sbornik, Gosstatizdat, Moskva, 1956, page 103, for the U. S. S. R. and Department of Commerce, Bureau of the Census, Statistical Abstract of the United States, 1956 edition, page 619, for the United States, unless otherwise noted.

Coverage

Agricultural land in the U. S. S. R. covers plowland, hayfields, pastureland, gardens, vineyards, and virgin land. Coverage of the United States data is roughly similar, except that they probably exclude virgin land—the exclusion would probably be quantitatively unimportant.

Agricultural land in farms in the U. S. S. R. covers all agricultural lands except those held in reserve by the state and not assigned to collective, state, or individual farms. Coverage of the same category in the United States refers to privately owned land in farms, plus about 2 million hectares of Indian and state land.

Plowland in the U. S. S. R. covers fallow and idle lands, as well as that actually plowed. Note that plowland in state reserves, not covered by this category, amounts to only 5 million hectares. Plowland in the United States covers the category of "cropland" plus plowable land currently in pasture.

Sown area in the U. S. S. R. covers harvested cropland, orchards, and home gardens, as well as areas of crop failures. The United States figure is harvested area only. The figure shown should be adjusted upward by about 2 million hectares to find sown area. The Soviet figure is from Narodnoe khoziaistvo SSSR, Statisticheskii sbornik, 1956, op. cit., page 108. The United States adjustment was reported in the 1954 agricultural census.

Public agricultural land in the U. S. S. R. refers to state reserves, including 97.1 million hectares in the land reserve (goszemfond), 19.3 million in the forest reserve, and 45 million hectares in miscellaneous agricultural lands. Most of the state reserves are usable by collective farms on a short-term basis. Public agricultural land in the United States is owned by Federal, State, or local governments. Almost all of it is pastureland, and it, too, is usable by private interests in many instances.

Nonagricultural land in the U. S. S. R. covers the state forest reserves (834.7 million hectares), much of which is in the permafrost zone; land held by collective farms and other agricultural enterprises (460.9 million hectares); state land reserves (221.8 million); and miscellaneous other lands. Nonagricultural land in the United States covers forest lands, waste lands, parks, roads, cities, etc.

Total land area in the U. S. S. R. is believed to exclude large bodies of water. Total land area in the United States definitely excludes such bodies. For further details see Department of Commerce, Bureau of the Census, Statistical Abstract of the United States, 1956 edition, page 158.

The productivity of land in the traditional Soviet agricultural areas is not as high as in the United States Corn Belt and Cotton Belt areas, even though the black soil belt in the U. S. S. R. is famous for its quality. When the additional factor of harsh climate is taken into account, the total usefulness of Soviet lands is reduced below that of agricultural land in the United States. This comparison takes into account the fact that both countries have a wide range of soil and climate conditions even in their agricultural zones. The areas in the Soviet Union to the east which have been added to Soviet cropland are quite definitely of lower physical productivity than the older Soviet agricultural regions. The contribution of their output in good years is important to bolstering total food supply, but there would be risks in relying on their yields in all years. As has already been implied, more important than the comparative composition of the soil is the generally inhospitable climate for agriculture in the U. S. S. R., especially in the newer areas. Because of its very northern latitude, more comparable to Canada than to the United States, the summers are short in most of the U. S. S. R. (though this is partially offset by longer hours of sunshine). And because of its continental size, the rainfall is moderate to negligible and the winters are unusually severe, with early-fall and late-spring frosts not uncommon.

The Soviet Union is so large that a full appreciation of its agricultural problem requires evaluation of regional food balances as well as total output. Some food imports, as to the Far East, are occasioned by the remoteness of deficit areas from the rest of the country.

The large increase in area sown to crops in the U. S. S. R., together with the huge size of the U. S. S. R. compared to the United States (its total land area is nearly three times as large) might suggest that Soviet agricultural lands are practically unlimited. Such an inference, however, would be incorrect. Nearly three-quarters of the Soviet land mass is nonagricultural, compared to only about one-third so classified in the United States. (See table 3.) Further, although parts of the nonagricultural areas in the U. S. S. R. are forest lands, some of which might be usable in agriculture in the future, large parts are tundra or desert which are completely unsuitable for agricultural use with present techniques.[5] As shown in table 3, Soviet agricultural lands are only a little larger than those in the United States, and its ploughlands are less than one-fifth larger. Other calculations, made before the current Soviet drive to cultivate virgin and largely semiarid steppe lands, and which exclude those and other as yet unutilized lands, show the Soviet Union as having only 349 million hectares of agricultural land, including both arable land and permanent meadows and pastures.[6]

2. Equipment, including draft power

(a) *Trends within the U. S. S. R.*—Soviet agriculture in 1928 had at its disposal total draft power equivalent to about 29 million horses,

---

[5] V. P. Timoshenko, in Bergson, Abram (ed.), Soviet Economic Growth, (Evanston : Row-Peterson) 1953, pp. 250–251, notes that about 312 million hectares are tundra and forest tundra, 90 million are semidesert, and about 210 million hectares are deserts.

[6] The official figures of table 3 include virgin lands as well as those into which cultivation has been recently extended, regardless of land quality. The smaller figure of 349 million was taken from the previous study prepared for the Joint Committee on the Economic Report by the Legislative Reference Service of the Library of Congress, Trends in Economic Growth, Joint Committee print, 83d Cong., 2d sess., p. 98 ; the citation given there was FAO, Yearbook of Food and Agricultural Statistics, I, Production, 1949, p. 13.

98 percent of which were in the form of workhorses and oxen.[7]   During the next 5 years, as a result of the peasant resistance to collectivization in the form of mass slaughter of livestock and improper care, including breeding, the number of horses and other draft animals dropped by 50 percent, so that despite some increase in mechanical power (tractors, combines, etc.), total draft power in 1933 was one-third less than in 1928.   In fact, it was not until 1938 that mechanical power increased sufficiently to offset the decline in draft animals since 1928.   In 1938 total draft power was once again at the 1928 level, with animal power accounting for only 40 percent of total power rather than 98 percent as in 1928.

> * * * However, the requirements for draft power increased materially after 1928 because of the expansion of cropped plowland, the disproportionate increase in the areas of such crops as cotton and sugar beets which require large use of power, additional work per hectare as a result of such practices as deeper plowing and more frequent harrowing, the replacement of human labor by mechanical or animal power, the enforcement of deliveries to the state at the peak of draft-power requirements, and so on.[8]

Therefore, relative to the requirements for it, there was quite possibly less draft power available in 1938 than 10 years earlier.

Further, in evaluating the shift to mechanical power, it should be noted that although the mechanical power appears to have been used a longer number of hours per year in the U. S. S. R. than in the United States, it was not as reliably available for work as was animal power. Allowance must be made for the time tractors are not available for work because of repair needs caused by overwork and abuse.   Few spare parts and poor fuel supply have added to difficulties.   It can also be observed that in a country lacking many private automobiles, both animals and trucks, even tractors, intended for farmwork have to be diverted to some errands performed in this country by automobiles.

Currently, total draft power in Soviet agriculture is about double that in 1928 and 1938, with mechanical power at about three times the 1938 level, and animal power considerably below it.[9]   The increase in total draft power relative to requirements, however, is again much less than the figures suggest.   The 1955 sown area increased by about two-thirds over 1928, and by about one-third since 1938 of which about 16 million hectares, or almost 12 percent of the 1938 total, was due to territorial expansion.   Further, much of the equipment, such as the case of tractors referred to below, is excessively large and of an unsuitable type even for use on the large Soviet farms.

(b) *Comparative levels of equipment and mechanization in the U. S. S. R. and the United States.*—Data on selected items of agricultural equipment and draft animals are given in table 4 below.   They indicate that United States agriculture has consistently had at its dis-

---

[7] Estimated in Jasny, Naum, op. cit., p. 458.   In accordance with Soviet usage, Dr. Jasny assigned values of 0.75 horsepower to workhorses, 0.5 horsepower to oxen, 7.5 horsepower to trucks and grain combines.   Mechanical draft power other than tractors, trucks, and combines was ignored, since Jasny concluded it was insignificant in 1928 and barely significant in 1938.

[8] Ibid., pp. 458–459.

[9] Based on data from Narodnoe khoziaistvo SSSR, Statisticheskii sbornik. 1956, op. cit., pp. 128, 144, and 155, and from Jasny, op. cit., p. 458 ; and patterned after Jasny. Note that animal power currently is probably much less than half its level 27 years ago.

posal more mechanical equipment than Soviet agriculture, together with apparently adequate numbers of draft animals. In 1928, for example, United States agriculture had considerably more mechanical power than the U. S. S. R., and 60 percent as many draft animals. The ratios changed through the period, but, despite the rapid mechanization in the U. S. S. R., the United States maintained its lead, so that by 1955 it had 5 to 6 times as many tractors and trucks, nearly 3 times as many grain combines, and still nearly half as many draft animals. If other forms of mechanical and electrical power could be taken fully into account, the United States lead would probably be increased further. As one analyst has noted—

* * * the mechanization of Soviet agriculture in general is limited to a few operations, while American agriculture is, to a large extent, mechanized through and through, in the field and around the house.[10]

TABLE 4.—*Agricultural equipment and draft animals in the U. S. S. R. and the United States: Numbers of selected items*

[In thousands]

	1928	1937	1940	1950	1955
Soviet Union:					
1. Tractors	27.	456	531	595	844
2. Grain combines		123	182.	211	338
3. Trucks and jeeps	0.7	146	228	283	544.
4. Draft horses	24,300	11,000	12,000	(¹)	(10,000)
5. Oxen	6,900	3,500	(¹)	(¹)	(¹)
United States:					
1. Tractors	827	1,368	1,675	3,940	² 4,750
2. Grain combines	61		190	714	1,000
3. Trucks (not including passenger cars)	840	1,042	1,095	2,310	2,800
4. Horses	13,200	9,600	9,600	4,700	² 2,900
5. Mules	5,300	4,100	3,700	2,000	² 1,400

¹ Not available.
² 1954 date.

NOTE.—Neither the equipment nor animals are strictly comparable in the two countries. Further, there were varying amounts of other equipment available in the two countries. (The United States is believed to have had a very considerable advantage in this respect in most of the years noted.) Therefore, the above comparison is offered only to establish orders of magnitude.

SOURCES AND COVERAGE

United States data are from the Department of Agriculture, Agricultural Statistics. The numbers of all items are given as of January 1, which are treated here as December 31 of the previous year, except where noted otherwise; 1955 data are preliminary. Row 1 data include garden tractors. Row 2 data for 1940 and 1950 are January 1 figures; and the figure shown for 1928 actually refers to the number of combines as of January 1, 1930. Row 4 and row 5 data use animals 2 years of age and older. U. S. S. R. data, unless otherwise noted, are as of December 31. They were taken or derived from the sources indicated below, by rows:

Row 1: Tsentral'noe statisticheskoe upravlenie pri Sovete Ministrov SSSR, Narodnoe khoziaistvo SSSR, Statisticheskii sbornik, Gosstatizdat, Moskva, 1956, p. 144. Data for 1955 may be as of July 1.

Row 2: Ibid, p. 145 for 1940, 1950, and 1955; Jasny, Naum, Socialized Agriculture of the U. S. S. R., Stanford University Press, 1949, p. 458, for 1937. Figure shown for 1955 is actually for 1954. If the increase in combines from 1954 to 1955 were proportionate to the increase in horsepower of tractors, the number of combines in 1955 would be about 360,000.

---

[10] Jasny, Naum, op. cit., p. 455.

Row 3: Narodnoe khoziaistvo SSSR, Statisticheskii sbornik, 1956, op. cit.,
p. 144. Data include tank trucks.

Row 4: Jasny, Naum, op. cit., p. 458, for 1928 and 1937 data; figure for
1940 estimated from data on pp. 458 and 797. Figure for 1955 estimated on
basis of horses in collective farms as of October 1, 1955, and other dates as
shown in Narodnoe khoziaistvo SSSR, Statisticheskii sbornik, 1956, op. cit.,
p. 128, compared to prewar data in Jasny, Naum, op. cit., pp. 458 and 797.

Row 5: Ibid., p. 458.

In interpreting the above quantitative comparison, several qualitative factors should be emphasized. On the one hand, it has been pointed
out that Soviet equipment is often less suitable to the purposes at hand
than United States agricultural equipment. For example, in the
U. S. S. R. in 1955 row-crop tractors accounted for only one-fourth
of the total compared to nearly all in the United States. As a consequence, Soviet agriculture has been very deficient in the number of
tractors of this type that it needs, while it has greater supplies of
certain other types, particularly the large heavy tractors.[11] On the
other hand, some of the larger Soviet machinery is suited to the tasks
at hand, and may take the place of several items of smaller equipment
in use in this country. Further, Soviet farm equipment must be used
more intensively on the average than is farm machinery in the United
States. However, one has to take into account the frequent complaints
in the Soviet press about farm equipment lying idle for lack of repairs
or other reasons.

On balance there is no question but that United States agriculture
is significantly better off with respect to both kinds and amounts of
farm equipment. And if the balance could be struck relative to respective needs, the scales would probably tip even further toward the
United States. For, owing to the greater danger in the U. S. S. R.
of late spring and early winter frosts, or in semiarid regions the
threat to spring crops of summer drought and scorching winds,
and the shorter growing season generally, it is even more imperative
for Soviet crops to be sown and harvested quickly. Such an imperative to be successfully carried out would require more equipment than
is currently available in the U. S. S. R., even according to statements
by Khrushchev and other Soviet authorities. Referring only to the
related but not identical problem of harvesting losses, in a speech
of January 25, 1955, Khrushchev attributed the harvesting delays
and resultant crop losses primarily to an insufficient number of harvesting machines, and he called for increased production of combines
and more efficient use of them.[12]

Although the purpose of machine tractor stations is to make a
limited number of machines do more work by serving several collective farms, undoubtedly there are disadvantages, too. There is in-
evitable conflict for the scarce services offered.

3. Manpower in agriculture

The question of manpower in Soviet and United States agriculture,
and in other parts of the economy, is taken up in some detail in chapter
IV. It should be noted here, however, that just 30 years ago the
U. S. S. R. employed about 85 percent of its labor force in agriculture,

---

[11] Figures on existing stocks of Soviet tractors were taken from Narodnoe khoziaistvo
SSSR. Statisticheskii sbornik, 1956, op. cit., p. 144. The estimate of stocks relative to
needs was given directly by Dr. Jasny.

[12] Pravda, February 3, 1955.

compared to less than 25 percent in the United States; and even in 1955 about half the civilian manpower in the U. S. S. R. was occupied in agriculture, compared to about 10 percent in the United States. In absolute terms, agriculture in the U. S. S. R. employed about 37 million persons [13] on an approximately full-time basis in 1955, compared to only 6.7 million whose principal occupation was agricultural in the United States. The comparative data on agricultural employment, when taken with the comparative data on agricultural output given in table 1, imply that labor productivity in agriculture in the U. S. S. R. in 1955 was between one-sixth and one-twelfth that in the United States.

The comparatively heavy use of manpower in Soviet agriculture is a result in large part of inefficiencies and other institutional defects, which are discussed in the following section; but it is also a natural concomitant of lower availability of equipment than in the United States, less use of fertilizers and lower natural productivity of the land. Unquestionably, the Soviet economy would benefit from increases in agricultural labor productivity—whether a matter of more output with the same labor force, or of decreases in labor force for the same output. However, except for increases in labor productivity through more efficient use of labor and other factors, there would be costs either in the form of (1) reduced agricultural output resulting from a withdrawal of labor without substitution of other factors of production such as equipment, fertilizers, irrigation, land, and even manufactured consumer goods as incentives to agricultural labor; or (2) increased use in agriculture of the above-mentioned production factors, which would then not be available to other economic sectors such as industry. A deliberate reduction in agricultural output, without compensating increases in imports of agricultural products, would now probably be an unlikely choice for Soviet authorities. Therefore, in determining how far it would be advisable to go in increasing the output per worker in Soviet agriculture, Soviet authorities would have to balance the benefits of potential increases in agricultural output, plus transfer of some farm labor to nonagricultural work, against the costs of the additional equipment and other factors to be used in agriculture, as measured in net output sacrificed in other economic sectors.

The very low levels of output per worker in Soviet agriculture correctly suggest that there are considerable opportunities for, and advantages to raising labor productivity so as to release farm labor for work in other sectors. The U. S. S. R. will probably find it profitable, on balance, to employ, for several decades to come, a much larger percentage of its labor force in agriculture than the United States does today, especially if after the current land-expansion program is essentially completed, the U. S. S. R. moves in the direction of more intensive farming, i. e., more intensive methods of growing grain, and increased emphasis on labor intensive commodities, such as meat and dairy products, vegetables, and industrial crops. Even if labor productivity in Soviet agriculture should continue to increase at the rate of approximately 33 percent each 5 years, as was officially claimed to have taken place between 1950 and 1955, it is interesting to note that

---

[13] Table 3 of ch. IV reports 41.6 million, but those figures have not been corrected for miscellaneous nonagricultural pursuits of the agricultural population. The 37 million figure is derived from Narodnoe khoziaistvo SSSR, Statisticheskii sbornik, 1956, op. cit., p. 187.

it would take Soviet agriculture until at least 1985 to 1990 to reach
the 1955 level of labor productivity in United States agriculture.

*4. Management, organization, and incentives in Soviet and United
   States agriculture*

The institutional or organizational makeup of United States agriculture is complex: There are numerous independently owned and operated commercial family farms, a comparatively small number of
privately owned large farms employing numerous hired workers, and
many farms rented for cash or a share of the crops, all of which provide
the great bulk of the marketed production. There are in addition numerous part-time and self-sufficing farms which have largely noncom-
mercial functions. However, because the institutional factors do not
appear to have inhibited agricultural output in this country, and because such factors are more familiar than the Soviet institutional
factors, this report will deal only with the organizational and management factors in the U. S. S. R. as they affect and have affected agricultural production.

Data on the proportions of total area sown by each type of farm
in the U. S. S. R. in 1955 are shown in table 5 below. Although they
significantly understate the share of privately farmed lands in total
value of Soviet agricultural output—because a large share of livestock
herds is still privately owned, and because of intensive use of plots for
vegetables, etc.—they do indicate clearly and accurately that the collective farm is the most important agricultural organization in the
U. S. S. R.; that state organizations, principally state farms, are still
relatively unimportant, although the trend is toward growth in the
production and marketing share of state farms; and that independent
farming in the traditional sense is now practically nonexistent.[14]

TABLE 5.—*Land utilization in the U. S. S. R. in 1955, by type of farm*

	Sown areas of all crops in 1955	
	Million hectares	Percentage of total
Collective farms (communal use only)	149.06	80.2
State organizations	29.37	15.8
Independent peasants	.04	.0002
Collective farmers (household plots)	5.79	3.1
Workers and employees (garden plots)	1.59	.9
Total sown area	185.85	100.0

Source: Absolute figures from Tsentral'noe statisticheskoe upravlenie pri Sovete Ministrov SSSR,
Narodnoe khoziaistvo SSSR, Statisticheskii sbornik, Gosstatizdat, Moskva, 1956, p. 108; percentages
derived.

The descriptions which follow reflect what generally has been true
since collective farms were established. Conditions since 1953 appear
to have eased somewhat, but this does not invalidate the picture given.
The Soviet collective farm is nominally a voluntary association of independent farmers who have joined together to farm nationally owned
lands, whose use is granted to them in perpetuity. In practice, however, coercion by party and Government officials has played a crucial

[14] Independent peasant households numbered somewhat more than 100,000 in 1955, according to Narodnoe khoziaistvo SSSR, Statisticheskii sbornik, 1956, op. cit., p. 99.

role in the formation and maintenance of the collectives. Aside from the original direct pressure to join, the economic pressures on private farming were so increased after 1930 that for all practical purposes there was no alternative to joining a collective—except that of working even more directly for the state. In theory, members of the collective farm direct their communal production program, except for the principal limitation that they must raise or otherwise obtain sufficient quantities of specific agricultural products to fulfill the plan for compulsory deliveries and sales, partly at confiscatory prices, partly at higher prices, to state purchasing agencies. In practice, however, Government and party officials select and remove collective-farm chairmen at will; they plan both the broad outlines of collective-farm work, such as types and amounts of crops to be sown, and until recently the most minute details, such as exact dates for harvesting and sowing. The collective farm delivers specified products to the state at prices so low that the deliveries are tantamount to exorbitant tax payments (this has been eased since 1953); it makes heavy payments in kind for the services of machinery operated by Government machine tractor stations (the collective is allowed to own only light equipment). Then after laying aside certain amounts for seed, capital, etc., collective-farm members in theory may divide the remainder, either in kind or in cash proceeds from sales, according to type and amount of work performed by each member. In practice, however, although the form of the procedure has been followed, the Government has managed in one way or another to exact increased deliveries whenever possible,[15] so that the collective-farm members could not rely on bigger rewards even for greater or more successful efforts. In a nutshell, Government controls over the collective farm have been so great that the principal difference between the average collective farmer and the average hired worker on a state farm is that the former is the residual claimant who bears the burden of crop failures with relatively little extra compensation in good years. Both collective farmers and hired state farmworkers are poorly compensated on the average, compared to nonagricultural workers. Each is entitled to, and does, farm a small plot of land privately in order to obtain crops and livestock products for his own family consumption or for sale on the free market at higher prices. Despite the limitations placed on what was intended as subsidiary farming, the collective-farm member or (to a lesser degree) hired state farmworker usually finds it so profitable compared to his "principal" farming activity that he devotes intensive effort to it— to the detriment of state interests.

Soviet authorities have by now spoken openly or by implication of such institutional deficiencies as those mentioned above; and they have recently moved to ameliorate some of them, as indicated below:

(1) Greater rewards for greater efforts of collective-farm members and regularization of payments to collectives: Compulsory deliveries are to be reduced and less closely geared to total output, so that a larger proportion of any increase in yields would stay with the collective farm and its members—to be sold at the higher free-market prices or consumed on the farm. Further, the prices paid for

---

[15] The procedure was to take a very large share of above-normal harvests—either by increasing the quota of compulsory deliveries or by arranging for "voluntary" deliveries above the original quota.

different types of state deliveries and purchases have also been raised,[16] so that the differential between prices of state-delivered products and those sold on the free market has been narrowed.

(2) Decentralization of agricultural planning: Soviet authorities have recently stressed the importance of expanding the role of on-the-spot planning by the leadership of the collective farm and the machine tractor station. Further, they have implied that they will restrain interference in collective-farm affairs by central and local officials of both the party and the Government and will reduce the mountains of paperwork required from the collective farms by administrators at all levels. It is interesting to note that in their efforts to achieve effective decentralized planning, however, they have dispatched by central pressures upward of 30,000 "trustworthy" individuals from the cities to the collectives to serve as chairmen or in other leading positions. Note, also, that when Khrushchev spoke at a conference of agricultural workers in Sverdlovsk on July 20, 1956,[17] he implied that at least initially there must be pressure on farm leadership to get them to devote more attention to raising corn. It seems that old habits are not easily broken!

These policy and personnel changes will take time to assess, for there is not yet any real measure of how competent the new managers are as farmers; it is more likely that they have been picked as politically reliable and that they may have more administrative drive than real knowledge of agriculture in specific terms of need. Their contribution at first may be spotty. It is also possible that much of the new plan of decentralization is still on paper rather than in practical effect.

(3) Changes in operations of the collective farm: Unquestionably, there has been resentment by collective-farm membership over their lack of control over farm policies, some of which may even be a residual of the forced collectivization drive of the thirties. There appears to be little feeling by the members that the farm belongs to them. Rather "it's not my cow or crops" seems to be a more prevalent attitude. The result is lessened attention to collective work as well as to communal property. Neglect and, outright thievery of communal property are not uncommon, so that in large part for that reason, collective farms employ an undue proportion of their personnel as guards and bookkeepers. Soviet authorities are aware of this deficiency of their agricultural institutions. For example, a recent Pravda editorial criticized a local Communist Party secretary for dismissing collective-farm chairmen arbitrarily. But this recognition probably implies only removal of the crudest aspects of undemocratic actions, of substituting leadership and persuasion for crude threats and punitive actions.

(4) Higher pay to permanent workers at Government equipment stations: Farmworkers who happened to be doing the work of driving tractors or combines equivalent to that of machine tractor station personnel have been transferred to machine tractor station payrolls. The better pay is likely to reduce turnover and is thus favorable.

---

[16] Soviet authorities are now in a better position than ever before to raise prices paid to farmers, and to satisfy the consequent greater demand by farmers for manufactured consumer goods.
[17] Sel'skoe Khoziaistvo, July 21, 1956, p. 2.

However, such personnel unless trained to perform other work in slack periods will be less productive on a year-round basis than when they were members of collectives.

(5) In conclusion, there has been some reversal of trend since the fall of 1953 in the previous policy to siphon off skilled workers from farms for industry. Now some former agronomists are being taken from city desk jobs, in particular, to return to agriculture, especially for the new regions in Kazakhstan. "Volunteers" have been moved back into agriculture by various means of persuasion, some rather compulsive.

It frequently seems to be the case that when the Soviet authorities move in the direction of concessions that these figurative carrots are accompanied by some use of the stick as well. Thus the very real easing of conditions in agriculture just described must be qualified. During the course of 1956 central pressure began to mount to have collective farms rewrite their rules so that private plots would be the privilege of conscientious collective farmers who performed full quotas of work. Those who devoted too much time to their private plots, and those who in some cases had actually left the collective farm for other employment were to have their plots reduced in size or eliminated. Part of the transfer of control to individual collectives was to include the right of the members to fix the size of plots. This was to provide no opportunity for the noncooperative holders of plots to ignore appeals for more work and to feel that the regional executive committees would protect them from the complaints of other members of the collective.

Along with these steps to limit size of plots and to limit who could hold plots, there was also a new pressure to limit the number of livestock which could be individually held. Also in response to central pressure, individual collective farms began to raise the number of work days required from able-bodied members. By putting this number high enough, the time left over for working private plots is made quite limited.

Much has been written about Soviet agricultural prospects in recent months. Soviet writings concede that all is not well in Soviet agriculture, and that the recent extensions of sown area, including the emphasis on raising production of corn, may not pay off in all years, owing to the marginal rainfall in most of the new areas. Even so, Khrushchev has stated that 2 good years and 1 medium year with 2 bad years out of every 5 would make this extension worth its cost. Western specialists share the misgivings of some Soviet writers and, in fact, put them forward in strengthened form together with others not conceded in the U. S. S. R. Whether or not the Soviet new-lands program itself will be permanently successful (harvests were unusually good in 1956), however, is only a part of a larger two-pronged question: Will Soviet agriculture as a whole be able to increase its yields per acre and consequently its total agricultural output, and eventually, also its product per worker? Or will the U. S. S. R. choose to concentrate its efforts on nonagricultural production and be able to vastly increase its imports of agricultural products?

For the immediate future, it is possible that the U. S. S. R. will in fact increase somewhat over present levels its imports of agricultural products; but these purchases are unlikely to be large relative to domestic production. For the longer future, imponderables preclude a reasoned, unqualified answer in which one can have confidence, although continued increases in such imports seem more likely under most conceivable circumstances than the reverse. At the same time, it also seems likely that Soviet agriculture in the next 5 years will be more successful in raising yields per acre and total output than in the past. For one thing, barring a change in international relations, the U. S. S. R. would be in a position to supply Soviet agriculture with more equipment and supplies than at any time in the past. For example, the high point of tractor production (excluding garden tractors) in the prewar period was 112,900 in 1936 although horses were more plentiful then; production in 1955 was 163,400, and the production planned for 1960 is 322,000.[18] Similarly, the high point of mineral-fertilizer production in the prewar period was 3.6 million tons in 1939; production in 1955 was 9.6 million; and it is planned to be 19.6 million tons in 1960.[19] Proportionately larger increases are planned for grain combines, and still larger increases for windrowers.[20] Plans are not reality, of course, and Soviet performance in this field has not been as successful as in heavy industry; however, there is little reason to doubt that the Soviet economy could provide agriculture with significantly greater quantities of the above mentioned industrial commodities in the future than it has in the past.

For the immediate future, it is believed, Soviet authorities are most concerned with raising total agricultural output quickly; and for that reason they have embarked on their extensive additions to sown area, even at the considerable risk of crop failures and stimulating a gigantic dust bowl in parts of the U. S. S. R., principally Kazakhstan. Once they have a somewhat larger total agricultural output to work with, however—as insurance against urban and rural dissatisfactions—it seems reasonable to expect that they will put forth more intensive efforts into the older agricultural areas. The increase of effort in the older areas appears already to have started, and it will probably be expanded into a major effort during the next 5 years or so. Initially, it seems reasonable that the major emphasis will be on raising yields, which would involve use of greater amounts of fertilizers, certain types of equipment, as well as the administrative changes already described. In fact, some of their efforts, such as raising milk output—in which significant successes were realized this past year (1956)—may require even more agricultural labor. Others, however, such as the introduction of more mechanical and chemical weeders, should release labor for both other agricultural and non-agricultural tasks, so that eventually the flow of labor from agriculture into the cities can be resumed on a heavier scale. This of course will depend on the availability of housing and other urban facilities. At that time, some of the new lands may very well be returned to permanent pasture, or at least farmed less frequently for grain.

Most Western specialists on Soviet agriculture believe the output increases planned to be realized by 1960 are unattainable, particularly those for grain and for animal products; and this belief seems supported by past Soviet performance. Nonetheless, it seems likely that

[18] Narodnoe khoziaistvo SSSR, Statisticheskii sbornik, 1956, op. cit., pp. 60, 75.
[19] Ibid., pp. 60 and 81.
[20] Ibid., pp. 57 and 60.

Soviet progress in agriculture during the next 5 years or so will, for the reasons discussed above, outstrip the poor results of the past.

This leaves unanswered the general question raised early in the chapter, the extent of agriculture's inhibiting effect on overall growth of the Soviet economy. To date, Soviet agricultural shortcomings have inhibited general economic growth chiefly through the holding down of living levels and the resultant deleterious effects on overall production. The necessity of investing large sums to make up for agricultural capital damaged during peasant resistance to collectivization and the war has also inhibited general growth in the past, just as the large current investments in agriculture to increase its output are and will be slowing up economic growth in other sectors. The costs of maintaining a large labor force in agriculture—in the past principally the physical costs of maintenance, and currently perhaps even more the lost production in other economic sectors—have also inhibited general growth. The inhibiting effects of agricultural shortcomings and the measures taken to ameliorate them have been and probably will continue to be significant; but they have not been and probably will not be so great as to be a predominant factor in slowing down overall economic growth of the Soviet economy.

Above all, it must be stressed that the Soviet state retains the capacity to allocate resources and to restrain demand. By these means industry, and especially military supply industry, can continue to rise despite a lagging agricultural sector.

CHAPTER IV

POPULATION AND LABOR FORCE

A. POPULATION

The U. S. S. R. covers an area nearly 3 times as large as that of the United States, more than 8.6 million square miles in contrast to about 3 million. Much of the Soviet area is virtually uninhabitable, owing to climatic and topographical conditions, so that the population density in the U. S. S. R. as a whole is only about 23 persons per square mile. In European Russia, including the Urals, where more than three-fourths of the population is concentrated despite official encouragement of eastward migration, population density is about 73 persons per square mile—a third greater than the approximately 56 persons per square mile in the United States as a whole.[1]

Perhaps the most economically significant point to note about the population trends (see table 1 below) is that the U. S. S. R. population is now barely above the prewar level, whereas the United States population has grown by 33 millions, an increase of 25 percent.[2] The sharply contrasting population trends are largely a result of the differential effects of World War II on the population in the two countries. Soviet casualties during that war were incomparably heavier among all segments of the population than were those in the United States;[3] and the Soviet death rates during the immediate postwar years were also certainly much higher.[4] Further, Soviet birthrates declined greatly during the war and postwar years, while United States birthrates increased significantly; so that the Soviet rates were lower than those in the United States during the war and immediate postwar years.[5] As a result, the Soviet population is now only 20 percent larger than that of

---

[1] Population densities in the U. S. S. R. were derived from data in Tsentral'noe statisticheskoe upravlenie pri Sovete Ministrov SSSR, Narodnoe khoziaistvo SSSR, Statisticheskii sbornik, Gosstatizdat. Moskva, 1956, pp. 252, 253; population densities in the United States were from Department of Commerce, Bureau of the Census, Statistical Abstract of the United States, 1956 edition, p. 5.

[2] Population of the United States in 1940 was nearly 132 million compared to a total of more than 165 million in 1955. In contrast to the data of table 1, both the above figures include Armed Forces serving overseas.

[3] The ratio of war-attributable deaths in the U. S. S. R. compared to the United States may have been as high as 50 to 1. Official data on the extent of war deaths in the Soviet Union are not available, but an estimate made by General Guillaume (Soviet Arms and Soviet Power, Washington, Infantry Journal Press, 1949, p. 111) places military deaths at about 7 million, civilian deaths at about 10 million, and totally disabled persons at about 3 million. By contrast, the official United States figures show 294,000 deaths as a result of combat activity.

[4] The crude death rate since 1950, however, may be somewhat lower in the U. S. S. R. than in the United States. Age-specific mortality, as opposed to the crude death rate, is undoubtedly far higher in the U. S. S. R.

Quantitative data are not available for the war or immediate postwar years in the U. S. S. R., but the conclusion in the text is supported by a variety of indirect evidence; data for other years were given in Narodnoe khoziaistvo SSSR, Statisticheskii sbornik, 1956, op. cit., p. 243, for the Soviet Union, and in Statistical Abstract of the United States, 1956 edition, op. cit., p. 58, for the United States.

[5] Soviet birthrates since 1950 have again become higher (by a small margin) than those in the United States, although they are still far short of prewar levels in the U. S. S. R.

Quantitative data are not available for the U. S. S. R. in the period 1941–49. Data for earlier and later years were given in Narodnoe khoziaistvo SSSR, Statisticheskii sbornik, 1956, op. cit., p. 243.

the United States, instead of about 45 percent as in 1940. It might be noted here that, although Western demographers were aware of the very large war losses and lowered birthrate in the Soviet Union during World War II, few of them apparently realized their full extent. Hence most Western estimates showed the Soviet population in 1955 as being from 15 to 20 million larger than the recently published Soviet . estimate shown in table 1.[6]

TABLE 1.—*Population of the U. S. S. R. and the United States, and its distribution by urban and rural areas, for selected years*

SOVIET UNION

	Population (in millions)			Percentage of total	
	Total	Urban	Rural	Urban	Rural
1913 (present boundaries)	159.2	28.1	131.1	17.6	82.4
1913 (boundaries on Sept. 1, 1939)	139.3	24.7	114.6	17.7	82.3
1926 (census of Dec. 17, 1926, interwar boundaries)	147.0	26.3	120.7	17.9	82.1
1939 (census of Jan. 17, 1939, interwar boundaries)	170.6	56.1	114.5	32.9	67.1
1940 (estimate, postwar boundaries)	[1] 191.7	60.6	131.1	31.6	68.4
1950 (estimate as of Dec. 31, 1950, postwar boundaries)	[2] 182.9	[3] 71.4	[4] 111.5	[4] 39.0	[4] 61.0
1954 (estimate as of Dec. 31, 1954, postwar boundaries)		[5] 84.6			
1956 (estimate as of April 1956, postwar boundaries)	200.2	87.0	113.2	43.4	56.6

UNITED STATES

	Total	Urban	Rural	Urban	Rural
1850	23.3	3.5	19.7	15	85
1870	39.9	9.9	28.7	26	74
1890	63.1	22.1	40.8	35	65
1910	92.4	42.0	50.0	46	54
1930	123.1	69.0	53.8	56	44
1940	132.0	74.4	57.2	57	43
1950 (old definition of urban)	151.2	88.9	61.8	59	41
1950 (new definition of urban)	151.2	96.5	54.2	64	36
1955	164.3	103.5	58.0	64	36

[1] The estimate of 191.7 million for midyear 1940 undoubtedly lacks precision. The annexations of population, the concurrent emigrations, the dislocations of population pursuant to Soviet occupation all apparently have made it difficult for the U. S. S. R. to provide a precise figure for 1940.

[2] Derived from figures for April 1956, and Khrushchev statement (Pravda, Feb. 15, 1956) that population had increased by 16.3 million during the fifth 5-year plan.

[3] Tsentral'noe statisticheskoe upravlenie pri Sovete Ministrov SSSR, Narodnoe khoziaistvo SSSR, Statisticheskii sbornik, Gosstatizdat, Moskva, 1956, p. 26.

[4] Derived by subtraction (col. 3) and by division (cols. 4 and 5).

[5] Ibid., p. 27; also ibid., p. 26.

SOURCE AND COVERAGE OF DATA FOR U. S. S. R.

Tsentral'noe statisticheskoe upravlenie pri Sovete Ministrov SSSR, Narodnoe khoziaistvo SSSR, Statisticheskii sbornik, Gosstatizdat, Moskva, 1956, p. 17, except for numbered footnotes above.

Coverage of U. S. S. R. data.—Data on total population cover roughly the present-day territory of the Soviet Union except when noted otherwise.

The Soviet estimate of population in April 1956, which is significantly smaller than population estimates previously accepted by most Western demographers, has been questioned by a few Western experts as being too low. It is provisionally accepted here, pending further inquiry and/or release of supporting evidence by Soviet authorities.

Urban settlements were said to have been defined similarly in all years (ibid., p. 26). Actually, there have been some changes which inflate the rate of urbanization, but the breakdowns into urban and rural components are believed to be sufficiently comparable for present purposes.

[6] This figure has been accepted for working purposes, with some reservations, by most Western specialists on Soviet population. The principal known exception is Dr. Demitri B. Shimkin, Bureau of Census, who doubts that the 1956 Soviet figure is correct and complete.

Total population data are from Department of Commerce, Bureau of the Census, Historical Statistics of the United States 1789–1945, p. 26 for 1850–1910; Department of Commerce, Bureau of the Census, Statistical Abstract of the United States, 1956 edition, p. 5 for 1930–55. Data are midyear population estimates for continental United States residents only.

Urban and rural population data are from ibid. p. 21 for 1850–1950, and ibid. p. 26 for 1955. Data refer usually to civilian population as of the census date, and, therefore, their total in some years does not equal the midyear estimates of total population in the United States. For a definition of the old (prior to 1950) and new (starting in 1950) standards of urban classification, see ibid. p. 2. The new definition is believed to be closer to the Soviet definition of urban areas.

Percentage distributions of the urban and rural population were derived from data in columns 2 and 3, and then rounded to the nearest whole percent. Use of the total in column 1 would have yielded a different result from the one shown—for reasons referred to in the immediately preceding paragraph—only in the years 1870 and 1955.

The predominantly rural character of the Soviet population is readily apparent from an examination of the data in table 1. In 1926, about the start of the Soviet planning era, approximately the same proportion of the population was in urban areas as in the United States just before the Civil War; and even currently, just as in the United States of the early 1900's, over half the population in the U. S. S. R. resides in rural areas. The rate of urbanization in the Soviet Union since 1926, however, has been extremely rapid—even with some allowance for upward bias owing to changes in definition of "urban"; and it has continued high during the postwar period. By contrast, the rural-urban population distribution in the United States has not changed significantly in the last 25 years (see table 1). Rather, suburbanization and the internal change of rural areas from farm to nonfarm have been the dominant processes.

Data on the age and sex distribution of the Soviet population have not been released by Soviet authorities since the 1926 census. However, estimates conforming to the official Soviet population totals and vital statistics have been prepared by the United States Bureau of the Census.[7] A comparison with similar data for the United States[8] suggests the following tentative observations:

(1) While the total population of the Soviet Union was about 20 percent higher than that of the United States in 1955, the number of persons in the working ages 15-59 was over 30 percent higher. This difference reflects the higher fertility of the Soviet population prior to World War II, offset in part by the heavy loss of men during the collectivization of agriculture and in the war. Because of these losses the ratio of men to women in ages 15-59 was only 84:100 in 1955, compared to 98:100 in the United States; the proportion of Soviet to American women in these ages being 1.4 to 1, in contrast to the male ratio of 1.2 to 1. Females outnumbered males in 1955 by only about 1 million in the United States, compared to about 12 million in the U. S. S. R. The deficit of males is particularly large in the 30 and older age group in the Soviet Union but as is usual in most countries, there is a small excess of males in the under-25 age group; that is, the

---

[7] Estimates furnished to the committee staff.
[8] Statistical Abstract of the United States, 1956 edition, op. cit., p. 26.

effect of World War II on males in that age group was not much if any greater than on females.

(2) In ages 60 and over, the Soviet population was only 70 percent as great as the American, a reflection of lower life expectancy and of the Soviet Union's stormy history.

(3) In the age group 5-14, which was heavily affected in the U. S. S. R. by the wartime decline in fertility and sharp rise in infant mortality, the population is less than 10 percent higher than the American. Restated, the proportion of the United States population in the age group 5 to 14 is larger than the Soviet. This suggests the possibility of proportionately larger increments to the United States than to the Soviet labor force during the next 5 or 10 years.

(4) However, the Soviet margin is reestablished in the age classes under 5, which aggregate a population about 25 percent higher than their American counterparts.

B. LABOR FORCE: UTILIZATION AND DISTRIBUTION

The civilian labor force in the Soviet Union is divided into 2 parts: "free" and forced. Reliable data are available only for the former. The subject of forced labor is discussed in some detail in a previous study for this committee,[9] and references to still more detailed sources are cited there. Two points should be emphasized, however. (1) There are significant differences among the groups usually classified under forced labor in the U. S. S. R. There is the very sizable but varying portion of forced labor which works and lives in concentration camps in remote areas, usually in very severe climates, under conditions so abominable and abhorrent as to defy full comprehension by free people. And there are those not so completely deprived of liberty, but still forced to work in undesirable areas and/or at reduced pay, and usually with some loss of social status. (2) "Free" workers in the U. S. S. R. are not free in the same sense that workers are free in the United States. For example, "free" workers in the U. S. S. R. have been legally restricted in several important respects during the period under review. Such restrictions included outright prohibition of or penalties for job transfers, heavy penalties for lateness or absence from work, transfer through force or heavy pressure to other jobs in other regions, obligatory overtime, and obligatory donations of time (sometimes with compensation at reduced rates) to road work and other civic improvements; "free" Soviet laborers have also never had the benefits of the right to organize freely, to bargain as equals with their employers, or to strike in support of those rights. The restrictions on "free" labor have been relaxed in recent years, particularly in April 1956,[10] and there have been some reports that conditions also have improved slightly for forced labor. Soviet authorities claim major reductions in number of labor camps and prisoners since 1953.

Forced labor in concentration camps, it should be noted, is covered by the estimated total labor force figures of table 2, but not by the

---

[9] A study prepared for the Joint Committee on the Economic Report by the Legislative Reference Service of the Library of Congress, Trends in Economic Growth, joint committee print, 83d Cong., 2d sess., pp. 234–246.

[10] Gliksman, Jerzy G., Recent Trends in Soviet Labor Policy, Monthly Labor Review, July 1956.

reported labor force data. At least part of the forced labor outside the camps, is apparently covered, however, by the data on the reported civilian labor force.

1. The labor force, in absolute terms and as a proportion of population

(a) *Reliability of Soviet labor force data.*—Data on the Soviet labor force have not been given fully and directly in Soviet sources since 1926, even for the segment called the "reported civilian labor force." It has not been possible, therefore, to determine with any precision labor force trends within the U. S. S. R. through time, or to make accurate comparisons between the U. S. S. R. and the United States. But the broad trends within the U. S. S. R. and the United States and the comparison between the 2 countries can be established with sufficient clarity for present purposes, and these data are given in table 2 below.

TABLE 2.—*Labor force and population in the U. S. S. R. and the United States*

SOVIET UNION

Year	Estimated reported civilian labor force	Inclusive estimated total labor force	Population (midyear)	Ratios	
				Estimated reported civilian labor force to population	Inclusive estimated total labor force to population
	Millions	*Millions*	*Millions*	*Percent*	*Percent*
1926 (interwar boundaries)	66.8	82.5	147.0	43	56
1940 (postwar boundaries)	78.2	100–105	191.7	41	52–55
1950 (postwar boundaries)	79.7	100–105	181.5	44	55–58
1955 (postwar boundaries)	85.9	105–110	197.5	43	53–56

UNITED STATES

Year	Civilian labor force	Total labor force	Population	Ratios	
				Civilian labor force to population	Total labor force to population
	Millions	*Millions*	*Millions*	*Percent*	*Percent*
1870	12.9	12.9	39.9	32.3	32.3
1890	23.3	23.3	63.1	36.9	36.9
1910	37.4	37.4	92.4	40.5	40.5
1930	49.8	50.1	123.2	40.4	40.7
1940	55.6	56.0	132.1	42.1	42.4
1950	63.1	64.6	151.7	41.6	42.6
1955	65.8	68.9	165.3	39.8	41.7

SOURCES AND COVERAGE

Soviet Union.—Estimated reported labor force includes salary and wage workers (other than domestic servants and day laborers) who are employed by civilian state and cooperative establishments (excludes civilians in certain military and security establishments); members of producers' cooperatives; independent craftsman; and agricultural workers on collective farms, independent farms, and private plots who are men aged 16–59 or women aged 16–54. Also included are those family members working on their private plots, but these are measured in man-years, probably meaning 265 man-days per year per standard worker. The other categories named earlier are mostly based on annual averages except for the agricultural workers who are measured in terms of end-of-year estimates of the number of able-bodied men and women of the ages specified above. Data for 1926 are from Gosplan SSSR, Vsesoiuznaia Perepis' Naseleniia 1926 g.

(All-Union Census of Population of 1926), völ. XXXIV, tables III and IIIg, Moscow, 1930. Data for 1940–55 from Tsentral'noe statisticheskoe upravlenie pri Sovete Ministrov SSSR, Narodnoe khoziaistvo SSSR, Statisticheskii sbornik, Gosstatizdat, Moskva, 1956, pp. 187–188, derived from percentage distributions on the basis of absolute information for components, for example, the numbers of workers and employees, and members of cooperatives.

Inclusive estimated total labor force includes, in addition to the coverage noted above, collective farm members aged 12–15, and the over-age workers; armed forces; domestics and day laborers; other miscellaneous employment; unemployed; party officials not elsewhere classified; and forced labor not elsewhere classified. Except for 1926, the totals given are estimates.

For 1926, 1940, and 1955 populations, see table 1. The 1950 midyear figure is estimated on the basis of the year-end figures shown in table 1.

United States.—Data on the civilian labor force in 1870–1910 are from Department of Commerce, Bureau of the Census, Statistical Abstract of the United States, 1956 edition, page 195; those for 1930–55 from ibid., page 197. Data for 1870–1910 cover "gainful workers" 10 years and older, while those for later years cover only persons 14 years and older. The earlier data are as of the census dates; those for later years were given as annual averages. Data for all years covered unemployed persons.

Data on the number in the Armed Forces in the United States are not readily available for 1870, 1890, and 1910. However, because such persons appear to have been included in the civilian labor force in those years, and because in any event their numbers were insignificant for present purposes, the number in the total labor force was estimated to have been the same as in the civilian labor force in those years. Data for the later years are from ibid., page 197. The total labor force differs from the civilian labor force in coverage only through inclusion of persons in the Armed Forces.

Population data for 1870–1890 are from Department of Commerce, Bureau of the Census, Historical Statistics of the United States 1789–1945, page 26; those for 1910–55 are from Department of Commerce, Bureau of the Census, Statistical Abstract of the United States, 1956 edition, page 5. Data are midyear estimates, with data for 1870–1910 referring to residents of continental United States, and those for 1930–55 covering also Armed Forces overseas.

(b) Soviet labor force trends, and comparison with the United States.—The estimated reported civilian labor force increased from 1926 to 1940 less than proportionately with the increase in population. The reasons are probably to be found in part in the reductions in labor force participation associated with urbanization and increased education. Proportionately fewer urban women are counted in the labor force than of those in rural areas. Attendance in schools beyond grade V rose about sixfold in the period 1928–29 to 1938–39 in the Soviet Union. The growth of military forces and the operation of forced labor camps by 1940 may have been contributing factors to the lower proportion of the reported labor force, as contrasted with 1926. The absolute increase in labor force shown in table 1 from 1926 to 1940 also takes into account the population which was acquired through territorial annexation. Were it not for the territorial change, the reported figures would show little increase for the period 1926–40.

Estimated reported civilian labor force participation in 1950 was higher than in 1940 despite the further increase of enrollment in grades V and above, of 80 percent from 1938–39 to the school year 1955–56. Thus despite continued urbanization, the reported utilization of the Soviet population of working age had become increasingly intensive. Although data are not available for the war years, the figures for 1950 showing intensive use may reflect a carryover of policies which prevailed during the war. The 1955 data reflect some easing in labor force participation as compared with 1950. Direct comparison with 1926 is complicated by the shift in proportions between rural and urban living.

The inclusive estimated total labor force as a proportion has been relatively stable over the whole period though showing the same general shifts and trends as the estimated reported civilian labor force. The inclusive figures reflect the Soviet effort to squeeze as much work as possible out of the population. The emphasis on agriculture, where labor participation traditionally is high, and the continuing efforts to raise the output of industry combine to explain the high ratios shown.

The proportion of the population in the United States in the civilian labor force appears to have increased substantially since 1870. However, because of the larger wartime and postwar birthrates, longer periods of schooling, the aging of the population, and the increases in numbers of military personnel,[11] there has been a reduction of the participation in the labor force during the past 10 to 15 years. (See table 2.) The proportion of persons of working age who are in the labor force has been relatively stable, however, while there has been a moderate increase in the proportion of working females between 1940 and 1955.

Compared to the U. S. S. R., the United States appears to have utilized a substantially smaller proportion of its population in the labor force in all years, although the disparity would be less in 1955 if the labor forces were shown as proportions of the total populations of working age in the two countries. A number of factors are or have been involved:

(1) A much larger proportion of the Soviet population resides in rural areas where the labor-force participation rate of women and of youth is high. As urbanization proceeds, it seems likely that the proportion of the Soviet population in the labor force will in the future decrease, though probably not to the United States level.

(2) A much larger proportion of the Soviet population at present is in the prime-working-age group of 16 to 60. This was probably not true before the war; but in those years, the Soviet population was even more heavily concentrated in rural areas.

(3) Extensive pressure—economic and other—has been exerted on women and the marginal working groups, in a determined effort by Soviet authorities to expand the labor force. By contrast, the United States has chosen to "produce leisure" rather than more goods and services in many instances, in part because the overall level of output per capita is already so high compared to that of almost any country. The choice of leisure instead of more goods and services in the United States is also reflected, it might be noted, in the shorter workweek and longer vacations of the American worker.[12]

2. Distribution of labor force into agricultural and nonagricultural work

Thirty years ago, only 16 percent of the reported labor force in the U. S. S. R. was devoted to nonagricultural work. By contrast, as early as 1850, more than double that percentage was employed in nonagricultural work in the United States. (See table 3.) During the past

---

[11] An offsetting factor has been the greater availability of part-time employment for youth.

[12] Increasing leisure in the United States coupled with many automobiles and powered household appliances has meant that many services once measured as part of the economy are now excluded. In contrast, some reported Soviet growth of activity is transfer into the measurable sector. Dr. Demitri Shimkin suggests that these two divergent trends are part of the explanation for apparent differences in growth rates of the two economies.

30 years the nonagricultural labor force in the U. S. S. R. has increased
to 3.5 times its previous size, with a nearly corresponding increase in
the percentage so employed.   This change has been faster than in any
comparable period in the United States, though even by 1955, the percentage of the Soviet labor force in nonagricultural work had not
reached the level attained by 1890 in the United States.   In terms of
total numbers reported as employed in nonagricultural work, the
Soviet Union is now at about the level of the United States in the
early forties and is still 20 percent below the current United States
level despite the greater overall labor force and population in the
U. S. S. R.

TABLE 3.—*Distribution of the civilian labor force between agriculture and nonagriculture, the U. S. S. R. and the United States for selected years*

SOVIET UNION

Year	Total	Agriculture	Nonagri-culture	Agriculture	Nonagri-culture
	Millions	*Millions*	*Millions*	*Percent*	*Percent*
1926	63.8	53.8	9.9	84	16
1940	78.2	47.0	31.2	60	40
1950	79.7	42.3	37.4	53	47
1955	85.9	41.6	44.3	48	52

UNITED STATES

Year	Total	Agriculture	Nonagri-culture	Agriculture	Nonagri-culture
1820	2.9	2.1	0.8	71.8	28.2
1850	7.7	4.9	2.8	63.7	36.3
1870	12.9	6.8	6.1	53.0	47.0
1890	23.3	9.9	13.4	42.6	57.4
1910	37.4	11.6	25.8	31.0	69.0
1930	48.8	10.5	38.4	21.4	78.6
1940	55.6	9.5	38.0	20.1	79.9
1950	63.1	7.5	52.5	12.5	87.5
1955	65.8	6.7	56.5	10.6	89.4

SOURCES AND COVERAGE

U. S. S. R.—Data for 1926 are from Gosplan SSSR, Vsesoiuznaia Perepis'
Naseleniia 1926g. vol. XXXIV, table III, Moscow 1930, and they refer to the
reported labor force only, as of the date noted in table 1.   Estimates for 1940,
1950, and 1955 were derived from data in Tsentral'noe statisticheskoe upravlenie
pri Sovete Ministrov SSSR, Narodnoe khoziaistvo SSSR, Statisticheskii sbornik,
Gosstatizdat, Moskva, 1956, pp. 188 and 190, and are intended to approximate
annual averages, excluding most of the work of children and other "non-able-
bodied" persons in agriculture.

United States.—Department of Commerce, Bureau of the Census, Statistical
Abstract of the United States, 1956 edition, p. 195 for all columns, 1820–1930;
p. 197 for 1940–55.   Data for 1820–1930 refer to gainful workers or experienced civilian labor force, 10 years and older, as of the date of census.
Data for 1940–55 are annual averages rather than as of a particular census
date, and they cover persons 14 years old and over.   The sum of "agriculture" and
"nonagriculture" from 1940 on does not equal the total because unemployed are
not assigned to either agriculture or nonagriculture.   The percentages have been
adjusted, however, to equal 100 percent.

Note that coverage of the labor force data in this table differs from that of
table 4, as indicated in the notes to the latter table.

3. *Proportions of population employed in nonagricultural work*

The comparison of utilization of population in nonagricultural
versus agricultural work can also be approached by comparing the percentages of the total population in each country employed in nonagricultural work.   Such a procedure avoids some of the statistical diffi-

culties involved in comparing labor force data of changing coverage.

The data shown in table 4 below indicate that the U. S. S. R. still employs less than 25 percent of its population in nonagricultural work—a proportion somewhat smaller than that in the United States in 1900. A comparison of proportions in industrial work alone would show the U. S. S. R. as somewhat more industrialized in one limited sense: about 40 percent of its (smaller) nonagricultural employment was engaged in industry in most years, in contrast to a proportion of about one-third of the larger number of nonagricultural employees so engaged in the United States through the past century. In another important sense, however, the U. S. S. R. is even less industrialized than the industrial employment data suggest: the U. S. S. R. provides to a far lesser extent the services of all kinds which are usually associated with urbanization and industrialization than the United States.[13]

In summary, the U. S. S. R. labor force and population were predominantly agricultural and rural just 30 years ago, with a labor force and population structure similar to that in the United States a century or more earlier. By 1955, the situation had changed radically in the U. S. S. R.—at rates more rapid than for similar changes in the United States—so that a bare majority of the Soviet labor force was then engaged in nonagricultural pursuits and over two-fifths of its population resided in urban areas. Despite these remarkably rapid shifts, however, the Soviet labor force and population taken as a whole would certainly be characterized as heavily rural in character, and at a stage approximating that of the United States at the turn of the century.

TABLE 4.—*Nonagricultural employment and population in the U. S. S. R. and the United States*

SOVIET UNION

Year	Civilian nonagricultural employment (millions) (1)	Population (millions) (2)	Ratio, col. 1 to col. 2 (percent)
1926	9.9	147.0	6.7
1939	28.5	170.6	16.7
1940	31.2	191.7	16.2
1950	37.4	181.5	20.7
1955	44.3	197.5	22.4

UNITED STATES

Year	Civilian nonagricultural employment (millions) (1)	Population (millions) (2)	Ratio, col. 1 to col. 2 (percent)
1870	6.5	39.9	16.3
1900	18.4	76.1	24.1
1930	34.5	123.1	28.2
1940	39.7	132.1	30.1
1950	50.3	151.7	33.2
1955	55.8	165.3	33.8

Sources: Soviet data from tables 2 and 3 with 1939 taken from Eason, Warren, in Bergson, Abram (editor), Soviet Economic Growth (Evanston: Row-Peterson), 1953, page 108. United States data from Redding, A. David, Comparison of Volume and Distribution of Nonagricultural Employment in the U. S. S. R.,

[13] For a further discussion of the utilization of labor in the two countries, see Redding, A. David, Comparison of Volume and Distribution of Nonagricultural Employment in the U. S. S. R., 1928–55, With the United States, 1870–1952, The Review of Economics and Statistics, November 1954, pp. 444–450.

1928–55, with the United States, 1870–1952. The Review of Economics and Statistics, November 1954, p. 445, for 1870–1950; and from Department of Commerce Survey of Current Business, July 1956, p. 20, for 1955. Data apply to contemporary boundaries.

Employment data rather than the labor-force data of table 3 are used for the United States, to obtain greater comparability with the Soviet data. The employment data for the United States are on a "full-time-equivalent" basis and were obtained from reports by employers, that is, by the "establishment approach." By contrast, the labor force data for the United States used in table 3 were based on population censuses. The population data for the United States include armed forces serving overseas.

C. QUALITY OF THE LABOR FORCE : EDUCATIONAL LEVEL AND TRENDS

There are a number of different ways to measure the quality of the labor force, none of which is completely satisfactory or unambiguous.[14] The decision to focus on formal educational levels and trends as an indication of the quality of the labor force was made in part because educational levels seemed at least as appropriate as any other single measure for the purposes of this report, and in part because of the interest attached to formal education per se. This focus was not intended, however, to deny the influence of the entire political-cultural-economic environment on both intellectual and physical achievements. It is recognized that formal education is but one element in the process of creating a mental and physical capacity for solving problems of all kinds—whether they are problems in physics, chemistry, sociology, or the sometimes less academic problems in production processes. Some of those factors, such as comparative levels of applied skills gained from work experience, have been introduced into the interpretation wherever possible and consistent with the objectives of this study. It should also be emphasized that the focus on formal education was not intended as a thoroughgoing coverage of the large and complex problem of the status of education per se in the two countries. Rather it was intended only to indicate the comparative quality of the two labor forces now and in the past.

1. Educational trends and levels

Data are presented in table 5 below on graduations, enrollments, and on current and past totals of living graduates in both the U. S. S. R. and the United States for selected years or periods. Several points emerge from an examination of these data.

(a) Starting from very low levels compared to the United States, the Soviet Union has increased its total (not per capita) enrollments and graduations at most levels of education to numbers approaching those in the United States.

---

[14] For example, the trends of labor productivity in each country could be measured and the levels compared at different points in time. But this would be unsatisfactory because there are many influences on labor productivity other than the quality of the labor force—influences such as quantity and quality of capital equipment. The question of labor productivity is taken up in another section of this chapter, in connection with future trends in the structure of the labor force.

Or, if the quality of output could be measured and compared, and account taken of extraneous influences, this also might indicate the quality of the labor force; but again such a measure would be ambiguous, as well as impractical for other reasons. Or, if the practical experience of the labor force in various skilled jobs could be measured and compared, this also would be relevant to a comparison of labor-force quality in the two countries.

(*b*) In view of its late start, the Soviet Union lags behind the United States in total numbers in the presently living populations who have finished elementary schools, or secondary schools, or colleges.[15]

(*c*) The Soviet Union has concentrated its efforts at the higher educational levels in the fields of physical and natural sciences and engineering, rather than the liberal arts, humanities, and social sciences. About half its current graduations are in the former fields, compared to about a quarter in the United States. Therefore, even though total graduations in the U. S. S. R. are currently somewhat fewer than in the United States, the level of current graduations in the scientific fields and engineering in the U. S. S. R. is significantly greater than in the United States—the extent of the difference depending on the definition of science. And in particular professions such as engineering, the numbers currently employed are probably somewhat greater in the U. S. S. R. than in the United States.

(*d*) Both enrollments in and graduations from the subprofessional schools in the U. S. S. R. have increased significantly during the period under review. Comprehensive data on subprofessional training in various technical schools in the United States are not available, so that a comparison of numbers of subprofessionals in the U. S. S. R. and United States cannot be drawn. However, there are in the United States a considerable number of subprofessional as well as in-factory schools, junior colleges, and Armed Forces training schools, which train such specialists as laboratory technicians, electricians, machinists, and nurses.

---

[15] Data were noted by the staff only for total graduates of higher educational institutions; but the above statement is consistent with the enrollment data for all levels shown in table 5, and it is supported by evidence on the median number of years of schooling completed by the Soviet population as a whole.

TABLE 5

PART I.—EDUCATION AND SPECIALISTS IN THE SOVIET UNION

[In thousands]

	Annual averages				1954–55	1955–56
	1929–32	1938–40	1946–50	1951–55		
I. Graduations:						
1. Higher education:						
(a) Total	[1] 42	[1] 109	[1] 130	[1] 224	[2] 256	[3] 265
(b) Engineering	(4)	(4)	[5] 32	(4)	[6] 59	[2] 71
(c) Other science	(4)	(4)	(4)	(4)	[6] 67	[2] 75
2. Subprofessional	[1] 73	[1] 226	[1] 256	[1] 312	(4)	(4)

	1927–28	1940–41	1950–51	1954–55	1955–56	1956–57
3. General secondary	(4)	[7] 285	[7] 220	[7] 750	[8] 1,400	(4)
II. Enrollments						
1. Higher education:						
(a) Total	[9] 169	[9] 812	[9] 1,247	[9] 1,730	[9] 1,867	(4)
(b) First year only	[10] 43	[10] 263	[10] 349	[11] 451	[10] 461	[3] 440
2. Subprofessional	[9] 189	[9] 975	[9] 1,298	[9] 1,839	[9] 1,961	(4)
3. General secondary (8 to 10)	[12] 130	[12] 2,370	[12] 1,500	[12] 5,140	[12] 5,250	(4)
4. Grades 5 to 7	[12] 1,330	[12] 10,770	[12] 12,030	[12] 11,600	[12] 9,300	(4)
5. Grades 1 to 4	[12] 9,910	[12] 21,370	[12] 19,670	[12] 12,700	[12] 13,600	(4)
6. Total	[13] 11,947	[13] 37,315	[13] 37,297	[13] 35,055	[13] 33,898	(4)

	1928	1940			1955	
III. Total number of specialists:						
1. Total professionals	[14] 233	[14] 908	---------	---------	[14] 2,184	---------
(a) All scientists	(4)	(4)	---------	---------	[15] 1,158	---------
(b) Engineers only	[16] 33	[17] 290	---------	---------	[17] 586	---------
2. Subprofessionals	[14] 288	[14] 1,492	---------	---------	[14] 2,949	---------
IV. Number of specialists per thousand population:						
1. Total professionals	[18] 1.5	[18] 4.6	---------	---------	[18] 11.0	---------
(a) All scientists	(4)	(4)	---------	---------	[18] 5.9	---------
(b) Engineers only	[18] 0.2	[18] 1.5	---------	---------	[18] 3.0	---------
2. Subprofessionals	[18] 1.9	[18] 7.5	---------	---------	[18] 14.9	---------

[1] Tsentral'noe statistichesko, upravlenie pri Sovete Ministrov SSSR Narodnoe khoziaistvo SSSR Statisticheskii sbornik, Gosstatizdat, Moskva, 1956, p. 229.

[2] Figures were provided by Mr. Nicholas DeWitt, author of Soviet Professional Manpower, from the following Soviet sources: Vestnik Vysshei Shkoly, 1956, No. 3, p. 4; Moscow News, August 15, 1956; and Pravda, April 25, 1956.

[3] Yeliutin, in Pravda, July 7, 1956, p. 2. Figure refers to anticipated enrollment.

[4] Not available.

[5] DeWitt, Nicholas, Soviet Professional Manpower, National Science Foundation, Washington, D. C., 1955, p. 164.

[6] National Science Foundation press and radio release, August 8, 1956. Science fields include agriculture, science teaching, university science (which probably would consist of students of physics, chemistry, etc., with emphasis on theoretical aspects), and an "other science" category which accounted for about 8 percent of the graduates in science in 1955.

[7] DeWitt, op. cit., p. 66.

[8] Pravda, editorial of August 7, 1956. Mr. DeWitt, in reviewing this chapter, noted that this figure is inconsistent with other data. Those data suggested to him that a figure of 1.1 to 1.2 million would be more nearly correct.

[9] Narodnoe khoziaistvo SSSR Statisticheskii sbornik, 1956, op. cit., p. 227.

[10] Ibid., p. 228. Refers to 1928.

[11] Yeliutin, August 31, 1954.

[12] Narodnoe khoziaistvo SSSR, Statisticheskii sbornik, 1956, op cit., p. 224. Data cover only students in the general school system, excluding those in labor reserve and adult education schools.

[13] Derived by addition of data in rows 1a, 2, 3, 4, 5, plus data on adult education given in ibid., p.221.

[14] Ibid., p. 193.

[15] National Science Foundation press and radio release, August 8, 1956. Total refers to the estimated number of living graduates, of which 566,000 were in engineering, 205,000 in agriculture, 240,000 in science teaching; 87,000 were university graduates in unspecified science courses; and 60,000 in other science fields. Note that the above estimate for living graduates in engineering is about 3 percent less than the figure given directly in ibid., p. 194.

[16] Estimated, on basis of figure of 40,700 given for 1929 in Dewitt, op cit., p. 239.

[17] Narodnoe khoziaistvo SSSR Statisticheskii sbornik, 1956, op. cit., p. 194.

[18] Derived from data in rows 1, 1a, 1b, and 2, shown under III, and from population data in table 1, ch. IV.

TABLE 5—Continued

PART II.—EDUCATION AND SPECIALISTS IN THE UNITED STATES

[In thousands]

	1929–30	1939–40	1949–50	1955–56
I. Graduations:				
1. Higher education:				
(a) Total	[19] 122	[19] 187	[19] 432	[20] 311
(b) Engineering [21]	10	14	53	26
(c) Other science [22]	[4]	[4]	63–98	33–66
2. Subprofessional	[4]	[4]	[4]	[4]
3. General secondary	[23] 667	[23] 1,221	[23] 1,200	[24] 1,319
II. Enrollments:				
1. Higher education:				
(a) Total	[25] 1,101	[25] 1,494	[25] 2,996	[26] 2,996
(b) 1st year only	337	[27] 418	[27] 583	[26] 683
2. Subprofessional	[4]	[4]	[4]	[4]
3. General secondary	[27] 4,812	[27] 7,130	[27] 6,435	[28] 7,747
4. Elementary, including kindergarten	[27] 23,740	[27] 21,127	[27] 22,225	[28] 28,514
5. Total [29]	29,653	29,751	31,319	39,257

	1930	1940	1948	1955
III. Total number of living graduates:				
1. Total professional	[4]	[4]	[4]	[30] 6,300
(a) All scientists	[4]	[4]	[4]	[31] 1,536
(b) Engineers only	[32] 215	[32] 261	[32] 350	[31] 575
2. Subprofessional	[4]	[4]	[4]	[4]
IV. Number of living graduates per thousand population:				
1. Total professional	[4]	[4]	[4]	[18] 38.1
(a) All scientists	[4]	[4]	[4]	[18] 9.3
(b) Engineers only	[18] 1.7	[18] 2.0	[18] 2.4	[18] 3.5
2. Subprofessional	[4]	[4]	[4]	[4]

[19] U. S. Office of Education, Biennial Survey of Education in the United States, 1950–52, ch. 4, sec. 1, p. 37.

[20] U. S. Office of Education, preliminary statistics.

[21] U. S. Office of Education, Engineering Enrollments and Degrees, 1955, Circular No. 468, p. 3, for 1949–50, and Summary Statistics on Engineering Enrollments and Degrees: 1956, Circular No. 491, p. 2. Figures for other years were supplied by that office. Note that if graduate degrees are included, the numbers would be changed for the years in question to 11,000, 16,000, 58,000, and 32,000, respectively.

[22] The smaller number of science graduates includes those in the fields of agriculture, biological sciences, physical sciences (including mathematics), and "sciences without major." The larger number of science graduates also includes those in the healing arts and medical sciences, anthropology, geography, and psychology. Data for all years are from U. S. Office of Education, Earned Degrees Conferred by Higher Educational Institutions, annual editions; figures shown under 1955–56 actually refer to 1954–55.

[23] U. S. Office of Education, Biennial Survey of Education in the United States, 1950–52, ch. 1, p. 22.

[24] U. S. Office of Education, Number of High School Graduates from Public and Nonpublic Schools, 1939–40 to 1953–54, and forecasts to 1969–70 (mimeographed, September 21, 1956).

[25] U. S. Office of Education, Biennial Survey of Education in the United States, 1950–52, ch. 1, p. 40. Data cover regular-session enrollment only.

[26] U. S. Office of Education, total enrollment estimated; first year only is fall enrollment from Circular No. 460. Enrollment covering the full academic year was 15 percent greater in 1954.

[27] U. S. Office of Education, Biennial Survey of Education in the United States, 1950–52, ch. 1, p. 7.

[28] U. S. Office of Education, press release of September 2, 1956.

[29] Derived by addition of data in rows 1, 3, and 4.

[30] Estimated, on basis of figure of 5,800,000 for 1953 cited by DeWitt, op. cit., p. 255, which appeared originally in Wolfle, D., America's Resources of Specialized Talent (New York, Harper, 1954). Graduates for 1954 and 1955 were added to this, and the figure was then rounded. The figure refers to the total number of living graduates, which would exceed the number actually employed in United States by a significant number.

[31] National Science Foundation press and radio release, August 3, 1956. Data on science graduates include those in engineering, natural sciences, psychology, and agriculture.

[32] U. S. Department of Labor, BLS Bulletin No. 968, Employment Outlook for Engineers.

NOTES TO TABLE 5

Data on Soviet and United States enrollments refer to the number at start of academic year. The number at the close of the academic year would be smaller.

Data on numbers of specialists in the U. S. S. R. are as of midyear 1928 and 1955, and end-of-year 1940; the date of data for United States is not specified.

All data on numbers of specialists, except those taken directly from Soviet sources, refer to the number of living graduates. Coverage of the data given directly in Soviet sources refers to census data on specialists.

Note further that in the United States the difference between numbers of specialists employed and numbers of living graduates might be very substantial.

Data on professionals in the U. S. S. R. refer to persons who have graduated from a university or higher education institute. Data on professionals in the United States refer to persons who have received a first-level professional degree. In most cases this would be a bachelor's degree; in some it would be a doctor's degree, such as D. D. S. or M. D. As noted in the text, the training of professionals covered is roughly comparable.

Data on subprofessionals in the United States were not available, so that no comparison could be made. Data are shown for the Soviet Union.

Since this table was prepared, there has appeared the Soviet publication Tsentral'noe statisticheskoe upravlenie pri Sovete Ministrov SSSR Kul'turnoe Stroitel'stvo SSSR, Moskva 1956 (Cultural Construction of the U. S. S. R.), which provides further breakdowns on Soviet education data and minor revisions of totals. Changes are not sufficiently great to warrant reworking this table, but additional comparisons are shown below, as prepared by Dr. Demitri B. Shimkin, Bureau of the Census.

TABLE 5A.—*Graduations from higher educational institutions by specialty, 1950 and 1955 (1st degrees only). Soviet Union and the United States*

Specialty	Soviet Union 1950 Total	Soviet Union 1950 From day divisions only	Soviet Union 1955 Total	Soviet Union 1955 From day divisions only	Index (1950=100) Total	Index (1950=100) From day divisions only	United States[1] 1950	United States[1] 1955	United States[1] Index (1950=100)
Total	176,869	145,817	245,846	179,229	139	123	433,734	[2]285,772	66
I. Engineering and physical sciences	30,749	28,975	60,229	56,046	196	193	[3]78,277	[3]38,720	49
1. Geology and geodesy	1,721	1,695	3,976	3,929	231	232	3,043	1,795	59
2. Mining	1,353	1,320	5,290	5,189	391	393	(4)	(4)	(4)
3. Energetics	2,380	2,262	4,957	4,457	208	197	(4)	(4)	(4)
4. Metallurgy	1,416	1,298	4,656	4,383	188	184	(4)	(4)	(4)
5. Machine and instrument building	9,101	8,256	15,736	13,078	173	158	(4)	(4)	(4)
6. Electrical machine and instrument building	1,433	1,403	2,981	2,830	208	202	(4)	(4)	(4)
7. Radio technology and communications	1,427	1,327	2,950	2,698	207	203	(4)	(4)	(4)
8. Chemical technology	2,586	2,513	4,954	4,774	192	190	10,619	5,920	56
9. Wood-products technology	727	717	1,885	1,784	259	249	(4)	(4)	(4)
10. Construction	4,873	4,560	9,440	8,916	194	196	(4)	(4)	(4)
11. Geodesy and cartography	294	293	540	533	184	182	(4)	(4)	(4)
12. Hydrology and meteorology	379	369	628	604	166	164	(4)	(4)	(4)
13. Transportation	3,059	2,962	4,236	3,971	138	134	(4)	(4)	(4)
II. Commerce and technology	13,638	12,412	19,685	14,369	144	116	[6]94,686	[6]55,269	58
1. Food technology	2,295	2,237	1,878	1,828	82	82	[7]7,976	[7]7,250	91
2. Consumers' goods technology	1,240	1,147	1,669	1,461	135	127	(4)	(4)	(4)
3. Economics	10,103	9,028	10,138	11,080	160	123	14,573	6,364	44
III. Agriculture, forestry, and biology	12,859	12,508	24,563	23,306	191	186	[8]28,716	[8]16,220	56
Of which, biology	(4)	(4)	(4)	(4)	(4)	(4)	13,717	9,050	66
IV. Health and physical education	20,747	20,623	16,943	16,404	82	80	[9]30,089	[10]32,497	108
V. Education and library science	78,529	54,413	98,249	50,944	125	94	[11]51,728	[11]47,482	92
VI. Law (and administration)	5,648	3,401	8,126	3,940	144	116	14,312	[12]9,061	63
VII. Drama and fine arts	2,376	2,371	2,491	2,314	105	98	[13]17,910	[14]14,736	82
VIII. Other[15]	12,323	11,114	15,560	12,806	126	115	[16]118,016	[17]71,787	61

[1] United States data are from 4-year institutions or more. Data on education and library science are for work in elementary and secondary schools only.

[2] Excludes military and naval science.

[3] Engineering, architecture, physical sciences (chemistry, physics, geology), and mathematics.

[4] Not available.

[5] Included with geology.

[6] Business and commerce, home economics, and economics.

[7] Home economics.

[8] Agriculture, animal husbandry, forestry, biology and zoology.

[9] Dentistry, medicine, nursing, optometry, pharmacy, and physical education.

[10] Healing arts, medical sciences, and social work.

[11] Education, industrial arts, and library science.

[12] Law, international relations, and public administration.

[13] Fine arts, music, speech and drama.

[14] Fine arts, except architecture.

[15] In the U. S. S. R., "education at university level," largely languages, history, and social sciences, including higher Communist Party courses, as well as small specialties, e. g., oriental studies. Some mathematicians, biologists, and other pure scientists are included here.

[16] English, history, journalism, modern languages, philosophy, political science, psychology, religious education, social sciences (not elsewhere classified), sociology, theology, and all other fields (not elsewhere classified).

[17] English, foreign languages, geography, journalism, philosophy, psychology, religion, social sciences (except for social work), and all other fields (not elsewhere classified).

Sources: Tsentral'noe statisticheskoe upravlenie pri Sovete Ministrov SSSR, Kul'turnoe Stroitel'stvo SSSR Statisticheskii sbornik (Moskva: Gosstatizdat) 1956, p. 217. Department of Commerce, Bureau of the Census: Statistical Abstract of the United States, 1951 (Washington, 1951), p. 112; ibid, 1956, p. 131.

TABLE 5B.—*The structure of graduate training in the Soviet Union, 1925–56, with comparative United States data for 1955*

Specialty	Soviet Union						United States	
	Persons completing graduate work		Graduate students				Graduate degrees conferred, by field	
	1925–1946		1951		1956		1955	
	Number	Distribution in percent	Number	Distribution in percent	Number	Distribution in percent	Number	Distribution in percent
Total	25,000	100.0	21,905	100.0	29,362	100.0	67,044	100.0
I. Natural science and engineering	8,875	35.5	9,085	41.5	15,336	52.2	10,723	16.0
1. Physical-mathematical sciences	2,550	10.2	972	4.4	2,855	9.7	[1] 2,429	3.6
2. Chemistry	1,750	7.0	1,319	6.0	1,318	4.5	2,178	3.2
3. Geology and mineralogy	550	2.2	503	2.3	1,260	4.3	661	1.0
4. Engineering	3,750	15.0	5,809	26.5	9,358	31.9	5,083	7.6
5. Architecture	[2]	[2]	154	.7	186	.6	183	.3
6. Geography	275	1.1	328	1.6	359	1.2	189	.3
II. Biological fields	7,440	29.8	4,798	21.8	6,154	20.9	7,950	11.9
1. Medicine and pharmacology [3]	4,170	16.7	1,386	6.3	2,164	7.4	3,442	5.1
2. Biology	1,400	5.6	1,247	5.7	1,426	4.8	2,603	3.9
3. Agriculture and veterinary medicine	1,870	7.5	2,165	9.8	2,564	8.7	1,905	2.8
III. Other	8,685	34.8	8,024	36.7	7,872	26.9	[4] 48,371	72.1
1. History and philosophy [3]	1,940	7.8	2,607	12.0	2,064	7.0	[6] 2,503	3.7
2. Law [7]	150	.6	748	3.4	367	1.3	907	1.4
3. Economics	750	3.0	1,366	6.2	1,810	6.2	[8] 5,104	7.6
4. Languages [9]	4,850	19.4	1,980	9.0	2,164	7.4	[10] 3,117	4.6
5. Education	275	1.1	864	4.0	1,037	3.5	[11] 27,758	41.4
6. Arts	720	2.9	459	2.1	430	1.5	3,257	4.9

[1] Mathematics, physics, and physical sciences (not elsewhere classified).
[2] Included with engineering.
[3] Includes physical education.
[4] Includes fields not elsewhere specified, e. g. religion, sociology, etc.
[5] Includes Communist Party theory in the U. S. S. R.
[6] Philosophy, history, and political science.
[7] Largely administrative; United States equivalent being law, international relations and public administration.
[8] Economics, home economics, and business and commerce.
[9] Includes literature, philology, and archeology.
[10] English, foreign languages, and anthropology.
[11] Excludes physical education, allotted to medicine (to accord with the Soviet tabulation).

Sources: DeWitt, Nicholas, Soviet Professional Manpower (Washington: National Science Foundation), 1955, p. 209.
Tsentral'noe statisticheskoe upravlenie pri Sovete Ministrov SSSR, Kul'turnoe Stroitel'stvo SSSR Statisticheskii sbornik, (Moskva: Gosstatizdat), 1956, pp. 256–7. Department of Commerce, Bureau of the Census, Statistical Abstract of the United States 1956 (Washington, 1956), p. 131.

TABLE 5C.—*Awards of higher degrees in the Soviet Union and the United States, 1934–55*

Year	U. S. S. R. Persons completing graduate work [1]	United States		
		Higher degrees awarded [2]	Of which—	
			Master's degrees in science and engineering [3]	Doctor's degrees in science [3]
1934	2,350	21,120	([4])	1,550
1940	1,978	30,021	([4])	1,812
1946	1,616	21,175	([4])	956
1948–55: Total	43,424	513,512	117,100	31,931
Ratio: 1955–48	(2.29)	(1.44)	(1.12)	(2.34)
1948	3,328	46,605	12,503	2,150
1949	4,528	56,120	14,689	2,767
1950	4,093	64,852	15,971	3,591
1951	4,895	72,470	17,100	4,212
1952	5,682	71,270	15,654	4,407
1953	6,495	69,332	13,782	4,721
1954	6,796	65,819	13,368	5,051
1955	7,607	67,044	14,033	5,032

[1] Considerable delays may take place in the date degrees are awarded, and in some cases, rejected. Hence, the series here is substantially different for the years 1940 on from that published by DeWitt, loc. cit.
[2] Excludes honorary degrees.
[3] Science defined, in accordance with National Science Foundation concepts, as agriculture, biological, medical and health fields, engineering, physical sciences (including mathematics and statistics), psychology, paleontology, anthropology, and geography.
[4] Not available.

Sources: DeWitt, Nicholas, Soviet Professional Manpower (Washington: National Science Foundation), 1955, p. 338.
Tsentral'noe statisticheskoe upravlenie pri Sovete Ministrov SSSR: Kul'turnoe Stroitel'stvo SSSR Statisticheskii sbornik (Moskva: Gosstatiz lat), 1956, p. 258.]
National Science Foundation: Scientific Personnel Resources (Washington, D. C.), 1955, p. 72.
Department of Commerce, Bureau of the Census, Statistical Abstract of the United States, 1946 (Washington, 1946), p. 134; ibid., 1949, p. 122; ibid., 1956, pp. 130–131.

(*e*) As a result of lower birth rates in the Soviet Union during and after the war years, and higher birth rates in the United States during the same and subsequent years, the number of students at the elementary levels has increased significantly in the United States while it has decreased in the U. S. S. R. However, owing to the efforts by Soviet authorities to increase the availability of secondary schools in all areas, there has been a very large increase in enrollments at the secondary levels in the U. S. S. R., despite the lower birth rates.

2. Relationship of education trends to the labor force in general

The statistics of table 5 leave no doubt that the Soviet Union has made significant progress in remedying its previously extremely low level of education. The quality of its education, which is not reflected in the statistics, seems also to have improved greatly since the mid-thirties, though by United States standards it is narrow in scope and more specialized, even at the lower levels.[16] Because of its low starting levels, in terms of formal education as well as in terms of numbers in the population having applied skills gained from experience in industrial work, the Soviet labor force as a whole is still far short of United States attainments—despite the heavy emphasis on expanding both general and technical education as well as in-factory and trade-

[16] See DeWitt, Nicholas, Soviet Professional Manpower, National Science Foundation. Washington, D. C., 1955. See also the comprehensive study by Collingwood, Harris. Engineering and Scientific Manpower in the United States, Western Europe, and Soviet Russia, prepared for the Joint Committee on Atomic Energy, Joint committee print, 84th Cong., 2d sess.

school training for the applied skills. It is the consensus of American students of the Soviet Union that for at least a generation to come the United States labor force as a whole (not just recent graduates of American schools) will be better educated as well as more skilled than its counterpart in the Soviet Union.

3. Relationship of education trends to the professional labor force

There are currently about three times as many persons in the United States with higher education degrees as there are in the U. S. S. R. (See table 5.) The lead of the United States in training professional manpower, however, is not nearly so overwhelming as it appears to be. For one thing, it is a specialized lead—in the social sciences and humanities rather than in the fields more directly related to production such as the physical and biological sciences and engineering. The number of engineers and other scientists [17] in the labor force, for example, appears to be of about the same order of magnitude in both countries. Second, there are a greater number of college-trained persons in the United States than in the U. S. S. R., who either do not work at all or work in positions unrelated to their field of specialization.

Both of the above qualifications are a reflection of the differences in general philosophy and in the aims attached to higher education in the two countries. In the U. S. S. R., higher education is an instrument of the state set up largely to increase Soviet material strength. As a consequence, Soviet graduates are obligated to accept employment in their chosen field of specialization—which is most often related fairly directly to production tasks. In the United States, on the other hand, more general aims are attached to higher education: such education may lead to employment in the same field of specialization, but it may be simply an extension of secondary education designed to round out the student's background, with no followup in specialized employment. Many secretaries and housewives in the United States, for example, have college degrees; and many college-trained men work as salesmen or in other fields which are not directly related to their college training.

Interpretation of the current situation of the professional labor force and past trends could be approached from several points of view. From an internal United States approach, demands for the services of professional graduates in the natural sciences, such as engineers, seem to be rising continually, as was reported by the Joint Economic Committee in a study on automation,[18] and as is amply illustrated by the want-ad section of any metropolitan newspaper. When contrasted with the declining trend in graduations of engineers between the periods 1949–50 and 1954–55,[19] a shortage of scientists and engineers seems self-evident; that is, demand for the services of such persons appears to exceed the supply at present salary levels. Such conclusions have been reached by a number of persons and groups, particularly with respect to future availabilities. Without intention of disagreeing with the central conclusions drawn by many of the in-

---

[17] See footnotes 6 and 22 of table 5 for coverage of this category in both countries.
[18] Automation and Technological Change, report of the Subcommittee on Economic Stabilization, committee print, 84th Cong., 1st sess., p. 7.
[19] All references in this paragraph to trends of engineering graduations since 1949–50 are based on data in U. S. Office of Education, Engineering Enrollments and Degrees, 1955, p. 3.

vestigations, or even of intruding on the broader question of whether or not the United States education system is performing and will be able in the future to perform its functions adequately, this report should like to note the following qualifications regarding the present "shortage" of engineers and other scientists: (1) Raising salary levels of such specialists might reduce some of the demand for their services and result in greater economies in their use, and in time also increase their supply. The effects of the resultant adjustments on the United States economy, however, would require further investigation. (2) The decline in engineering graduates since 1950 is a result of abnormal factors, so that it need not indicate a potential shortage. Graduations in the academic year 1949–50 were at a peak because of the large number of war veterans who entered the universities after the war. The decline in engineering graduations simply reflects the completion of formal education by this special group. Further, the downward trend was halted in 1954–55, and there was a 15 percent increase in engineering graduates in 1955–56. (3) Soviet authorities also have stated publicly that their industry needs more professional men such as engineers,[20] so the question becomes a relative one: Who needs them the more?

The last-named qualification suggests that investigation of the comparative needs for professionals in the United States and the Soviet Union as those needs relate to production is a more relevant approach for the purposes of this study. Firm answers to such a question could be arrived at, however, only if preceded by a detailed examination of the structures of the economies and educational systems of the U. S. S. R. and the United States, including a study of the pattern of utilization of professional manpower in the two countries; a thorough evaluation of the differences in cultural-political backgrounds; and a specification of assumptions and purposes. The following observations, however, using engineers as a case study for professionals in the natural sciences and engineering, seem important:

(a) Differences in the economic structure may result in greater use of engineers for the same end results in the Soviet Union. First, design and production appear to be separated to a far greater extent in the Soviet Union than in the United States.[21] Second, it may be that a larger proportion of engineers are required in or gravitate toward administrative work because of the proliferation of control levels in the Soviet Union; because of an alleged tendency, noted often in Soviet writings, on the part of some professional men and even semiprofessionals to avoid contact with work at the production levels, especially if it is dirty or otherwise unpleasant; and because of an apparent tendency on the part of Soviet administrators to call on engineers to take part in endless conferences, in part, perhaps, because competent administrators with technological or engineering backgrounds may be rarer in the U. S. S. R. than in the United States. The evidence on some of the above points is convincing.[22]

---

[20] For example, Yeliutin, in Pravda, July 7, 1956, p. 2, refers to certain specific shortages.
[21] See De Witt, op. cit, p. 252.
[22] For example, see Khrushchev's speech at a conference of coal miners in Stalino, in Pravda, August 18, 1956.

(*b*) Differences in the educational system and in education levels probably have resulted in greater need for engineers in the U. S. S. R. Although the quality of engineering and other scientific training appears to be high in the Soviet Union (actually, the length of training in most courses is greater, and the study requirements appear to be heavier), the training is narrower in scope. Therefore, in many instances the broader training of the American professional might enable one man to function often in two related fields where two professionals might be required in the Soviet Union. This is not intended as a denial of the advantages of occupational specialization; rather it is intended to suggest only that the occupational specialization may have gone further than is advantageous at the present stage of specialization of production in the Soviet Union.[23] Perhaps more important, the generally lower educational level of the Soviet labor force would probably increase the need for supervisory personnel, including engineers.[24]

(*c*) Differences in the cultural-political background and current environment may also have resulted in greater use of professionals per unit of output in the U. S. S. R. The evidence suggests that the Soviet engineer has been encouraged throughout his home and school training to accept authority rather than to think critically and independently; and after completion of formal training to look to top planners for directions rather than push new ideas—either his own or those of others. Further, the Soviet system in many ways inhibits innovations by engineers and others through its failure to provide ample rewards for success, coupled with heavy penalties for failure. In the short run, any innovation is likely to reduce output, and this is especially true if much time is required to install it or to familiarize workers with new methods. If after the initial difficulties the innovation turns out to be successful, the extra profits are usually shortlived and the pressure to increase output further is just as great, because Soviet planners usually increase the output plan. (The extra profits come mostly from above-plan output.) If it turns out to be a failure, however, the penalties range from censure to demotion or discharge; and in the past even imprisonment and execution have been the price of failure. For these reasons, the factory managers and others at higher levels often prefer to "play it safe," with the result that even proved innovations are slow in being adopted. Managers may receive special rewards for extra accomplishments, but this stimulus is often offset by a stifling bureaucratic atmosphere. The question is too complex to treat in detail here, but such conditions would seem to inhibit efficient utilization of engineers and, for that matter, of all factors of production.

On the basis of the above observations, it could be argued that, when viewed from such a standpoint as production needs, the U. S. S. R.

---

[23] For a discussion of specialization of production in industry, see ch. 2.
[24] A reviewer of this report noted: "Evidence appears to indicate that Russian engineers and scientists are assisted and supported by more and better trained technicians than American professional workers. This may lead to better utilization of Soviet than American engineers * * *." If true, the greater need for supervisory personnel may be met in the U. S. S. R. by the subprofessional group; and there may not be any need for more engineers to supervise production. In fact, fewer engineers might be required. The evidence is, however, inconclusive.

today is more in need of all kinds of professional men than the United States; for, with roughly the same number of engineers and other professionals in the natural sciences, the U. S. S. R. produces only about one-third as many goods and services as does the United States. The above argument undoubtedly attaches too much importance to the influence of engineers on production levels, but it may be a useful balance to the recent emphasis on numbers of professionals, especially engineers. On the other hand, numbers are also important: for example, because of increased numbers of new engineers, it is possible that the U. S. S. R. is now in a better position than it was previously to compete with the United States and West European countries in providing technical aid to the presently underdeveloped countries; and the greater the numbers of professionals as a whole, the higher is the probability that among them there will be persons of top rank.

Before attempting to present and interpret the problem of future requirements for, and availability of, professionals in the United States and the Soviet Union, a word should be said about the numbers and quality of professionals employed in high-level research in both countries. The number of scientists engaged in basic and applied scientific research at the higher levels may currently be larger in the United States than in the U. S. S. R.[25] Nonetheless, some observers have argued that the number of scientists rather than the size of available funds to hire them is the greater bottleneck in research and development programs in the United States (cf. supra for discussion of personnel shortages). Numbers in this context also may be less important than the quality of the researchers; although, again, the greater the numbers, the higher the probability of finding creative genius. In that connection, qualified observers have stressed that the bulk of Soviet scientists no longer simply copy or modify Western accomplishments, as in the past; that instead, they are increasingly capable of conducting independent high-quality and high-level research. It should be noted that there have always been top level Soviet scientists in the U. S. S. R. who compare favorably with top level scientists in the West.

4. Future requirements for, and availability of, professionals in the United States and the Soviet Union

The United States lead in total numbers of currently living college graduates will probably persist for several decades to come, in view of the size of the lead and the currently greater number of persons graduating each year from professional schools. (See table 5.) By 1960 the annual rate of graduations from Soviet professional schools as a whole might equal that in the United States, but it is not likely to exceed it substantially.

In the scientific and engineering fields, however, the picture is quite different. The U. S. S. R. is expected to graduate about 420,000 engineers and 125,000 other professionals in the natural sciences during the years 1955–60, so that by 1960, the number of engineers and other

---

[25] Allen Dulles, Director of the CIA, estimated in U. S. News & World Report, May 11, 1956, pp. 124–127, that the United States currently employs about 240,000 scientists in all research in the physical and biological sciences, in contrast to about 120,000 so employed in the U. S. S. R.

scientists will be about 800,000 and 260,000 respectively.[26]   By contrast, only about 143,000 engineers and 85,000 scientists are expected to graduate in the United States during the same period, so that the numbers of such professionals in 1960 will be about 750,000 and 320,000 respectively.[27]

Some of the differences between the structures of the two economies, such as the greater availability of capital equipment in the United States, are expected to diminish; the general educational level in the Soviet Union is gradually approaching that in the United States, although probably at least another generation will be required to close the gap for most currently living persons; the gap in applied skills is also being closed; and Soviet authorities are making fresh and determined efforts to improve incentives to all "classes" of people in the U. S. S. R.   Therefore, the apparent ability of the United States to produce more with fewer engineers will in all probability also be lessened.

Finally, scientific research careers have recently been made even more attractive to qualified persons in the Soviet Union.   Such careers have normally been attractive to exceptionally gifted students because of the relatively greater freedom in most scientific research unrelated to political economy, compared to careers in administration, party work, etc. The Soviet Union has also for a number of years granted exceptionally high status and salaries to scientists, has paid living stipends to students at higher educational institutions, and has provided more openings at those institutions for students in the physical and biological sciences.   A few months ago it abolished tuition fees at the secondary level, so that the only fees still charged are those for boarding schools, and it has increased the availability of secondary schools in rural areas. For the past few years, since Stalin's death, the U. S. S. R. has further enhanced the attractiveness of scientific work by somewhat easing the restrictions on choice of scientific research problems and on communications with Western scientists.   Such encouragement has borne fruit and is likely to bear even more fruit in the future, according to Western scientists.[28]   Of course, it would not be realistic to report that Soviet citizens have an equal opportunity based on merit to share these benefits.   But whatever the remaining discriminations to individuals, the system is producing results for the Soviet state.

On the basis of the above observations it is hard to avoid the conclusion that whatever the relative positions of the two countries are today, the relative superiority in numbers of engineers and other pro-

---

[26] Estimate of N. DeWitt given at the Symposium on Manpower at the 10th Annual Convention of the Air Force Association, New Orleans, La., August 3, 1956 ; the address was made available in mimeographed form.

The increase in graduations compared to previous 5-year periods in the U. S. S. R. may seem, at first glance, inconsistent with the drop in enrollments at the elementary levels. See table 5.   However, current acceptances to Soviet professional schools are only about one-third as numerous as the number of general secondary-school graduations ; so that, even in the unlikely event that secondary-school graduations fall below the level of openings in professional schools in the future, a considerable backlog of applicants—though probably not the most gifted—will be available.   Such considerations, as well as the present stage of very keen competition for the limited openings, may well be behind the recent urgings by Khrushchev and other Soviet leaders, that secondary-school graduates go directly into production jobs so that they can later make a more mature choice of professions.   (For example, see Pravda editorials of June 9, 1956, and August 7, 1956.)

[27] Estimate of Dr. Hower Meyerhoff, Director, Scientific Manpower Commission, cited by DeWitt, op. cit.

[28] See, for example, an article by Dr. Freeman Dyson, Institute of Advanced Studies, Princeton, N. J., reprinted from the Baltimore Sun in the Washington Post and Times Herald, July 25, 1956.

fessionals in the United States vis-a-vis that in the Soviet Union will decrease in the future. This may adversely affect relative production levels, although for some time to come the United States should be able to maintain a very substantial lead; it could affect the ability of the United States to compete with the U. S. S. R. in providing technical aid to the presently underdeveloped nations—although willingness to provide such aid, as well as economic maturity, is undoubtedly a rather important factor;[29] and it could affect the ability of the United States to compete with and stay ahead of the U. S. S. R. in some phases of research.

D. FUTURE POPULATION AND LABOR FORCE TRENDS

1. Population

The Soviet population currently is increasing at a rate somewhat greater than that in the United States, so that by 1965 the Soviet population is expected to exceed that of this country by about 45 million persons, or nearly 24 percent, instead of the 32.5 million and nearly 20 percent excess in 1955. (See table 6.)

TABLE 6.—*Population projections for the U. S. S. R. and the United States*

[In millions]

Midyear estimates	U. S. S. R.	United States
1955	197.5	165.3
1960	216.0	178.0
1965	235.0	190.0

SOURCES

U. S. S. R.—Projections for midyear 1960 and 1965 are based on recent population trends and an assumption that approximately present fertility levels and death rates will continue through 1965. A Soviet estimate of about 218 million persons as of an unspecified date in 1960 can also be derived from the per capita-output and total-output goals for that year, as given in Voprosy ekonomiki, No. 3, 1956, page 36, and Tsentral'noe statisticheskoe upravlenie pri Sovete Ministrov SSSR, Narodnoe khoziaistvo SSSR, Statisticheskii sbornik, Gosstatizdat, Moskva, 1956, page 60. The figure for actual population as of midyear 1955 is from table 2, this chapter.

United States.—Department of Commerce, Bureau of the Census, Statistical Abstract of the United States, 1956 edition, page 6, for midyear population projections for 1960 and 1965, based on assumption that 1950–53 fertility level will continue through 1965. Projections based on different fertility assumptions range from 176.5 to 179.4 million for 1960, and from 186.3 to 193.3 million for 1965. Projections include all citizens regardless of whether or not they are residing in continental United States. The figure for actual population as of July 1, 1955, is from table 2, this chapter.

The rate of urbanization in the U. S. S. R. is expected to slow up during the next 5 or 10 years, owing in large part to Soviet difficulties in providing housing and other urban facilities,[30] as well

---

[29] The Soviet Union may also have an advantage in being able to assign technicians abroad for specified periods, with less consideration of personal desires and without the necessity of paying large premiums. The advantage need not, however, prove overriding; and it might even be offset by Soviet difficulties in finding "politically reliable" personnel.

[30] Khrushchev stated in a speech at the 20th Communist Party Congress (Pravda, February 15, 1956) that the recruitment of workers for the large cities should be stopped, and he called for more housing in suburban areas. This discouragement of rural-urban migration appears to apply mainly to the larger centers. But there have also been some reports that collective farmers must show a release order from collective farm management in order to get a job in the city; and even with this they are barred from settling in particularly overcrowded metropolitan centers such as Kiev, and instead are directed to satellite towns in the suburbs.

as, temporarily, the need for retaining and even selective recruiting of manpower for agriculture. Therefore, although net rural-urban population movements have continued in the postwar period at rates greater than in the United States, apparently even during 1954 and 1955 (see table 1), it seems likely that for some time to come the percentage of Soviet population in urban areas will be considerably below that in the United States.

2. The civilian labor force as a whole

Estimates of the Soviet civilian labor force in 1960 and 1965 are not available, so that detailed comparisons between the two countries are not possible. The annual net increase in the Soviet labor force as a whole, however, is expected to decline somewhat between 1955 and 1960, with sharp declines in the increase expected between 1960 and 1965. The primary reasons for this are the lower birth and higher infant-mortality rates during the war and early postwar years, together with the current large-scale increases in secondary school enrollments, the effect of which is to reduce or delay the number of new entrants into the Soviet labor force. The participation rate of women in the labor force may also decline, especially during the second half of the period, because of expected continuing urbanization and an increase in the number of males of marriageable age. The future effect of urbanization is clear from past experience; but the effect of increased numbers of males is indeterminate. There were 12 million fewer males than females in the Soviet population in 1955, so that increased numbers of marriages, and consequent withdrawal of women, especially of mothers, from the labor force could be expected. This would be offset in part, however, by the usually greater participation rates of males than females in the labor force. There may also be a gradual retirement of over-age or otherwise marginal workers from the labor force if Soviet living conditions continue to improve; however, the recent introduction of a new pension plan [31] may affect the rate of withdrawals in a direction which cannot yet be determined.

By contrast, although the net increase in the United States labor force between 1955 and 1960 is expected to be somewhat below that of 1950–55, the increase between 1960 and 1965 is expected to be significantly greater than during either of the 2 preceding 5-year periods. As a result of those differential movements in the U. S. S. R. and the United States, the absolute increases in the labor force will probably be larger in the U. S. S. R. than in the United States during the first half of the 10-year period, and smaller during the second half.

3. Distribution of the labor force between the agricultural and non-agricultural sectors

Reflecting the shift of manpower from agricultural into nonagricultural pursuits, the nonagricultural labor force increased significantly faster than the total labor force in both the United States and the Soviet Union during the periods under review (see table 3). Such shifts (or, alternately, direction of new entrants into the labor force) into nonagriculture are expected to continue in the United States for some time to come. For about the next 5 years it is unlikely that these shifts will take place on a large scale in the Soviet Union; but after that

---

[31] A draft of the new law on pensions is available in Pravda, May 9, 1956.

time it seems probable that they will once again occur—at rates which will depend in part on the increases in agricultural labor productivity and production; in part, perhaps, on changes in international trade patterns; and in part on the extent to which urban services, principally housing, are expanded in the U. S. S. R.

Labor force and output data can be compared in each country to provide crude estimates of relative labor productivity in the U. S. S. R. vis-a-vis the United States. The data indicate that labor productivity in Soviet agriculture is probably between one-twelfth and one-sixth as great as in the United States, in contrast to Soviet-United States ratios of about one-fourth for labor productivity in the output of all goods and services, and between one-third and one-half for nonagricultural goods and services, or for industrial production alone in the U. S. S. R. vis-a-vis the United States. Or, using the data shown in chapter VI for a comparison of labor productivity in the different economic sectors within the U. S. S. R., it appears that labor productivity in Soviet agriculture is about one-fifth as large as labor productivity in Soviet industry or transportation.[32] These calculations, whether shown as a single estimate or as a range, are, it should be noted, of the crudest nature; they are subject to a wide but unknown margin of error; and they may not be entirely consistent with each other.

The low levels of output per worker in Soviet agriculture suggest, as was noted in chapter III, that there are considerable opportunities for significant increases in agricultural labor productivity, and consequent release of farm labor for work in other sectors. And, in fact, output per worker in Soviet agriculture is alleged to have increased by about a third since 1950.[33] A prerequisite for rapid increases in labor productivity and withdrawal of agricultural workers in the future would seem to be the raising of agricultural output to a level which would allow steady, though perhaps small, increases in per capita food consumption plus some additions to food reserves. Otherwise, the withdrawal of even the least productive labor would diminish total agricultural output at a time when it could not be afforded. Once output has been sufficiently increased, Soviet authorities would be in a position to tackle seriously in its own right the problem of raising labor productivity in agriculture.

It should be noted that some of the measures already taken to increase agricultural output, and more particularly, those which are planned to be taken, are expected to raise labor productivity at the same

[32] The above ratios were derived as follows: The U. S. S. R., according to estimates in ch. VI, produces about one-third as many goods and services of all types as does the United States, and has a total labor force of about 100 million persons, if account is taken of those working part time in agriculture and other undernumerations, compared to about 66 million in the United States. The labor productivity ratio is derived by dividing the output ratio (1/3) by the labor force ratio (3/2).

Similarly, in agriculture Soviet production is probably about half as large as that in the United States, especially if adequate account could be taken of this country's much greater production of the more valuable meat and dairy products as well as vegetables and fruits; and the agricultural labor force in the U. S. S. R. is probably significantly more than six times as large as in the United States.

In the case of total nonagricultural goods and services, the U. S. S. R. was estimated to have produced about one-third as much as the United States, with a labor force about 78 percent as large; and in the case of industry alone, the estimated ratio of output was again about one-third, with a labor force of about the same magnitude.

The comparison of labor productivty ratios within the U. S. S. R. in the various sectors was based on estimates derived by dividing the share of income originating in the various sectors (see ch. VI) by the estimates of the labor force in the various sectors (given in Narodnoe khoziaistvo SSSR, Statisticheskii sbornik, 1956, op. cit. p. 190).

[33] Ibid., p. 102.

time.[34] The extent of the Soviet effort to increase labor productivity
in agriculture as a goal in itself (rather than as a concomitant of
efforts to increase agricultural output) will depend, however, on the
alternative uses to which labor-saving equipment and materials can
be put in other economic sectors. The relative scarcities of labor,
capital, and land in the Soviet Union are different from those in the
United States, so that there is no apparent reason why Soviet authorities should attempt to raise labor productivity in Soviet agriculture in
the short run to the levels in the United States, even if they could.
Rather, because labor in Soviet agriculture appears at this time still
to be relatively more plentiful than capital equipment, it would probably be a better overall allocation of their resources to use proportionately more labor in agriculture than is done in the United States and
to conserve capital.

An alternative method by which Soviet authorities might reach a
position where they could shift labor out of agriculture is suggested by the comparisons of labor productivity in the various
economic sectors; that is, the exchange on a large scale of certain Soviet
industrial products for agricultural products from other countries
willing to engage in such trade. Soviet authorities may already have
embarked on such a policy in a limited way, but the evidence to date
is inconclusive. Although it might make sense to do so, from a narrow economic viewpoint in the long run, there are several reasons why
such trade might not materialize on a large scale: (1) in the short run
the Soviet Union would have to give up some of the industrial products
which it needs either for its own further growth in heavy industry or
for consumer satisfaction at home; and (2) the Soviet Union in the
past has preferred not to become dependent for any supplies on other
countries not under its control.

Pursuit of either of the above methods (raising agricultural labor
productivity or increasing purchases of agricultural products abroad)
would lead to the possibility of substantial releases of Soviet
agricultural labor. However, in order for that labor to be able to
move to the cities in significantly larger numbers, a prerequisite would
be construction of new housing and other urban facilities. Not only
would housing have to be provided for the newcomers, but the pent-up
demand by present urban residents seems too strong to be completely
ignored. Only to the extent that these measures are undertaken would
Soviet authorities once again be in a position to encourage a large-
scale shift of farm labor to nonagricultural sectors of the economy.

---

[34] See ch. III for supporting data on, and discussion of this subject. Some of the new
agricultural measures might require more manpower on the farms, even though labor
productivity were raised—e. g., programs for expanding dairy farming and livestock raising, and even greater use of fertilizers. Other programs for providing more and better
harvesters, sowers, weeders, etc., would probably raise labor productivity by more than
output. In other words, some agricultural-improvement measures would be primarily
yield-raising, others would be primarily labor-saving.

CHAPTER V

LEVELS OF LIVING

Levels of living and allocations to consumption in most Western societies are considered to reflect the effectiveness of the economic system in providing for the material needs of individuals of the society. To Soviet planners, however, security and enrichment of state power are paramount, with allocations to individual consumption viewed not as an ultimate goal of the economy but rather as an expense necessary to preclude disaffection and to induce required growth in productivity of labor. This basic difference between the United States and the Soviet Union must be kept in mind along with the usual cautions about international and intertemporal comparisons of levels of living.

Measurement and evaluation of levels of living [1] is a complex and difficult task and the answers vary widely according to the yardstick chosen. This is true whether the yardstick is that of some previous time in the history of a nation or that of some other nation, or whether it is food or all goods and services actually consumed or produced, or simply measurement of purchasing power of the average worker (real wages). The variations are especially large if, as is true here, there have been very significant changes in the consumption pattern within one or both of the nations (particularly the Soviet Union in this case), or if the consumption pattern of the nations compared is significantly different. Even though quantities of goods and services can be put into a common price system, the social valuations put upon them cannot be made comparable. This assessment, therefore, must be remembered as being viewed in United States values.

In approaching the problem, this study has used several yardsticks, resulting in these findings: (1) Soviet living levels are far below those in the United States; they have been widely reported to be significantly or noticeably below those in Europe; and they appear to be considerably higher than those in neighboring countries of Asia. (2) Soviet levels of living in 1955 were not necessarily above those of 1928 at the start of the Soviet planning era, even though they have risen sharply during the past 5 and 10 years, recovering from wartime losses. By contrast, although levels of living in the United States have not risen as rapidly during the last 5 years as those in the Soviet Union they are half again the levels of 1928. (3) There is no apparent reason why living levels should not continue to rise in both countries. The rise in Soviet living levels seems unlikely to continue at the high rates achieved during the period 1950–55, but the rate is likely to be

---

[1] Reference is to the actual levels of living, not to any standard or norm, so that only "living levels" is rigorously correct in this context. Living standards in the sense of expectations, based on foreign experience of Soviet troops, a better educated population, and promises of government leaders, may have risen in recent years. It is the gap between a still low level of living and rising standards which, though not subject to quantitative measure, would spell trouble for Soviet authorities.

higher than in the United States for some time to come, because the Soviet base is so much lower. No conceivable rise, however, could result in Soviet living standards approaching those of the United States within the next decade or two. The Soviet authorities boast that they can win a straight per capita production race with the United States, as Khrushchev claimed in late May 1957. Secretly, they probably believe that a collapse of the United States economy in the doctrinaire Marxist sense would provide their only hope. But our economy has no intention of collapsing.

A. COMPARISON OF SOVIET LEVELS OF LIVING WITH THOSE IN THE UNITED STATES AND OTHER COUNTRIES IN 1955

International comparisons of living levels must be approached with a healthy skepticism. However, questionable though the quantification of results may be, the mere attempts often reveal significant points that otherwise might be overlooked in less detailed analysis. One approach to international comparisons is by means of purchasing power comparisons of respective currencies for significant commodities or categories.

In 1955 an estimated 670 billion rubles were expended in the U. S. S. R. on goods and services for private consumption,[2] in contrast to about $270 billion so spent in the United States.[3] As a result of a series of recent studies of Soviet and United States prices by the Rand Corp.,[4] the ruble expenditures can now be converted into United States dollars. Naturally, the dollar purchasing power of each ruble varies according to how it is spent. For example, in the purchase of foods, a Soviet ruble would purchase from about a penny's worth of lard to about 25 cents worth of carrots; in manufactured consumer goods, from $1\frac{1}{2}$ cents in the purchase of a rayon dress to about 33 cents in a thermometer; and in services, a ruble was worth from 3 cents in dry cleaning to about 50 cents in a haircut. For that reason, it makes a great difference how much weight is given to each of the commodity-price-relatives in computing an average ruble-dollar price index. The procedure followed in the Rand studies was to weight the individual price ratios by the proportion each represented in Soviet consumption to obtain an average ruble-dollar ratio based on Soviet consumption habits; and then to repeat the process using United States weights to obtain a ratio based on United States consumption habits.[5] For the purposes at hand, it can be assumed that a "true"

---

[2] The ruble consumption figure derivable from table 1 in ch. VI was about 620 billion rubles in 1955. That figure, however, was in 1953 prices, and because it was designed to measure the value of consumption expenditures at approximately factor costs, it excluded most turnover taxes. Because the ruble-dollar price ratios given below include turnover taxes in the U. S. S. R., as well as excise taxes in the United States, about 85 billion rubles in turnover taxes which were removed for the purposes of ch. VI, should be added back for present purposes, and about 5 percent should be deducted from the total so derived in order to convert the figure from 1953 to approximately 1955 prices.

[3] The United States figure on consumption is normally given net of Government expenditures for public education and health. However, because these are included in the Soviet figures, their magnitudes in the United States were estimated for 1955 and added to the consumption figure for that year.

[4] A recent study in the series is by Norman M. Kaplan and Eleanor S. Wainstein, A Comparison of Soviet and American Retail Prices in 1950, RM-1692-1 (The Rand Corp.), May 1, 1956. Other studies are referred to in the above paper.

[5] The Rand studies used consumption patterns in 1937 and in some years as late as 1952 for the Soviet Union, and a consumption pattern only for the year 1950 in the United States. These studies were most complete for 1950, then were tentatively extended to 1954 through various adjustments. This report assumes 1955 to be similar enough to 1954 to warrant extending those preliminary estimates, if it is understood they cannot be exact.

ruble-dollar index lies somewhere between the two averages computed, but the Rand Corp. itself would probably be more cautious in stating such a conclusion, considering the coverage uncertainties and gaps in some of the underlying data, as well as the for-some-purposes insoluble conceptual and methodological problems involved.

Based on Soviet consumption habits, a ruble in 1955 was worth not more than about $0.10½, contrasted with a purchasing power of not more than $0.07 based on a United States consumption pattern. Total Soviet personal-consumption expenditures in 1955, therefore, amounted to from about 46 billion to 70 billion United States dollars, depending on the price index chosen—or only about one-fourth to one-sixth the household consumption expenditures in the United States. When converted to a per capita basis, the personal consumption in the U. S. S. R. turns out to be only about one-fifth to one-seventh as great as personal consumption in the United States.[6]

About the same results on comparative levels of living were obtained through a crude comparison of real wages of nonagricultural employees in the U. S. S. R. and the United States. That is, division of the U. S. S. R./United States ratio of average money earnings in 1955 by the ruble-dollar price ratios indicates that the Soviet wage or salary earner could buy on the average only from about one-quarter or one-fifth to one-seventh as much as the average United States wage or salary earner. (See table 1). The similarity of results is not surprising because of the basic similarity of the underlying data. However, it conceals some important coverage differences which tend to be offsetting. First, the real wages approach covers basically only nonagricultural employees, plus the relatively few hired farm employees in each country; that is, it excludes the very large number of collective farmers in the U. S. S. R. and the independent farmers in the United States. Second, government services are included in the personal consumption, but not the real wages approach. Finally, the ratios of wage earners to dependents are different in each country.

TABLE 1.—*Ratio of Soviet to United States real wages of urban workers*

1. Average ruble-dollar price ratios in 1955:
    - (*a*) Using U. S. S. R. consumption pattern—not less than 9.5 rubles equals $1
    - (*b*) Using United States consumption pattern—not less than 14.0 rubles equals $1
2. Average annual money earnings in 1955:
    - (*a*) U. S. S. R: worker and employee group—about 8,300 rubles
    - (*b*) United States: wage and salary earnings, full-time equivalent employee—about $3830
    - (*c*) U. S. S. R./United States money earnings ratio—2.2
3. Ratio of U. S. S. R./United States real wages:
    - (*a*) Using U. S. S. R. consumption pattern—1 to 9.5/2.2 equals 1 to 4.3 or higher
    - (*b*) Using United States consumption pattern—1 to 14.0/2.2 equals 1 to 6.4 or higher

Sources: Figures on ruble-dollar price ratios shown are actually the tentative findings for 1954 by Kaplan, Norman M., and Wainstein, Eleanor S., A Comparison of Soviet and American Retail Prices in 1950, RM–1692–1 (Santa Monica: The Rand Corp.), May 1, 1956, p. 30.
Figures on average annual money earnings are from table 3, this chapter.
Ratios of real wages are derived from the preceding parts of the table.

[6] The exact ratios computed were as follows: from 1/3.9 to 1/5.9 for total U. S. S. R./United States personal consumption; and from 1/4.7 to 1/7.0 per capita consumption.

Although the ratios of real wages and salaries given above cannot be used as precise measures of relative levels of living in the two countries, they indicate, as do the estimates based on gross national product data given in chapter VI of this study, that the average consumption level in the U. S. S. R. is far below that in the United States.[7] The orders of magnitude are supported by the reports of nearly all Western visitors to the Soviet Union, and are supported (though not quantified as to extent) even by statements in the Soviet press. Further, it is supported by inspection of relative production and consumption figures on individual items of consumer goods in the U. S. S. R. and United States in 1955. (See table 2 below.)

Relative to the United States, Soviet per capita consumption of consumer goods is greatest for soft goods and food products, except animal products. They lag the furthest behind (and are improving the fastest) in expenditures for such durable consumer goods as passenger automobiles, washing machines, and television sets.[8] The amount and quality of housing available is miserable but, unlike consumer durables, is difficult to improve. The comparison of bare figures in table 2 may seem more real if illustrated. Suppose, for example, that an average-size house in the United States, of about 1,000 square feet or 93 square meters, housed about 20 persons; or suppose about 40 persons were crowded into one of the middle-class or older homes. That degree of crowding would approximate the housing situation in the U. S. S. R. where most families have only a single room in which all members sleep.

---

[7] The fact that the two different approaches to levels of living yielded nearly identical results—i. e., that Soviet per capita consumption and real wages are from one-quarter or one-fifth to one-seventh as great as those in the United States—should not be interpreted as confirming either result, for, in view of the similarity of underlying data, contradictory results should not have been expected.

The methods of estimating total and components of gross national product also are such that firm conclusions cannot be drawn from the dissimilarity between the ratios of Soviet/United States GNP and Soviet/United States consumption. Ch. VI concludes that the various factors of production (principally labor, but also capital and management) were probably relatively more productive in investment than in consumer goods, using the United States as the standard. The results of this comparison of total consumption are at least consistent with that provisional conclusion, since the Soviet/United States ratio was higher for GNP as a whole (one-third) than for consumer goods alone (one-fourth to one-sixth).

[8] The Soviet pattern of priorities with respect to types of consumer goods differs less from the "early-capitalist" pattern than does the concentration of Soviet industry on producer rather than consumer goods. Goods essential to a minimum subsistence have received greatest priority in the past, and the balance has only recently begun to shift slightly to "superior" food products and consumer durables.

TABLE 2.—*Levels of living: Per capita availability, consumption, or stocks of goods in 1955*

Commodity	U.S.S.R.			United States, 1955	Per capita, 1955			Per capita ratios, 1955, U.S.S.R./United States
	Unit	1955 sales	1955 production		Unit	U.S.S.R.	United States	
FOODS								
Meat	Million metric tons	(4.874)	4.0(2.522)	12.050	Kilogram	20.2	72.9	0.28
Fish	do	1.990	2.498	0.744	do	10.1	4.5	2.24
Poultry meat	do	(?)	(?)	1.951	do	(?)	11.8	(?)
Eggs (number)	Billions	(2.281)	(?)	60.500	Number	(12)	366	}0.35
Milk fat solids	Million metric tons	(?)	29.8 (13.5)	44.118	Kilogram	150.7	266.9	
Milk nonfat solids	do	(?)		26.398	do			
Fluid milk and cream	do	0.439	(0.459)	0.661	do	2.2	159.7	0.55
Butter	do	0.461		0.595	do	2.3	4.0	0.64
Margarine	do	(1.998)	(1.156)	2.347	do	10.1	3.6	0.71
Other fats and oils	do			11.240	do		14.2	(?)
Fruits	do			14.348	do	(?)	68.0	(?)
Vegetables	do			12.844	do	(?)	86.8	(?)
Potatoes	do		67.000	8.463	do	338.7	51.2	6.62
Grain, dry pulses	do			12.844	do	230.0	77.7	2.96
Coffee	do			1.141	do	(?)	6.9	(?)
Tea	do	0.051		0.050	do	0.3	0.3	1.00
Cocoa beans	do			0.298	do		1.8	(?)
Peanuts	do			0.331	do		2.0	(?)
Confectionery items	do	1.706	1.382	(?)	do	8.6	(?)	(?)
Salt	do	4.467	6.200		do	22.6		
Sugar	do	(11.141)	3.419	7.224	do	17.3	43.7	0.40
CLOTHING AND TEXTILES								
Cotton fabric	Billion linear meters	(?)	5.90	11.9	Linear meters	29.8	72.0	0.41
Wool fabric	do	(?)	0.25	0.4	do	1.5	2.4	0.63
Linen fabric	do	(?)	0.31	0.05	do	2.5	0.3	5.00
Silk fabric	do	(?)	0.53	0.05	do	(?)	0.3	8.33
Rayon, acetate fabric	do	(?)	0.11	2.2	do	0.5	13.3	}0.03
Synthetic fabric	do	(?)		0.9	do		5.4	
Hosiery	Million pairs	(?)	772	1,811	Pairs	3.9	11.0	0.35
Knit underwear	Million pieces	(?)	345	940	Number	1.7	5.7	0.30
Shoes	Million pairs	(?)	275	639	Pairs	1.4	3.9	0.36

See footnote at end of table, p. 112.

Table 2.—Levels of living: Per capita availability, consumption, or stocks of goods in 1955—Continued

Commodity	U.S.S.R. Unit	U.S.S.R. 1955 sales	U.S.S.R. 1955 production	United States, 1955	Per capita, 1955 Unit	Per capita, 1955 U.S.S.R.	Per capita, 1955 United States	Per capita ratios, 1955, U.S.S.R./United States
DURABLE MANUFACTURES								
Automobiles	Thousands	64	108	7,763	Number	0.0003	0.047	0.006
Motorcycles	do	216	245	40	do	0.001	0.0002	5.00
Bicycles	do	2,801	2,884	2,900	do	0.014	0.018	0.78
Sewing machines	do	1,647	1,611	2,200	do	0.008	0.013	0.62
Electric irons	do	(1)		2,900	do	(1)	0.048	(1)
Washing machines	do	83	87	4,300	do	0.0004	0.026	0.02
Clothes dryers	do	(1)		1,400	do	(1)	0.008	(1)
Refrigerators	do	144	151	3,700	do	0.0007	0.022	0.03
Vacuum cleaners	do	121	(1)	3,400	do	0.0006	0.021	0.03
Clocks and watches	do	19,193	19,700	43,000	do	0.097	0.260	0.37
Cameras	do	971	1,023	5,900	do	0.005	0.036	0.14
Radios	do	846	848	(1)	do	0.004	(1)	(1)
Record players	do	3,474	} 4,024	14,100	do	0.018	0.085	0.21
Television sets	do	483	}	7,800	do	0.002	0.047	0.04
Electric shavers	do	(1)	(1)	4,600	do	(1)	0.028	(1)
Room air conditioners	do	(1)	(1)	1,200	do	(1)	0.007	(1)
Electric blankets	do	(1)	(1)	1,300	do	(1)	0.008	(1)
HOUSING								
Living space, total available					Square meters	4.8	32.0	0.15

1 Not available.

Coverage

There are not available adequate and comprehensive data on actual consumption in the two countries. Therefore various approximations have been used to show representative items of consumption in real terms.

Food consumption is estimated for the Soviet Union by deriving sales in 1955. Production is also shown for 1955 for general comparison purposes. United States total consumption for 1955 is derived from available per capita information. Soviet per capita food consumption is calculated by dividing 1955 sales by 197.5 million people. To the extent that persons in the military services or in slave labor camps do not draw on these same stocks, there may be a tendency to understate civilian consumption; no figures are available to allow an accurate correction for such institutional populations.

Certain categories are most likely to be understated through incomplete reporting, and these have been shown in parentheses. These include meat, butter, some edible fats, eggs, and dairy products. Where a better estimate was available for comparison purposes, it has been shown, and is described below in the section on sources.

It should be remembered that all per capita figures have the failing of not distinguishing among different groups in the population, as for example by not showing the generally different levels of living of rural population as compared with the urban. Differences in patterns of consumption also appear in the table. It is striking that the Soviet authorities do not include in their sales data the two biggest items in the national diet—grain and potatoes—as well as not reporting vegetables or fruits. Data on grain consumption and on potato production have been derived independently as noted below.

The table can give no adequate measure of the greater variety of processed foods available in the United States including fresh and frozen items purchasable in all parts of the country even when out of season locally.

Clothing and textiles sales data are not available for the Soviet Union. But judging from comparisons of sales and production on other manufactured goods, use of production data seems adequate for order of magnitude comparisons. The 1955 per capita consumption is derived from 1955 production.

United States data are production figures corresponding to those used in chapter II, but with adjustments for imports and exports. As explained in chapter II, a further correction is needed to reflect the greater average width of United States fabrics, and this has been made. The sample of items cannot measure qualitative differences, nor does it cover the great variety of related manufactured products.

The items selected to show as durable manufactured goods also represent a very small sample, not indicating the greater variety and better styling and quality of furnishings and appliances available in the United States. For a few examples, there is no reflection of United States use of foam rubber mattresses, modish furniture, adequate lighting fixtures. Many Soviet radios receive only the local official Soviet broadcast, perhaps on a single channel; in contrast large numbers of United States radios include such added features as electric clocks, timing devices to control appliances, record players, FM channels, or shortwave reception. Likewise, fully automatic washing machines represent the greater part of current production in the United States while the Soviet models almost certainly resemble earlier types. The table only suggests a few of the extra appliances available to American consumers—room air conditioners, electric blankets, clothes dryers, and electric shavers; there are statistics available on more than 25 additional classes of appliances which do not appear to be manufactured yet in the Soviet Union.

Perhaps even more important, the United States is at a replacement stage for many items which the U. S. S. R. is producing for the first time.

As in the case of food, Soviet sales and production are contrasted. The data seem to give a measure of diversion of automobile production away from consumers either to export or to official use.

United States data correspond to those reported in chapter II, but have had adjustments made to add imports and to subtract exports.

Housing alone is reported in terms of available total supply rather than in current production or sales. It is difficult to make more than a general order of magnitude comparison, but the contrast is very striking, as discussed in the text.

Sources

Soviet production data are from the pages noted below in the Tsentral'noe statisticheskoe upravlenie pri Sovete Ministrov SSSR, Narodnoe khoziaistvo SSSR, Statisticheskii sbornik, Gosstatizdat, Moskva, 1956, except as specifically noted: Meat, page 59 (but supplemented by a better estimate from table 2, in ch. III) ; it represents a slight overstatement even in corrected form by including lard. Fish, page 89; this is a gross catch figure and may not be comparable. Milk equivalent, page 59 (but supplemented by a better estimate from table 2 in ch. III). Butter, page 59; but this is known to be incomplete. Other fats and oils, page 59; but this is known to be incomplete at least to the extent of understating the lard component. Potatoes, see chapter III, table 2; this almost certainly is a gross figure not directly comparable. Confectionary items, page 59, but possibly incomplete. Salt, only a total production figure is available as given in chapter II, table 1. Sugar, page 91. All clothing and textile items, page 58. Automobiles, page 56. All other durable manufactures from page 59.

Soviet sales data for 1955 on all items where shown are from Tsentral'noe statisticheskoe upravlenie pri Sovete Ministrov SSSR, Sovetskaia Torgovlia, Statisticheskii sbornik (Moskva: Gosstatizdat) 1956, pages 80–81. They have been derived by relating the data shown on stocks on hand times turnover, and can be considered only to approximate actual annual sales. For most items, the data are consistent. For meat and sugar, particularly the latter, the derived sales seem out of line. The data on durable manufactured goods represent the quantities allocated to state and cooperative trade for sale to the population, as given in the same place, pages 56 and 57.

Soviet per capita human consumption of grain was arrived at by consultation with Western specialists.

Housing living space per capita was estimated by Dr. Timothy Sosnovy, and furnished in advance of publication. Figure refers to urban housing only, but for the order-of-magnitude purposes of this report, the estimate is believed to portray satisfactorily the housing situation in both urban and rural areas. See his The Housing Problem in the Soviet Union (Research Program on the U. S. S. R.), 1954, for estimating procedures in earlier years, as well as for an excellent discussion of Soviet housing conditions.

United States per capita food consumption was taken from Department of Agriculture, The National Food Situation (NFS–78) November 2, 1956, page 4. Only the data on milk solids were supplemented with a figure more nearly comparable to the Soviet by making a rough calculation for total fluid milk equivalents by assuming each fluid weight unit contains 4-percent fat and 9-percent nonfat solids.

Total United States consumption of foods was found by multiplying the per capita data by 165.3 million. This makes no slight correction for military personnel, many of whom draw their food from normal civilian channels, in any case.

Production data on clothing and textiles are from Department of Commerce, Bureau of the Census, Statistical Abstract of the United States, 1956 edition, as follows: Fabrics, page 816; knit underwear, page 819; hosiery, page 821; shoes, page 820 for leather shoes, plus a figure for canvas shoes with rubber soles given in Leather and Shoes, November 1956, page 30. Production data on appliances are given in Department of Commerce, Bureau of the Census, Statistical Abstract of the United States, 1956 edition, on page 838 for the following: Television sets, refrigerators, washing machines, vacuum cleaners, air conditioners, electric blankets, clothes dryers (electric or gas) ; electric irons, and electric shavers. Production data on automobiles, radios, cameras, bicycles, clocks and watches, and sewing machines are from table 1 of chapter II.

All of the above data were given adjustments for international trade though these changes made no marked change in the orders of magnitude, except in the cases of motorcycles, bicycles, sewing machines, and clocks and watches. The sources used to make these adjustments were:

Department of Commerce, United States Imports and Merchandise for Consumption (Rept. No. FT 110), calendar year 1955; and Department of Commerce, Quarterly Summary of the Foreign Commerce of the United States, January–December 1955 (issued June 1956).

Housing in the United States does not require central control, so only partial data are available for purposes of estimating living space per capita. The estimate provided is probably close enough for order of magnitude purposes. It was arrived at by consulting the Department of Commerce, Census of Housing, 1950, volume I, part 1; the Department of Commerce, Statistical Abstract of the

United States 1956 edition, page 782; and the Housing and Home Finance Agency, Eighth Annual Report (1954), pages 218–21; the resulting figure is probably conservative.

Soviet standard cans of food (subcomponents of the sales data on meat and fish) were converted at 400 grams each, based on the capacity measure of 353.4 cubic centimeters.

If quality could be taken into account, the differential is further increased, because the quality of Soviet housing is notoriously low. Judged from reports and pictures made by Western observers, as well as statistical data,[9] most United States housing is incomparably better built and maintained. Further, nearly three-fourths of all dwelling units in this country (rural plus urban) have inside bathrooms; about the same percentage have hot and cold running water; 80 percent have mechanical refrigerators; and an additional 11 percent have iceboxes. By contrast, except for a small proportion of the new urban housing, most Soviet housing—both new and old—has been widely reported by Westerners as rivaling the houses in our slum areas. Although many of the newer urban units have individual inside bathrooms, such "luxuries" are practically unknown in rural areas, and bathrooms shared among a number of families are the rule even in urban areas. Kitchen facilities in the U. S. S. R. also are usually shared by a number of families, and such items as refrigerators are luxuries still beyond the reach of the bulk of Soviet citizens.[10]

The frame of reference of this study is one of Soviet and United States comparisons. However, in view of Soviet activities in Asia, it would be more relevant to compare Soviet living standards with those of countries other than the United States. United States living standards are much higher than those in any other country, so that the U. S. S. R.-United States comparison is interesting but not as relevant to policy problems as certain other comparisons. A provisional conclusion, based on reported observations of many competent Westerners, is that Soviet levels of living are significantly lower than those of industrialized nations such as England and France, but observably higher than those of the neighboring countries of Asia.[11] This conclusion, probably accepted in most of the uncommitted nations of Asia, is of more than academic interest, since a great deal of the reported attractiveness of Soviet communism to some Asians is based on their belief that the Soviet way of industrialization is more adaptable to their circumstances than is the free-competitive-enterprise method. These people ignore the heavy human costs and center their attention on the alleged results of communism in raising living standards in the U. S. S. R. They are not aware that per capita consumption on the average has improved very little in the 1928–55 period in the Soviet

[9] In addition to the sources cited in the footnotes to table 2, data on housing in the U. S. S. R. and United States were taken or derived from Department of Commerce, Bureau of the Census, Statistical Abstract of the United States, 1956 edition, pp. 775–783, and Tsentral'noe statisticheskoe upravlenie pri Sovete Ministrov SSSR, Narodnoe khoziaistvo SSSR Statisticheskii sbornik, Gosstatizdat, Moskva, 1956, pp. 162–164.

[10] It is also interesting to note that whereas approximately two-thirds of the dwelling units in the United States are single-family, detached houses, most Soviet housing, even in rural areas, is multiple unit; and whereas 60 percent of all United States dwelling units are owner-occupied, less than a third of Soviet housing (in terms of floorspace) was built by or for individual citizens for occupancy by them. However, the fact that as many as nearly a third of the urban Soviet dwelling units are privately owned is a matter of some interest.

[11] The evidence is admittedly fragmentary, and the observations in the U. S. S. R. were confined mainly to European Russia; but they seem consistent with statements in the Soviet and Asian press. The conclusion probably applies also to the Asiatic areas of the U. S. S. R., judged from Justice Douglas' recent reference to higher living standards in Soviet Asia than in the neighboring areas of Iran and Afghanistan (New York Times, June 10, 1956, review of William O. Douglas' Russian Journey).

Union. Any increase in opportunities for Soviet citizens to compare higher levels of living in Europe with their own lower levels can cause trouble for the Soviet authorities, too, if this is added to previous comparisons restricted to the Soviet economy.

B. TRENDS IN LEVELS OF LIVING WITHIN THE U. S. S. R. AND THE UNITED STATES

Analyses of trends of levels of living within the U. S. S. R. and the United States are of interest, as were the comparisons of present Soviet-United States levels made above, principally because such trends are the standards normally used by the so-called uncommitted nations in evaluating progress within the Soviet Union, and also because comparisons with his own experience over time probably dominate the judgments of material satisfaction or dissatisfaction of the Soviet citizen toward his government. Reliable information for the first purpose has not usually been available to the uncommitted nations, so that evaluations have often been made on the basis of unsupported Soviet claims or a limited number of Communist-directed visual observations. It is relevant to note, regarding the second purpose, that although Soviet citizens are allegedly very interested in comparing their living levels with those in other countries, they have had little opportunity to do so in most years; but they have always been able to compare their own living levels at any time with that which they remember from some earlier year, or with that related to them by others. Such recollections, incidentally, may not always coincide with reality.

TABLE 3.—*Trends in average real wages and salary earnings of Soviet and United States urban workers, 1928(29) and 1950 to 1955*

	U. S. S. R. indexes		United States indexes	
	1928=100	1950=100	1929=100	1950=100
Average money earnings in 1955	1071	------------	273	127
Cost of living in 1955	900–1300	------------	156	111
Average real wages in 1955 before taxes	82–119	------------	175	114

INTERPRETATION

The temptation to read broad meaning into this table should be resisted. It is not a measure of the whole economy nor of per capita incomes in the economy. It is simply one small additional measure restricted as described in the table heading. What other adjustments might be made to add to understanding of the figures are described below.

Calculation of money-earnings index

Primary reliance was placed on the detailed calculations made by Janet Chapman, in Real Wages in the Soviet Union, 1928–52, Review of Economics and Statistics, May 1954, pages 134–156. Her estimates of money wages in 1928 were 775 rubles and in 1952 were 8,050 rubles. It was necessary to find a 1955 equivalent, and only an approximate calculation could be made.

In 1940 the average wage was calculated at 4,070 rubles on the basis of a wages fund figure of 123.7 billion rubles and employment of 30.4 million, given in Voznesensky, Growing Prosperity of the Soviet Union, 1941, pages 9 and 29. The 1953 ratio on the 1940 base was given as 2.01 in Akademiia Nauk SSSR. Institut Ekonomiki, Politicheskaia ekonomika Uchebnik (Moskva: Gospolitizdat), 1954, page 462, yielding a wage figure of 8,180 rubles, not inconsistent with the Chapman figure for 1952. Between 1953 and 1955, only small wage increases took place, principally due to upgrading of workers rather than general increases, estimated at 120 rubles, or giving a 1955 average of 8,300 rubles.

Corresponding United States information was more simply found. Wages and salary disbursements for 1929, 1950, and 1955 were taken as given in the Department of Commerce, National Income, 1954 edition, pages 162, 163, 196, 197 and Survey of Current Business, July 1956, pages 10, 11, 19.

Calculation of cost-of-living index

Janet Chapman in the work cited develops cost-of-living indexes including one for all markets and all commodities, using 1928 as a base, but obtaining different results depending on whether the index is in terms of the 1928 pattern of consumption or 1937 is used as the pattern. The fact that the resulting range is so wide is a reminder of the difficulty of comparing two time periods. If a 1955 weighting system were available, undoubtedly the range could be changed again. Her 1952 indexes are 1444 (1928 pattern) and 1005 (1937 pattern). These 1952 indexes were extrapolated to 1955 by using price information given in Tsentral'noe statisticheskoe upravlenie pri Sovete Ministrov SSSR Narodnoe khoziaistvo SSSR, Statisticheskii sbornik, Gosstatizdat, Moskva, 1956, pages 210 and 215, and also volume statistics for the different types of markets given in Voprosy Ekonomiki 1956, volume 2, page 68. It is a crude estimate because official prices in state retail trade have been cut, collective farm market prices have moved up, and less information is available about black market prices. The estimate used is that the 1955 index should lie in the range between 1,300 (1928 pattern) and 900 (1937 pattern).

The United States cost of living index is that issued by the Bureau of Labor Statistics, and reprinted by the Joint Committee on the Economic Report in the 1955 Historical and Descriptive Supplement to Economic Indicators, page 49. The data for 1929 and 1950 are drawn from there. The 1955 data are from Economic Indicators, December 1956, page 23, which contains a continuation of the same series.

Calculation of real wages index

In the case of 1928 and 1955 for the Soviet Union, the index of earnings has been divided by the index of prices. The year 1950 presents a different problem, however. If one assumes that the Soviet official real wages index since 1950 is reasonably valid for general order of magnitude comparisons, directly as given in Narodnoe khoziaistvo SSSR, Statisticheskii sbornik, 1956, op. cit., page 37, the index for 1955 is 139, taking 1950 as 100.

In this instance, choosing the Soviet calculation, does not impute to the present any absolute value for 1955. Further it has been partially matched by two other calculations. These are as follows:

Janet Chapman estimated 1948 wages as 7,600 rubles and 1952 as 8,050 rubles. By simple interpolation, 1950 would be 7,825 rubles, if wages moved up at a steady increment each year. This would mean 1955 wages were 1.06 of 1950 wages. Price index data, weighted by the relative importance in 1950 and 1955 of State prices and collective farm market prices give an overall index that 1955 prices were 77 percent of 1950 prices. The wage and price indexes applied to the interpolated actual wage estimate then yield a real wage index for 1955 in terms of 1950 of 138. Kaplan and Wainstein in the work cited, page 33, estimated 1950 wages at 7,700 rubles. Applied to the price index calculated above, the 1955 real wages in terms of 1950 would be 140.

Narodnoe khoziaistvo SSSR, Statisticheskii sbornik, 1956, op cit., gives price index numbers for state retail trade on page 210, and for collective farm market retail trade on page 215. The proportion of total trade in each kind of market is given on page 206. The calculation used to find the overall price index is:

1.38 (1955 index, state retail prices) ×0.909 (1955 state and cooperative trade share) =1.25442

1.11 (1955 index, collective farm market prices) ×0.091 (1955 collective farm share) =0.10101

1.84 (1950 index, state retail prices) ×0.880 (1950 state and cooperative trade share) =1.6368

1.04 (1950 index, collective farm market prices) ×0.12 (1950 collective farm share) =0.1248

$$\frac{1.2544 \text{ plus } .1010}{1.63868 \text{ plus } .1248} = \frac{1.3554}{1.7616} = 0.769 \text{ overall price ratio for 1955 in 1950 terms}$$

Some reviewers regard as fantastic that average Soviet real wages of urban workers could have risen by 39 percent in the years 1950–55, even though this may have been partly recovery to 1928 levels. They point out that considering the easing of conditions in rural areas such an increase for urban workers does not lie within the capacity of the Soviet economy already under strong pressure. These criticisms are probably justified, but no alternate calculation has been offered, so the table does not carry a figure.

Further adjustments which might have been made

Janet Chapman makes calculations for various years including 1952 to report real wages after taxes. Assuming slight reductions in taxes since that time, the corresponding range for 1955 on 1928=100 would yield 74 to 107 percent. Also following her calculations, but reflecting the improvements in educational services by extending schooling, the indexes on 1928=100 recalculated to include the imputed value of education and health services would yield a range of 84 to 122 percent.

Some reviewers have suggested that these rates should be recalculated once again to reflect changes in dependency ratios from 2.0 in 1928 to 1.4 in 1955. This would raise the index markedly. But it also implies an accuracy of consumer welfare measures which is not possible in the scope of the data.

All of these further adjustments would be difficult to make on the United States side. Here, too, big shifts would be occasioned by subtracting taxes and adding the value of imputed services. But the calculation still would reveal no measure of the substantial transfer payments and the income from property which even wage and salary earners may have in the United States.

The one general conclusion from these calculations is that there is a strong implication that Soviet real wages on the average have improved very little in real terms since 1928, but have made a sharp recovery from the low levels prevailing during and after World War II. United States real wages have gone up by a very substantial amount since 1928, and even since 1950. None of these measures, however, actually tells much about the availability of goods, as contrasted with their prices.

Measurements of price movements within a single country, especially when there have been significant changes in consumption habits during the period, are subject to difficulties at least as great as those described above for international comparisons of price levels. There is also an additional complication in this instance, inasmuch as the average money earnings exclude those of collective farmers and independent peasants in the Soviet Union, and of self-employed farmers in the United States, and the BLS consumer price index covers only families of urban wage earners and clerical workers. For all practical purposes, therefore, the results may be interpreted as referring only to urban workers.

Changes in urban real earnings are not equivalent to changes in urban consumption levels. First, the number of wage earners per family appears to have increased during the period in both the U. S. S. R. and the United States so that increases in consumption levels would be greater than indicated. Also, there have been changes in hours of work and leisure time available. In the Soviet Union, on the other hand, new direct taxes and near-compulsory bond purchases must be subtracted from the apparent improvements.[12] There was also during this period a tremendous flow of people to urban areas; and since living levels in rural areas were lower, even a maintenance of urban living levels would indicate an increase in overall living levels,

---

[12] In April 1957 the bond subscription program for future years was halted ; simultaneously, a 20-year moratorium on redemption of bonds was declared.   On net balance these measures will increase the disposable incomes of workers but will freeze substantial assets of bondholders, thus enhancing governmental planning and control of current monetary flows.   In May 1957 a new bond drive was instituted again "just for one more year."

unless rural levels declined correspondingly. And finally, the questions of availability of consumer goods at the prices indicated during the years compared, as well as the stocks of goods in the hands of consumers—especially housing—may be fully as important in indicating changes in living levels as the indexes of real wages.

Despite the qualifications referred to, however, the indexes of average real wages shown in table 3 reflect the general order of magnitude of changes since 1928 and 1950. For the period, 1928 to 1955, as a whole, Soviet money wages increased very sharply, but price inflation may have been even greater; so that, by 1955 the estimated range of real wages in the Soviet Union had only just reattained a zone which straddled the 1928 level, meaning they could as easily be below the 1928 level as above it. By contrast, during approximately the same period, real wages of the United States urban workers increased by nearly 80 percent. The possible bare reattainment of Soviet real wages after 27 years of Soviet planning and economic controls—especially when contrasted to the United States record—illustrates the lopsided character of Soviet economic development. During this period, the U. S. S. R. increased its total industrial production about eightfold, and, partly because of newly acquired territory, increased its agricultural output by perhaps 35 to 50 percent. The increases, however, were largely in goods not available for personal consumption, so that increases in output of consumer goods barely kept pace with the increases in population. The peasant population fared even more poorly than the average for the U. S. S. R. By contrast, the increases in United States industrial production (of "only" 136 percent) during the period 1929 to 1955, and in agricultural output of about 50 percent, were reflected in roughly proportionate increases in levels of living. (Further, in 1929 production in the United States was at a peak.)

Of interest, too, is the trend in real wages during the past 5 years. Real wages increased, according to Soviet statistics, by about 39 percent in the Soviet Union, compared to an increase of about 14 percent in the United States from 1950 to 1955. The Soviet claim is almost certainly too high in light of other evidence, even though it would be an admission of abysmally low levels in 1950. Juxtaposition of the longer-term trends in both countries from 1928 (29) to 1955 and the United States trend from 1950 to 1955, together with an examination of other aspects of the U. S. S. R. economy, suggest that the real wage trends in the U. S. S. R. during the past 5 years were not normal in any sense of the word. In 1950, at a time when overall reconstruction of war damaged areas had been largely completed and prewar industrial production levels exceeded, Soviet real wages were significantly lower than in any late prewar year, and were possibly only somewhere in the range of from 60 to 85 percent as high as in 1928. Obviously, then, the rapid rise to approximately 1928 levels by 1955 represented something of a dramatic effort to regain lost ground rather than a necessarily continuing and stable phenomenon of Soviet growth. It reflects both the increased domestic output of manufactured consumer goods by the early and middle fifties, and also the woefully low postwar level of Soviet real wages in 1950.

C. CHANGES IN PER CAPITA CONSUMPTION

Data on per capita consumption of products important to Soviet living standards have been compiled in table 4 below for the years 1928, 1950, and 1955.[12] For reasons alluded to at the start of this section [13] changes in real wages would differ from changes in per capita consumption, so a comparison of the two (see tables 3 and 4) is only a partial check, even with the best of data; and since the data for 1928 are understated in the case of shoes, and undoubtedly understated in the case of a few other commodities,[14] the comparison also has statistical limitations. For example, urbanization in the Soviet Union has increased the need for many products over those of an agricultural era, and the table does not correct for this type of change. The comparison at least suggests that the previous measures of trends in real wages are probably fairly correct in general order of magnitude. Per capita consumption of grain, meat, and dairy products all declined during the period, the decline being approximately offset by increases in consumption of such products as fish, potatoes, sugar, soap, fabrics, and perhaps shoes. The decline in grain could be expected if consumption of meat, dairy, and other food products had increased correspondingly. But these more desired products did not increase sufficiently overall to assure the unimportance of the grain decline. Urban housing in being also declined by about 20 percent, per capita, during the period. There are new consumer durable goods being turned out today which were not made in 1928, but the limited amounts available must be spread over so many people as not yet to enter very seriously into the calculations. Services of education and health protection improved, although they are not measured with these commodity data. Even so, the data suggest overall, as did the trends in real wages, that Soviet living standards have improved little if at all during the past 27 years.

---

[12] For 1955 data on per capita consumption in the United States, see table 2.

[13] The reasons are spelled out in more detail by Janet Chapman, op. cit., pp. 148–149.

[14] In 1928 small-scale enterprises—some privately owned and consisting of an independent artisan with sometimes a few employees, some owned cooperatively by several artisans, and some owned and operated by the state—produced a large share of the consumer goods. There is reason to believe that some of this output, especially that by independent artisans and peasants for their own use or for sale, was not included. The unrecorded output was probably large in the case of shoe production in 1928, and may have been significant in certain textiles, soaps, etc.; it would have been insignificant in 1955.

TABLE 4.—*Per capita availability, consumption, or stock of goods in the U. S. S. R., contrasting 1928, 1950, and 1955*

	Unit	1928	1950	1955
FOODS				
Meat, including lard	Kilogram	24. 4	17 1	20. 2
Fish	do	5. 5	7. 0	10. 1
Milk and milk products	do	198. 8	138. 0	150. 7
Butter	do	(. 5)	(1. 8)	(2. 2)
Margarine	do		1. 1	2. 3
Other fats and oils	do	(3. 0)	(6. 3)	(10. 1)
Potatoes	do	306. 5	462. 5	338. 7
Grain, dry pulses	do	251. 0	(1)	230. 0
Tea	do	(1)	. 2	. 3
Confectionery items	do	(. 7)	5. 4	8. 6
Salt	do	(1)	21. 3	22. 6
Sugar	do	8. 5	13. 9	17. 3
(Soap)	do	(2. 1)	4. 5	5. 4
CLOTHING AND TEXTILES				
Cotton fabrics	Linear meters	(17. 7)	21. 5	29. 8
Wool fabrics	do	(. 6)	. 9	1. 5
Linen fabrics	do	(1. 1)	1. 5	1. 5
Silk fabrics	do	(. 1)	. 7	2. 5
Rayon and synthetic fabrics	do	. 01	. 1	. 5
Hosiery	Pairs	(. 4)	2. 6	3. 9
Knit underwear	Number	(. 05)	. 8	1. 7
Shoes	Pairs	(. 4)	1. 1	1. 4
DURABLE MANUFACTURES				
Automobiles	Number	----------	. 0001	. 0003
Motorcycles	do	----------	. 0006	. 001
Bicycles	do	. 00007	. 004	. 014
Sewing machines	do	. 002	. 003	. 008
Washing machines	do	----------	. 000002	. 0004
Refrigerators	do	----------	. 00001	. 0007
Vacuum cleaners	do	----------	. 00003	. 0006
Clocks and watches	do	. 006	. 045	. 097
Cameras	do	----------	. 001	. 005
Record players	do	----------	. 002	. 004
Radios	do	----------	. 005	. 018
Television sets	do	----------	. 0001	. 002
HOUSING				
Living space, total available	Square meters	5. 9	(1)	4. 8

[1] Not available.

Sources

All 1955 data and calculations as given in table 2, this chapter, except for soap, see below.

The 1928 and 1950 data for meat, milk, and potatoes, are from table 2 of chapter III, divided by the estimated 1928 population of 151.4 million or the estimated 1950 population of 181.2 million as appropriate.

All other 1950 sales and production data have been found in the same source pages as the 1955 data of table 2, this chapter, adjusted to per capita terms by dividing by 181.2 million people.

Similar divisions of production data by population for other 1928 data have been made for the following items, all drawn from Tsentral'noe statisticheskoe upravlenie pri Sovete Ministrov SSSR, Narodnoe khoziaistvo SSSR, Statisticheskii sbornik, Gosstatizdat, Moskva, 1956, with pages noted as follows:

Page 57: Automobiles
Page 58: All clothing and textiles
Page 59: All durable manufactures, plus butter, other fats and oils, and confectionery items, soap (the 1950 and 1955 data are from the same page).
Page 89: Fish
Page 91: Sugar

As in the case of table 2 of this chapter, a special estimate had to be used for measuring human consumption of grain. It was found in Jasny, Naum, Socialized Agriculture of the U. S. S. R. (Stanford University Press), 1949, page 751. The figure actually refers to 1927–28.

As in the case of table 2 of this chapter, a special estimate had to be used for measuring living space available. It was found in Sosnovy, Timothy, The Housing Problem in the Soviet Union (Research Program on the U. S. S. R.), 1954, page 106. Both this figure and the 1955 one now appear in Sosnovy, Timothy, Housing in the Workers' State, Problems of Communism (November–December 1956, No. 6), page 32.

Interpretation

It cannot be emphasized too strongly that in a long list of products, the 1928 to 1955 comparison is more one of the transfer of small-scale and cottage industry to state control and regular factories. It definitely does not measure how consumption has changed. The table also reveals in some small measure the shift in the nature of consumption patterns as new consumable durable goods have been added, even though still at a low level. The figures which are most vulnerable to misinterpretation have been put in parentheses.

The future

Reliable forecasts of future trends are particularly hazardous in the case of Soviet living standards, because of their direct dependence upon planning decisions of the central government. There is little question but that the Soviet economy could double or triple its output of manufactured consumers goods (that is, those not dependent upon agricultural materials) in a relatively short time, say, a single decade, if it were willing to forego increases in output of the producer and defense goods to which it has always given priority. This is not an astonishingly large increase simply because such a small percentage of industrial resources are presently devoted to consumer needs. The increase referred to is not an overall measure of consumer levels of living, which are much harder to improve rapidly. Even after a 2- or 3-fold increase, Soviet output of such manufactured goods would still lag far behind the United States. All the indications point to continued emphasis on investment goods, if one places any credence in the statements of Soviet leaders. But even slight shifts in emphasis would produce significant percentage results in the consumer-goods sector. Large increases in personal consumption of foodstuffs must be predicated, also, on greatly increased availability of agricultural products, either through imports or increased domestic production, which will not be easy, despite the boasts of Khrushchev in late May 1957.

However, further intensification and rationalization of Soviet economic activity in the course of further rapid growth of the industrial sector will inevitably require allocation of additional increments for consumption. The tendency to substitute incentives for coercion to achieve the desired placement of labor throughout the economy, while it persists, is an important factor working to reinforce this requirement. Preferential allocations of scarce consumer goods to those retail outlets serving priority sectors of the economy serve to tie consumption to priority production activities in much the same way that company-provided fringe benefits augment nominal wages in attracting labor to a particular plant in the United States. That the Soviet planning authorities and leaders consider this aspect of consumption significant is clear from their attempts to induce what is called material interestedness of the worker in production, and is reflected in the relative importance of the Directorates of Workers' Supply for the various economic ministries in retail trade distribution (almost a fifth of state and cooperative retail sales were through these outlets in 1955).[15] An important reason for the current emphasis on housing construction especially in new industrial complexes remote from existing urban centers, is the need to attract adequate labor by the provision of housing facilities. Thus, increments to consumption are increasingly apportioned in a manner consistent with the desired distribution of the labor force—and are considered, therefore, by Soviet leaders as a necessary "cost" of increased labor productivity arising from "better" distribution of the labor force.

On balance, it seems likely that Soviet levels of living will continue to rise in the foreseeable future. The rise has already slowed down during the past 2 or 3 years, so that future increases are unlikely to be nearly as high as the average increases attained while principally recovering from low postwar levels. On the other hand, they are unlikely to be anywhere near as low as the average increase, if any, for the entire period 1928–55. (The trends of both these periods should be ruled out, unless similar circumstances could occur in the future: Forced industrialization and the "agricultural revolution," war devastation and extremely low consumption levels even by Soviet standards, and rapid recovery once the more "basic" production goals had been met.)

In summary, given the present disparity in levels of living between the United States and the U. S. S. R., the prospect of Soviet living levels approaching those of this country in the foreseeable future seems very remote. Soviet authorities know that they lag far behind the United States in providing consumer goods with little prospect of catching up in a straight production race. They take comfort in the doctrinaire assumption that the United States will collapse into economic depression, affording the U. S. S. R. an opportunity to surpass us. This hope should certainly be in vain.

---

[15] See Tsentral'noe statisticheskoe upravlenie pri Sovete Ministrov SSSR, Sovetskaia Torgovlia, Statisticheskii sbornik (Moskva : Gosstatizdat), 1956, pp. 33–34, 36.   Separate statistics on certain rural sales of this sort are given on p. 58, as well.

CHAPTER VI

NATIONAL INCOME AND PRODUCT

A. INTRODUCTION

The purposes of this chapter are: To provide a clearer understanding of the structure of the Soviet and United States economies at various points of time; to examine the trends in total production of goods and services in each of the two countries, with some reference to a broad-level comparison of current levels in each; and to provide an indication as to likely rates of economic growth in each country.

National income and product calculations have enjoyed a great deal of popularity in recent years as a means of measuring the economic progress of a country or comparing its economy with those of other countries. Because of the diversity of production in any one country, a listing and comparing of all the quantities produced is beyond comprehension, nor would it yield an unambiguous result. The sum of goods and services produced in a given year, however, can be expressed in money values. "National product" is a convenient measure for summarizing such production; and "national income" measures the incomes generated in that process.[1]

In addition to their use as summary measures, national income and product calculations can also provide insights into the structure of an economy: For example, they can indicate the relationship among different uses of total product, uses such as private consumption, investment, and government, including defense; the relationship of different sectors where national income originates, sectors such as agriculture, industry, services, and so forth; and the relationship of such income-generating and product-consuming parts of the economy as private households, business enterprises, government, and so forth.

Data on national product by final use are presented to indicate the percentage allocation of resources to production for particular uses such as consumption and investment; and the data on national product by sector origin are presented to indicate the share of such economic sectors as agriculture and industry in total production. Data or estimates presented for the purposes of comparing trends in the two countries and likely rates of economic growth will refer only to total production, not to its uses or sector origin.

B. STRUCTURE OF THE SOVIET AND UNITED STATES ECONOMIES

1. National product by final use categories

A breakdown of national product by expenditures for private consumption, civil government, investment, and national security can be

---

[1] Note that there are other summary measures which would be more useful for other purposes. For example, if we were concerned here with a measure of goods which could be shipped to underdeveloped nations, a measure of agricultural surpluses or of industrial production might be more relevant.

a useful approximate indicator of a country's allocation of resources to various uses, provided certain adjustments are made. These are discussed below.

(a) *Coverage of the data.*—Coverage of the Soviet and United States data (see table 1) differs, but is sufficiently comparable to show in a table together when accompanied by qualifying notes.

Consumption is shown in two parts: expenditures by households (line 1a) and expenditures by governments on behalf of households, mostly for education and health (line 1b). The latter expenditures are not normally reported separately from other government purchases in the United States, but they have been estimated as explained in notes accompanying the table.

Government administration represents those expenditures of government for goods and services not specifically listed elsewhere in the table.

Gross investment is shown in two parts; a figure for private investment plus net foreign investment (line 3a) and a figure for public investment (line 3b). It is gross in the sense that it includes expenditures for capital used up in production (that is, depreciation and capital losses) as well as capital going into new investment.

TABLE 1.—*Gross national product by use in the U. S. S. R. and the United States* [1]

[Percentages only, from current prices, partly adjusted]

	1928 U.S.S.R.	1929 United States	1937 U.S.S.R.	1937 United States	1940 U.S.S.R.	1940 United States	1944 U.S.S.R.	1944 United States	1948 U.S.S.R.	1948 United States	1950 U.S.S.R.	1950 United States	1955[2] U.S.S.R.	1955[2] U.S.S.R. modified	1955[2] United States
1. Consumption	71.5	78.6	66.3	78.1	64.3	75.4	48.8	53.9	56.8	73.2	59.4	71.7	57.0	57.0	68.6
(a) Household expenditures	66.3	75.7	55.7	74.1	55.3	71.5	41.2	51.9	45.2	69.0	48.6	68.0	48.7	48.7	65.0
(b) Government services to households	5.2	2.9	10.6	4.0	9.0	3.9	7.6	2.0	11.6	4.2	10.8	3.7	8.3	8.3	3.6
2. Government administration	2.4	1.6	1.8	3.5	1.8	3.5	1.8	1.5	2.0	1.6	2.6	1.4	1.9	1.9	1.6
3. Gross investment	23.2	18.9	22.9	16.6	16.6	18.4	13.5	6.4	25.6	18.9	23.3	20.0	28.5	26.9	18.7
(a) Private domestic, net foreign	6.4	16.3	(3)	13.0	(3)	14.6	(3)	2.4	(3)	16.8	(3)	17.2	(3)	(3)	15.1
(b) Government domestic	16.7	2.6	(3)	3.6	(3)	3.8	(3)	4.0	(3)	2.1	(3)	2.8	(3)	(3)	3.6
4. National security	2.8	1.1	9.0	1.8	17.5	2.9	35.8	38.2	15.6	6.3	14.7	6.9	12.6	14.2	10.9
(a) Defense	2.5	.6	7.7	1.1	15.6	2.2	34.2	37.8	11.7	4.5	11.9	5.0	11.1	13.4	10.0
(b) Other security										1.5		1.4			.4
(c) Internal security	.3		1.3	.7	1.9	.7	1.6	.4	3.9	.3	2.8	.5	1.5	.8	.5
5. Gross national product	100.0	100.0	100.0	100.0	100.0	100.0	100.0	100.0	100.0	100.0	100.0	100.0	100.0	100.0	100.0

[1] Details may not add to totals because of rounding.
[2] 1955 Soviet data were calculated in 1953 prices.
[3] Not available.

U. S. S. R.

1928 from Hoeffding, Oleg, Soviet National Income and Product in 1928 (New York: Columbia University Press), 1954, pp. 19, 46.

1937–48 from Bergson, Abram, and Heymann, Hans, Soviet National Income and Product 1940–48 (New York: Columbia University Press), 1954, pp. 95, 99.

1950–55 estimated by staff following same pattern as preceding in consultation with specialists experienced with these data. The second U. S. S. R. 1955 column similarly arrived at, but departs from the earlier pattern to estimate more nearly categories corresponding to those used in the United States. Soviet 1955 data are based on 1953 prices.

The sources should be reviewed for the details of calculation of the data which are percentages of current prices, adjusted in each year to subtract turnover taxes, adding the amount of subsidies paid, and taking account of multiple prices of farm output. The purpose of these adjustments is to approach factor costs implied by the output shown.

United States

Percentages shown derived from current dollar values as follows:

All basic categories from Department of Commerce, Survey of Current Business, July 1956, pp. 10–11, with additional adjustments as follows:

Gross investment includes private investment and net foreign investment as shown in Idem. Added to these were estimates of public construction and durable goods purchased by the Government, estimate supplied to staff by National Income Division, Department of Commerce.

National security total corrected downward by estimates of National Income Division, Department of Commerce, by subtracting sales of military equipment in 1944–55, and adding the full amount of public construction and public purchases of durable goods in 1944, which were assumed for that year only in this table to be mostly military, or related to defense.

National defense figures for 1948–55 corrected downward by exactly the same amount as the national security figures. In the period 1948–55, it was possible to show separately as "Other security" the expenditures for foreign aid not labeled as military, and the expenditures of the Department of State. Defense still includes in United States practice not only the costs of the Armed Forces, but also all foreign military aid (much of it indistinguishable from economic aid), atomic energy costs, expenses of economic stabilization agencies, costs of stockpiling essential materials, and subsidy costs for the merchant marine through 1948. Data for 1950–55 include merchant marine subsidy costs as "Other security."

Internal security costs estimated by staff through review of State and local costs for police and fire protection in Department of Commerce, Historical Statistics of the United States, 1789–1945, p. 316, and Department of Commerce, Statistical Abstract of the United States, 1956, p. 404. This figure covers normal protective services only, while the Soviet measure is more inclusive. It is useful to show these data in conjunction with defense because the Soviet internal security figure is believed to hide atomic energy development costs, at least in part. The Soviet internal security category also includes border guards and paramilitary forces which have no equivalent in the United States. The Soviet figure may also involve administration of the slave labor system which has no counterpart in the United States.

For the United States, government services to households and government administrative costs were found by subtracting national security, public construction, and public purchases of durable goods from the total for government. The division between government services to households and government administrative costs was made by a series of trial calculations of State and local expenditures for education, hospitals, schools, libraries, and recreation (the latter two being small items). To these figures were added postwar expenditures by the Federal Government for veterans education and veterans hospitals, plus a small figure for other Federal services not paid through the States as shown from studies of sample budgets. These costs brought a total which had to be adjusted downward to remove capital expenditures already included elsewhere in the table. This was found both by restudying the amount of total public works expenditures by local and State governments and by analyzing State payroll data and non-construction purchases of goods. Testing of the data showed that approximately two-thirds of State and local payrolls and goods purchased is a fair approximation of local and State services to households. A total 1955 estimate for Federal as well as State and local government services to households was supplied by the National Income Division, Department of Commerce, and it checked closely against independent estimates of the staff. This worked fairly well except for 1950, when apparently the estimate of veterans benefits included transfer payments which had to be removed, and consequently were.

National security is a broad category which involved several estimates as explained in the notes accompanying table 1. Defense (line 4 (a)) represents military goods and services actually purchased, normally exclusive of investment in defense plants; it also excludes military pensions. However, the Soviet figure shown is only that recorded as such in the budget. This is a very important qualification for there is strong evidence that other defense expenditures are hidden by Soviet authorities, or institutional differences otherwise make the category much narrower in the U. S. S. R. United States national accounts on defense include not only expenditures for the Armed Forces (except defense plants and pensions) but also atomic energy, merchant-marine promotion (through 1948), stockpiling essential materials, economic stabilization agencies, and foreign "military" aid (which in some cases may be indistinguishable from general economic aid).

In the United States, a broader category called national security (shown in the table in incremental form as "other security", row 4 (b)), is reported. It includes in addition to defense the expenditures of the Department of State, all foreign economic aid, and after 1948 the promotional expenses for the merchant marine on the part of Government. Before 1948, it was not the practice to distinguish between defense and this broader category of national security.

Internal security (line 4 (c)) in the case of the United States is a simple estimate of police- and fire-protective services. It is important not to equate these services in function or scope with the Soviet category which includes in addition the dread activities of the security police. This line has been placed under national security rather than under government administration because Soviet internal-security expenditures include those for border troops which in the United States would be part of defense. Further, it is suspected that a good part of atomic-energy expenditures for the U. S. S. R. are hidden under internal security rather than reported as part of defense as done in the United States.

There may be other ways in which the national security estimates of the two countries are not comparable. United States data include the cost of maintaining forces overseas, while the large Soviet garrisons in Eastern Europe have most of their costs billed against the captive countries and not the Soviet defense budget. Also Soviet military research and development carried on outside the military establishment are apparently not included in the Soviet defense category.

All of the qualifications above, which cannot really be overcome because of lack of specific data, tend to overstate United States defense expenditures as compared with the U. S. S. R.[2] A very crude correction has been estimated, however, for 1955, and explains the second U. S. S. R. column shown in the table. This trims the estimates for gross investment and for internal security, adding correspondingly to

[2] For further details of the Soviet and United States categories, see notes accompanying the table, and Bergson, Abram, and Heymann, Hans, Soviet National Income and Product (New York : Columbia University Press), 1954, ch. II and pp. 99–101.

defense (rough estimates for the costs of border troops, military research and development, and atomic energy).

All expenditures in the main part of the table are shown in percentages based on current prices of each year.   The Soviet data were adjusted, however, by estimates which removed the turnover taxes, added the value of subsidies, and took into account the multiple prices of farm output.   The purpose was to approach the identification of output in terms of costs of factor services used in production (i. e., labor, land, and capital).   Under certain assumptions, such adjusted data would indicate more nearly than the unadjusted figures that Soviet authorities could increase expenditures in any sector by decreasing their expenditures by an equivalent amount in any other sector.[3]   The adjustments are separate and distinct from any price deflator changes required over time because of variance in the price level.

Such an adjustment to a so-called factor cost basis was not performed on United States data because the percentage data shown probably would not shift enough to warrant the estimations which would be required.[4]   The principal reason for this difference is the unequal effect in the U. S. S. R. among sectors of turnover taxes and subsidies, both more widely used in the Soviet Union than in the United States where the income tax is used to a greater degree.

(b) *Comparative structure and trends (see table 1)*.—In percentage terms, the United States allocated more of its gross national product to consumption than did the Soviet Union in all years studied.   In both countries, consumption as a share is smaller than it was before World War II, even though there has been some recovery from the lows of the war period.   This recovery has been more rapid and greater in the United States than in the U. S. S. R.   This continued lower share in both countries is largely a reflection of the heavy responsibilities to meet the needs of national security.   In both countries, too, government services to households are greater than they were at the start of the period studied, with the Soviet Union not surprisingly using public services to a greater extent in relation to the size of the economy.

Data on Government administration are not certain enough, because of their residual character and small share of the total, to warrant trend conclusions or very specific international comparisons.

---

[3] The calculation of these adjustments is arduous, and the results, though better than the raw figures, must be considered provisional.   Ideally, they should also have removed an arbitrary amount called planned profits, but added imputed amounts for interest, more adequate depreciation, and the imputed value of land rent.   Some of these changes probably either cancel each other, or have a smaller differential effect among sectors of the economy than the other adjustments which were made, and therefore have not been attempted.   The adjustments which have been made, however, are important.   For example, in some years, sales taxes accounted for more than 50 percent of the retail value of all consumer goods sold in state and cooperative trade, whereas the tax on investment goods was relatively insignificant.   In contrast, subsidies were relatively small on consumer goods and relatively large on investment goods.   Without making adjustments, the data would overstate the apparent share of consumption and understate investment and defense.   The details of analysis are to be found in ibid., pp. 71, 90, 219, and 222 ; and also in Hoeffding, Oleg. Soviet National Income and Product in 1928 (New York : Columbia University Press), 1954, p. 46.

[4] Trial adjustments to United States data showed that in 1944 the burden of indirect taxes and of subsidies on the various sectors of the economy had very little differential effect on the results.   Consumption would have to be cut about 2.5 percent. In 1948, the cut in consumption would be about 1 percent. and in 1937 and 1940 by even less than 1 percent. See Bergson, Abram, and Heymann, Hans, op. cit., note, pp. 103–104.

Generally the United States share seems smaller than the Soviet, although the data for 1937 and 1940 are not consistent in this respect.

Except in 1940, gross investment in the U. S. S. R. has run as a higher share than in the United States.[5] The two economies are contrasted, where data are available, by the great reliance on private investment in the United States except in war, and upon public investment in the U. S. S. R. even at the start of the planning period. The United States data are influenced by the addition or subtraction in particular years of net foreign investment which has a less important and less well-known role in the U. S. S. R.

Soviet gross investment as a share was down in 1940 and 1944 when defense expenditures pressed on available resources. The United States investment share was low in 1944, but the table does not show the peaks of private investment in 1941 and of Government investment in 1942 when war conversion efforts were dominant. The Soviet figure for 1944 reflects battle area reconstruction.

The problems of comparing defense and other security shares in the two countries have been discussed at length above. Nonetheless, some trend comparisons are possible. The Soviet defense category rose sharply by 1937, doubled again by 1940, and by 1944 accounted for about a third of all output. This was at the expense of consumption as early as 1937 and later hurt investment, too. There was less letdown after World War II, compared with the United States. Soviet expenditure shares ran at levels not too different from the mobilization period of 1940, particularly if one keeps in mind the probable hidden amounts, as estimated in the second 1955 column for the U. S. S. R. United States disarmament relative to the U. S. S. R, after World War II is quite apparent. The United States share ran well above prewar levels partly because this country was not a major military power in 1929 and 1937, and because the postwar reports include foreign aid and atomic experimentation which was very expensive. Only the heightening of the cold war and the experience in Korea led to a partial rebuilding of the share of military expenditures which clearly is still well below the Soviet level, especially when one takes into account incomparability of data as presented in the first U. S. S. R. 1955 column and as tentatively corrected in the second column. The disproportionate Soviet increase in 1948 of expenditures for internal security may be compounded of several elements. It may include the transfer of paramilitary functions including border troops to the MVD; it may reflect a great atomic-development program, which is primarily military.

All the foregoing analysis, it must be remembered, has been in terms of current prices, partly adjusted for taxes, subsidies, and multiple pricing. There is a great danger in trying to read too much into the comparisons, and no one comparison is capable of conveying the full meaning of the trends in the two countries. Percentages were used to indicate shares in terms of prevailing values of outputs (measured at factor costs) in each year studied. As students of national income and product concepts and methodology have noted, percentage shares of total resources allocated to different sectors such as consumption, investment, etc., do not necessarily indicate the output

[5] The Soviet category of investment may be somewhat more comprehensive than the United States category. See Bergson, Abram, and Heymann, Hans, op. cit., p. 103.

share of such goods in total production. Therefore table 1 does not necessarily indicate the trends either of output of goods by sector, or the physical volume of resources allocated to sectors. On the other hand, the difficulties of converting to absolutes for purposes of studying trends in shares of goods and services in question are extremely great and are not treated in this study.

Allen Dulles has stated that in real terms, the United States may be producing currently about three times as many goods and services as the Soviet Union;[6] and in some earlier years the ratio was probably even greater. Therefore, except perhaps for military expenditures in certain years, the real magnitude of expenditures in all sectors has probably been greater in the United States than in the U. S. S. R., in all the years studied. Many economists, however, balk at even attempting to state such comparisons on the grounds that they are meaningless when two countries have different economic structures.

With respect to comparative real output in the military and investment sectors, it should be noted that Soviet resources are thought to be significantly more efficient in producing these goods than consumption goods. Therefore, real investment and military output in the U. S. S. R. almost certainly has been significantly greater than is indicated by the U. S. S. R./United States ratio of total output given above and the proportions of approximate resource allocations shown in table 1. That is, military and investment goods in the Soviet Union probably require a smaller input of resources per unit of output than do consumption goods, and this is apparently true of figures which of course have been adjusted to minimize the distortions of turnover taxes and subsidies.[7]

With respect only to comparative military expenditures, it should also be noted that, because of the elimination of certain useful but costly features in Soviet military equipment, and greater standardization for mass production, the ruble's purchasing power in military goods is higher than in consumption goods. Not only does standardization of weapons without refinements pay off in lower resource costs, but the very best of new machinery and trained manpower is made available to the production of military goods. The Soviet Union gains certain economies as compared with the United States because it moves more often to early production of items instead of testing many possible prototypes. Its logistic support costs are lower, too, both because it provides fewer amenities and because its armed forces are expected to be closer to home bases or to live off the land. Each of these differences has its sound reasons in the two countries, but the balance of their effect is to provide the U. S. S. R. with larger apparent military forces than the comparative statistical tables on national product suggest. Real output in the military sector in the U. S. S. R. may have been as great as that in the United States in 1955. In any event, it would be grossly incorrect to calculate from the proportionate data shown in table 1 either the size of real military

---

[6] Dulles, Allen, Russia's Growing Strength Could Be a Weakness, in U. S. News & World Report, May 11, 1956, p. 124.
[7] The conclusion is suggested by the lower ruble-dollar price ratios for investment than consumption goods. The ratios, inclusive of turnover tax, were compiled by the Rand Corp. and the Stanford Research Institute principally for the year 1950. The relationship seems to hold, however, even after crude adjustments for this tax. This hypothesis, however, cannot yet be proven with available data.

output in the U. S. S. R. compared to the United States in 1955, or the size of military forces maintained, or their combat effectiveness.[8]

Except for the orders of magnitude indicated above, the extent of the difference in real output among the various economic sectors in the United States and U. S. S. R. has been estimated in this report only for consumption expenditures (see ch. V). This was the only sector where sufficient ruble/dollar price ratios were available to convert the expenditures into a common currency.

2. National product by sector of origin

(a) *Coverage of the data.*—The national product data in the U. S. S. R. and national income data in the United States are believed to be sufficiently comparable in coverage for the present limited purpose of an overall comparison.

As in table 1 of this chapter, the Soviet data are derived from current price, adjusted basis, rubles. The corrections for turnover taxes, subsidies, and multiple prices have resulted in a near approximation of national income equivalents, aiding comparison with the United States data. Difficulties of establishing identical coverage in the two countries should not be considered surprising, and this hazard must be kept in mind while reviewing table 2. More thorough review of the problems associated with these comparisons can be found in the sources used for constructing the table. The 1955 estimates of net national product (U. S. S. R.) and national income (United States), are supplemented by gross national product estimates for both countries as well.

TABLE 2.—*National product (or income) by industrial sector*
[In percentages]

Sector	1928	1929	1955			
	U. S. S. R. net product	United States national income	U. S. S. R.		United States	
			Net product	Gross product	National income	Gross product
Agriculture, forestry, and fisheries	42	9	28	29	5	6
Industry, mining, and construction	28	34	40	41	40	43
Transportation and communications	7	9	9	9	7	7
Services, Government, trade	23	48	23	21	48	44
Total national income		100			100	
Net national product	100		100			
Gross national product				100		100

NOTES CONCERNING THE TABLE

Gross national product equals net national product plus allowance for capital used up in production.

Net national product less indirect taxes plus subsidies equals national income.

Soviet percentages are derived from current price, adjusted ruble figures which correct for turnover taxes and subsidies and for multiple pricing of farm

[8] For these purposes a more correct picture could be obtained directly from published information on the military strength of the two countries—which indicates that the U. S. S. R. has consistently maintained a much larger army (now perhaps 175 divisions as contrasted with about 19 in the United States), together with a modern navy and air force which today approach the size and the effective equipment of the corresponding forces of the United States, even if each of these forces differs in composition and missions assigned.

products.   Therefore their net national product figures are not too different from what could be labeled national income.

U. S. S. R. 1928 data are as given in Hoeffding, Oleg, Soviet National Income and Product in 1928 (New York: Columbia University Press), 1954, p. 47.

U. S. S. R. 1955 data are staff estimates arrived at in conjunction with specialists experienced with the data.

United States national income data are from Department of Commerce, Survey of Current Business, July 1956, p. 16.   United States 1955 gross national product data are estimated by staff in conjunction with specialists.

(b) *Structure and trends in the two countries.*—If one can read limited meaning into table 2, the Soviet Union devoted a somewhat smaller share of its resources to industry and construction in 1928 than did the United States in 1929; about 5 times as large a percentage to agriculture; and about half as large a percentage to services, government, and trade.   By 1955, owing to a substantial shift of Soviet resources from agriculture into industry, the industry and construction sector in the U. S. S. R. used about the same proportion of national resources as was used in the United States.   However, owing to a similar shift of United States resources, agriculture in the U. S. S. R. still required about five times as large a share as did the United States. The proportions and the relationships attributable to the services, government, and trade sectors in 1955 were about the same as in 1928 and 1929, and the changes in proportions attributable to transportation and communications were not large enough to warrant special attention in as approximate a comparison as this.

A review of information in chapter II on industry and in chapter III on agriculture can provide an approximate yardstick to suggest the increases in real output which have occurred in the period 1928–55. Industrial output was about 8 times as large in 1955 as in 1928 (see ch. II), and although the volume of construction output was crudely estimated to have increased by less than that of industry, with the preponderance of industry in the combined total for industry and construction, the increase for industry alone can be used as the approximate increase for both sectors; agricultural output was only about a third to a half greater than in 1928 (see ch. III); and the output of services in the remaining 2 sectors (transportation-communications and services-government-trade) can be crudely estimated to have increased to about 6 times its 1928 level.   The reliability of the estimated increases, especially in the services-government-trade sector, is not very high; but the increases are believed to be accurate enough to indicate the orders of magnitude of output of the various economic sectors.

C.   TRENDS AND COMPARISONS OF GROSS NATIONAL PRODUCT

1. *Comparative levels in 1955*

In real terms the U. S. S. R. may be currently producing about one-third as many goods and services as the United States.[14]   This ratio, if read with great emphasis on the "about" preceding it, is probably satisfactory as an overall measure.   Using this ratio together with the rates of growth given below, it would be possible also to derive the relationship of Soviet to United States output in 1928 and 1950.   Such derivations are avoided here, because they would involve specific cal-

---

[14] Dulles, Allen, op. cit., p. 124.

culations of ratios which should not be granted so great a degree of implied exactness. The hazards of such translations in the face of structural and price changes have already been made clear in this study.

2. Rates of growth

(a) *Choice of a period for Soviet-United States comparison.*— The question of selection of periods for comparison has been discussed at length in chapters I and II. The same considerations make difficult the choices for national product and income comparisons. In consistency with other parts of this study, the following two comparisons are offered: (1) The entire period 1928–55, from the start of the 5-year plans through the last complete year for which data are available in both countries; and (2) the period 1950–55 after reconstruction had been essentially completed in the U. S. S. R.

As has been explained earlier, concurrent periods do not provide an ideal comparison between nations because of differences in their stage of development, and different exogenous forces which may be at work, as well as the structural differences which make all international comparisons difficult under any circumstances. It is possible to seek other time periods which may overcome in part the problems of differing stages of development, but all the other difficulties remain. If simply to illustrate the point that rates of growth do change over time in most countries, it is possible to select other time periods to show these differences, provided one does not try to read significance into the comparisons. Such illustrations may or may not be truly representative, as was discussed in the earlier chapters which sought to find good periods for comparison.

(b) *What growth in the U. S. S. R. and the United States has been.*—The temptation to provide a table setting forth categorically previous growth rates is resisted here, lest they be misunderstood as being definitive judgments. In the case of the United States, a measure of gross national product in constant prices is available. In the period from 1929 to 1955 the annual average growth rate can be calculated at 3 percent, and from 1950 to 1955 the corresponding rate is 4 percent.[9] These measures are commonly presented, although they, too, have limitations. There is no adequate counterpart of information covering all sectors of Soviet output. If our estimates of changes in real output by sector have any validity, then each sector could be brought into combination by some set of constant prices, if good ones were available; but the comparison would still involve arbitrary decisions about the importance of each sector. From various attempts which have been made by Western students of the problem [10] and from staff

---

[9] Department of Commerce, Survey of Current Business, July 1956, pp. 24–25.

[10] For the period 1928–37, when the official Soviet rate was 16 percent, Colin Clark computed the 4.4 percent annual average rate of growth in United States dollar prices of 1925–34; and Julius Wyler calculated the 5.6 percent figure in 1940 United States dollars. Both indexes valued the Soviet products whose output increased the most at prices which were considerably below those used by either the official Soviet index or the third Western-computed index. Naum Jasny computed the average rate of growth at from 7.5 to 9 percent, when valued in actual or estimated Soviet prices of 1926–27. His rates of growth are significantly lower than the official rate apparently because goods introduced into production after 1926–27 were valued at prices more nearly approaching those which would have prevailed for those items had they been produced in large quantities in that year. By contrast, the official production index, also in prices of 1926–27, valued such goods in the inflated prices of later years with "some" adjustment alleged to have been made in some instances to correct for this inflation. All of the above indexes were cited in a summary report, National Income of the Soviet Union, prepared by Abram Bergson for the Council for Economic and Industry Research, November 1954, p. 27. Original sources are given there.

estimates based on material available in this study, a range of answers results, with no way to say which is best because of the incompleteness of information and the structural changes which have occurred. If one were to quote a rate for the period 1913–55, the annual average would be modest, but would not reveal too much about the present Soviet economic machine. From 1928 through 1955 most of these calculations yield results of at least a 4-percent annual average increase. A calculation for the period 1950–55 suffers less from structural changes, but suffers more for lack of adequate data and from the fact that it may be of limited value in measuring long-term trends. Such calculations of limited significance seem to yield a rate of about 7 percent.

(c) *Interpretation of the data.*—It must be emphasized repeatedly that overall comparisons of growth rates between two countries of different structures and at different stages of development under the best of circumstances present very great hazards. It must also be recognized that past rates of growth are not a guaranty that such rates will be continued in the future. (See below.)

The information available in this study and discussions by students of Soviet economic growth do not answer definitely whether in fact the overall Soviet long-run growth rate has been higher than that of the United States in the period of this study. Use of different base years in price calculations might be enough to explain any difference in rates. Many arguments can be made that the great costs accepted by the U. S. S. R. in order to grow should have yielded higher overall growth rates, as well as accomplishing the admitted growth in certain branches of industry which has been large. But industrial forced growth has had its costs to other sectors of the economy.

Perhaps what is of greater significance to the United States is the Soviet effort to expand gross national product in the period since World War II. Most measurements for the period 1950–55 show that the probable rate of growth has been higher than in the United States. This is not surprising in the light of the great effort made to invest in industries conducive to growth, the earlier stage of development, and the exploitation of the captive countries. We must keep in mind this is still a contrasting of two quite different economies, as indeed this entire study has made clear. Soviet agriculture has increased output moderately since 1950, in contrast to its very limited rate of advance over the entire period 1928–55. This, coupled with the growth of population, again under way, the effort to industrialize, and the improvement of technology by borrowing from the West and by providing more training, all unite to provide a rate which for the 5-year period has yielded a good-sized spurt.

It is worth repeating, too, that growth rates are only a part of the comparison between countries. If indeed the Soviet economy is only a third the size of that of the United States, then the absolute increments to output in the United States each year are still larger today and will be for many years, even though the current rate of Soviet growth is possibly higher. The absolute gap between the two countries has been widening. But as was pointed out in chapter II on industry, there can be no permanent solace in this widening if there is any likelihood that the U. S. S. R. growth rate will continue to be higher than that of the United States. In time, the absolute gap would begin to narrow sharply, under such circumstances.

3. Likely future rates of growth of the Soviet and United States economies

The economic future cannot be regarded as fixed or determined by present levels or past rates of growth, since it will be influenced by a whole range of human decisions, by changes in nature, by new discoveries, as well as by predictable shifts in the availability of human and material resources which may be different from those available in the past. These resources, including trained manpower and capital equipment in industry and agriculture, have been assessed in turn in earlier chapters.

Recent events in the Soviet Union should certainly urge great caution in making predictions about future Soviet output. This study is being completed at a time when Soviet authorities face some markedly different circumstances which undoubtedly will have their repercussions on future growth. The captive countries are restive, and they are much less likely to make a net contribution to the economic well-being of the U. S. S. R. as they did in earlier years after World War II. Instead, the price of maintaining Soviet control may be more concessions in trade, and a heavier Soviet defense expenditure than otherwise would be required in order to replace politically unreliable satellite armies. The political and social ferment within the U. S. S. R. itself may lead in several possible directions with varying effects upon economic goals and the distribution of the gross national product.

By now it seems clear that the Soviet rate of growth is falling relative to the very high rates which prevailed shortly after World War II. It is not equally clear that these lower rates are down to the rate the United States has been able to sustain for the postwar years.

Soviet leadership has been compelled in the last few months to accept a considerable reduction in the rate of industrial growth. They can no longer ignore cumulative pressures which have been developing over the last several years. The most dramatic among these have been the recent uprisings in the captive countries. In general these pressures represent factors which cannot be easily surmounted and will have the effect of reducing future economic growth below the high rates achieved in the past several years.

Certainly there should be no complacency about the poor ability of the U. S. S. R. to produce goods in sufficient quantity to affect the national security of the United States so long as the Soviet authorities persevere in any drive to extend their control over a larger part of the earth, with the multiple weapons of military, political, economic, and psychological warfare.

Whatever their immediate difficulties in the economic sphere through too ambitious planning, it is the fact of their accomplishments of the recent past, and their continued ability to elect pursuit of several alternate courses, inimical to the interests of the United States, which must be a dominant consideration in the problems reviewed by this study.

The United States has an encouraging economic future, which this study has not explored in its particulars. The staff of the Joint Economic Committee developed estimates in 1954 which made assumptions about the economic outlook of this country, looking to the decade ahead.[17]   Nothing has happened since that time to bring much disagreement with the projections offered, which in effect showed a sound basis for believing the United States economy will be able to continue growing at a rate not too different from that which has prevailed since 1950.

In the case of the Soviet Union, any projection must somehow balance the continued drive to expand production as a goal in itself, the still less developed nature of that economy which can continue to draw upon the experience of the more advanced countries, and the growing Soviet population, against the emerging pressures on limited resources in agriculture, of less favorably situated industrial resources, of a growing need for replacement capital, and of internal and captive country disaffection.   Where that balance ultimately will lie, only time will tell.

---

[17] Materials prepared for the Joint Committee on the Economic Report by the committee staff, joint committee print, 83d Cong., 2d sess.   Potential Economic Growth of the United States During the Next Decade.

CHAPTER VII

SUMMARY AND CONCLUSIONS

A. INTRODUCTION

It has been over 2 years since the Joint Economic Committee sponsored a thorough review of the economic growth of the Soviet Union. During that time both new events and much more available data have made appropriate a fresh look.

This study has chosen two time periods for major consideration: 1928–55, taking as a starting point the beginning of comprehensive economic planning in the Soviet Union, and 1950–55, the postwar period after reconstruction in the U. S. S. R. was essentially complete.

The study has found comparisons difficult for several reasons. Outside events affecting both countries in the span of the study have made it hard to know what development trends might have been in the abstract. Territorial changes in the U. S. S. R. invalidate some of the apparent trends which seem to apply. Conceptual difficulties are inherent in trying to compare 2 countries whose economic structures are so different, where values in the 2 societies defy common translation, and where matters of definition plague most comparisons.

There have been statistical problems as well. Figures are not collected in the same way or kept for the same reasons. Different categories, the failure of statistics to measure qualitative differences, and gaps in information have added to the problems. There has been some falsification in Soviet statistics, but this study like all others has to be based fundamentally on Soviet records. They are, however, sufficiently internally consistent, and important enough to Soviet planning authorities that they can be taken as a useful starting point to analysis.

B. INDUSTRY AND TRANSPORTATION

Soviet industry today may be gaged as roughly one-third the size that of the United States, but its composition is quite different. The Soviet government has given first place to heavy industry and producers' goods to the neglect of consumer products, particularly of the durable type. It is a system under extreme pressure to grow and one where shortages constantly appear. Quality of output varies with the importance of the product in the eyes of Soviet authorities. They are capable of turning out advanced machines and good equipment; they are also prone to turn out shoddy goods for consumers.

Physical indexes, rather than value-based statistics, give the best indication of Soviet production trends to compare with those of the United States. A review of individual commodities shows that often the Soviet production quantities of 1928–55 are more akin to United States ranges of 1890–1920, and the Soviet period 1950–55 in many ways is easier to compare with the United States period 1922–27 than any more recent.

139

The Soviet Union has been able to borrow Western technology on a large scale, has shifted great amounts of manpower from agriculture, and has sacrificed most other goals to the single goal of growth of industrial and military power. Rates of growth have been influenced by the periods of collectivization and great purges, by war and territorial seizure, and by conquest and exploitation of the captive countries. In the same period of time the United Staes has had a long period of depression, a world war, and a phenomenal boom. Because of the artificial pressures for growth of industry and borrowed technology and experience, it seems probable that Soviet industry (as contrasted with other sectors of the Soviet economy) has grown faster than United States industry did at comparable stages of development, although periods can be found in United States industry with very high spurts of growth under special conditions.

United States and Soviet comparisons can be made in terms of absolute gaps as well as rates of growth. In many industries, the gaps have been widening as the United States forges ahead. But this of itself is not grounds for complacency, and would turn out to be a temporary phenomenon if the differential in percentage growth rates favorable to the Soviet Union were to be maintained long enough.

Soviet growth (where it has occurred) has been achieved by subordinating other goals, by a high rate of investment in industry, by the forced shift of labor out of agriculture, by borrowing technology, by accepting a smaller variety of goods, often of lower quality; and at the human costs of famine in some years, a system of forced labor and police repression, and low levels of living at all times.

For the future, many factors must be balanced and weighed in judging the outlook. On the one hand, continued high rates of investment should continue to yield more output. There is still much room for improving efficiency through better methods. Improved training of labor and the provision of some more incentives may raise productivity. Once the low decade is past, a new upsurge of numbers in the labor force should add to output of industry, too. But these gains must be weighed against the heavy needs to mechanize auxiliary processes if further gains in efficiency are to be made. More accessible ores and other resources are being exhausted, and the shift to new sources will take capital. The decline of labor inputs relative to capital may lead to smaller increases in capital efficiency. Resources may have to be diverted to building more housing, to improving agricultural output, and to replacing wornout and obsolete equipment. Instead of there being fresh capital windfalls from occupied territories, there may be a net drain of capital exports required to keep the captive countries and China within the bloc. Probably the net balance of all of these factors would make a rate of industrial growth possible that is higher than the likely United States rate, but not as high as the Soviet rate in many of the years since World War II.

Both countries have active programs for the peaceful use of atomic energy. The United States base of experience is more substantial, but Soviet research and programed power development warrant close attention.

Soviet transportation facilities are improving, but relatively they are neglected. A railroad system still relying principally on steam power, and still not uniformly equipped with four-axle cars, air-brakes, and automatic couplers provides about four-fifths of the service. Roads are very inadequate, and even waterways development is lagging, particularly as contrasted with publicity given schemes for improvement. Pipeline transport and transport aviation lag, too, although development of new jet and turbine-propeller aircraft may narrow the gap in the years ahead. Railways are in the early stages of dieselization and large-scale electrification of trunklines, as well as improvements in signaling and roadbed. For the passenger, travel is like war conditions with tremendous crowding, not to mention unspeakable conditions for prisoners in freight cars. Automobiles still are not a serious factor in Soviet transportation. Soviet transportation is retarded and could hold back general industrial progress. The new Khrushchev plan of May 1957 to regionalize some economic controls is designed in part to reduce dependence on inadequate transportation facilities.

C. AGRICULTURE

This is a retarded sector in Soviet development, partly because of natural limitations of soil and climate, and partly because Soviet authorities have not set a high priority on improvement, so long as enough food was raised to support industrial growth and feed military forces. Soviet authorities have viewed agriculture as a source of labor for industry, and at some points in time, of products for export which could pay for imported machinery. The desire to control the rural population and to control their output without having to pay more than a minimal amount for this product was a reason for the collectivization program which was so costly. In contrast to the United States, constant worry about raising enough food has been a feature of the Soviet scene. Over the course of the period under review, United States agricultural output has increased by 50 percent. Soviet output increases probably have been less, and even these have been aided by territorial acquisition. Meat and dairy product output actually may be lower today than in 1928.

The Soviet Union has about 30, percent more sown area than the United States, while in 1928, the position of the two countries was reversed. Productivity of the land is much lower than in the United States. The period of collectivization was accompanied by great livestock losses including draft power. Farm mechanization has largely been a matter of replacing animals, and even today equipment is in short supply as contrasted with the United States.

The output per worker of Soviet farmers averages only one-twelfth to one-sixth of their counterparts in the United States. They have farm-management problems; at the moment Soviet authorities see the need for greater rewards to farmers to encourage output for the general market, more decentralization of planning and reorganization of management of collectives.

Agricultural prospects are limited by the quality of the land and climate, but farms may be able to do somewhat better than in the period reviewed providing more machinery and fertilizer are made available. Now that needs to replace draft animals have been largely overcome, future capital investment in agriculture may pay bigger dividends in output. But the new areas put under cultivation may turn into a great dustbowl if a spell of dry years appears, shifting emphasis back to the more traditional areas.

Because of the Soviet capacity to allocate resources and to restrain consumption, expected continued lags in agriculture are more likely to limit consumer welfare than to hold back industrial growth in marked degree.

D. POPULATION AND MANPOWER

The Soviet Union's population is about one-fifth larger than that of the United States. The distribution by age and sex is unbalanced particularly as a result of World War II. Low birth rates were a characteristic of both the war and postwar periods.

Data on the labor force are incomplete, and there is no exact information on the number of persons held as slave labor. The labor force seems to be growing fairly slowly partly because of the effects of World War II, alluded to above, partly because with increased urbanization fewer women and children join the labor force, and partly because extended schooling is delaying entry. The most marked trend has been the shift from about 84 percent of the labor force in agriculture in 1926 to only 48 percent in 1955, as contrasted with the United States which had 21 percent in 1930 and 11 percent in 1955. But since 1950, to all intents and purposes, the Soviet shift was at an end. The combination of a much larger proportion of agricultural employment and the drive to raise industrial output, however, tend to force a larger share of the population into the labor force than is the case in the United States.

Educational levels in the Soviet Union for most of the population have been very low, with only 4 years of schooling commonly provided. Today, however, a major effort is changing the outlook markedly. Higher education as well as secondary education is under great pressure to expand, and in the fields of engineering and the physical sciences, enrollments exceed those of the United States. A considerable program for training technicians is also underway. If current trends are continued, the Soviet Union will add each year a larger supply of well-trained people in the above-named fields than the United States is adding. The quality of Soviet training varies from very good to mediocre and limited in scope. Technicians are attracted to their endeavors because of the differentially higher pay and special privileges accorded this group in the Soviet Union.

E. LEVELS OF LIVING

It is apparent from the record of Soviet behavior that the goal of the system is not primarily to better the life of the consumer, but to enhance the power of the state. Consumers receive improved benefits only as the rulers believe more goods or shorter hours will increase productivity and keep unrest within manageable limits.

The Soviet level of living was little better in 1955 than it was in 1928. However, conditions were so bad in some intervening years that the progress from 1950 to 1955 was very considerable.

Soviet consumer expectations of better living may have increased in recent years, and failure of the economy to live up to these expectations may cause trouble, and indeed it seems to have done so recently.

Although it is extremely difficult to compare living levels, the real wages of Soviet workers appear at the very best to be only one-fourth to one-seventh as high on the average as those in the United States. Supplies of soft goods and food are less inadequate than anything else. Consumer durable goods are being increased in output quite rapidly because they are starting from very low levels. At best the impact of these new so-called luxury items is very small on the level of living of the average Soviet citizen. Perhaps the most acute shortage is in urban housing, with the share of each person only 15 percent that applicable in the United States. And this does not measure the great qualitative differences which also exist.

It should not be overlooked that some Asiatic neighbors of the Soviet Union do not view Soviet levels of living as depressed, but rather as high. This means a comparison with the United States is not the only important one, even though our levels of living are not rivaled.

The trend in urban real wages in the two countries contrasts the problematical increase since 1928 in the U. S. S. R. with the 75 percent improvement in the United States. Since 1950, the United States has gained 14 percent more, in contrast to a probably larger gain in the Soviet Union, which started from a level low even by Soviet standards.

In the future, Soviet levels of living should continue to improve, although at nothing like the rate for 1950–55, but there is no readily foreseeable time when they will approach the levels of living of the United States.

F. NATIONAL INCOME AND PRODUCT

Very roughly, the Soviet national product can be said to be about one-third that of the United States. But this is a comparison which is particularly difficult to make because the structure and the value judgments of the two countries are so different. The absence of an adequate measure for translating ruble values into dollars adds to the difficulties of such comparisons. Data are too incomplete on the Soviet side to prepare a really comprehensive comparison.

Measuring the comparative structures in current prices only, without translation into a common currency, a larger relative share of United States resources seems to be devoted to consumption, and a larger relative share of Soviet resources to investment and to military activities. Illustrative of the difficulties of comparing the 2 economies is that any simple comparison of a share of resources devoted to military output when compared with the total output of the 2 economies in real terms is highly unrealistic. The size of Soviet military forces currently maintained in real terms is considerably larger than, perhaps even double, what might be indicated even by their larger relative share of their much smaller gross national product.

The sources of Soviet income by industrial origin have shifted over time. Measured in current price terms, the share of agriculture has shifted from 42 percent in 1928 to 28 percent in 1955. The shift in the United States has been from 9 percent to 6 percent in the same general years. Soviet industry has grown from a share of 28 percent to 40 percent, and United States industry from 34 percent to 40 percent. Most of the difference between the two countries is accounted for by the larger role of services in the United States.

It is not easy to measure precisely what the growth rates of national product have been in the two countries, and even when this has been done, unlike things are being compared. What limited evidence there is, shows a possibly higher Soviet growth rate over the whole period, but it is not demonstrably so. In the postwar period, the Soviet growth rate appears to have been definitely higher than that of the United States, but it has been declining. The absolute gap between the two countries is still widening, but the time may come when the differential in growth rates may also bring a narrowing of the gap.

The reasons for Soviet growth are not hard to find. They relate to the great effort to expand industry through new investment and through sacrifice of consumer living standards. They rest, too, in the earlier stage of development, and in the opportunities to borrow the experience and the technology of the West.

As for the future, the Soviet Union must reckon with trouble in the captive countries and ferment in the Soviet Union itself, with pressure on the most accessible natural resources, and with previous mistakes in planning. Even with these handicaps, whose total effect is beyond measurement, Soviet growth rates may continue enough higher than those of the United States that in time the gap between the levels of output in the two countries could begin to close. This is hardly to be expected in the near future. Therefore the Soviet hope probably is pinned upon their doctrinaire view that our economy will suffer either stagnation or collapse. We have no intention of affording them this opportunity, and their continuing disappointment in our economic prosperity is evident.

G. CONCLUSION

The economic growth of the Soviet Union has been at great cost to the Soviet people, and they have shared little benefit from the development of a great industrial plant. On the other hand, even the temporarily widening gap between the output of the United States and the Soviet Union leaves no room for complacency. Soviet economic capabilities are already great enough to support a formidable military machine and to engage in international activities inimical to the interests of the non-Communist world. It will be up to the United States to demonstrate the progress of which it is capable in partnership with other non-Communist nations if the Soviet power and influence is to be restrained.

APPENDIXES

APPENDIX A

A COMPARISON OF THE CONCLUSIONS WHICH WERE PRESENTED IN THE PREVIOUS REPORT ON THIS SUBJECT BY THE LEGISLATIVE REFERENCE SERVICE, AND THE CORRESPONDING FINDINGS OF THE PRESENT REPORT

I. *Old.*—The present economic capacity of Western Europe, the United States, and Canada is significantly greater in terms of absolute magnitudes, diversity, and flexibility than the combined strength of the Soviet bloc. This conclusion emerges from comparisons of statistics relating to such basic indexes of economic strength as manpower, agriculture, steel capacity, transportation, and power potentials.

New.—The present economic capacity of the United States is significantly greater in terms of absolute magnitudes, diversity, and flexibility than the strength of the Soviet Union. This conclusion emerges from comparisons of statistics relating to such basic indexes of economic strength as agriculture, steel capacity, transportation, and power production.

(The two conclusions differ only because the geographic areas encompassed are not the same. Neither comparison includes the potentials of the Communist bloc countries of the Far East, or of other free world countries.)

II. *Old.*—In the period 1938–53, as a whole, the national product of the United States increased about three times as rapidly as that of independent Europe, and almost twice as rapidly as that of the Soviet Union. To a substantial degree, this difference reflects the varying effects of World War II. Between 1948 and 1953 the national product of the United States grew not quite 30 percent faster than that of independent Europe, and only two-thirds as fast as that of the Soviet Union.

New.—In the period 1928–55, as a whole, the national product of the United States increased at approximately the same rate as that of the Soviet Union, with any statistically apparent Soviet advantage lying well within the range of error for such crude calculations. Between 1950 and 1955 the national product of the United States grew statistically only three-fifths as fast as that of the Soviet Union. To a substantial degree the parallel rates of the longer period reflect the varying effects of World War II on both countries, the depression of the 1930's in the United States, and the waste associated with collectivization and purges in the 1930's in the Soviet Union. Soviet growth generally in the past (when not at war) has been greater than that of the United States because of the strenuous efforts to spur investment in growth-inducing industries, with a willingness to accept great human costs and lopsided results. Also factors are the earlier stage of development, and the ability to borrow technology from the West.

(The two conclusions differ only because of the changes of time periods included, plus the difference in geographical coverage. Neither report takes into account growth in Communist bloc countries of the Far East, or other countries of the free world.)

III. *Old.*—An examination of the various factors of production (growth of labor input, agriculture, housing, etc.) in the United States and in the Soviet Union today gives strong grounds for expecting that the absolute gap in the size of the 2 economies will widen over the next 2 decades, although the rate of growth in the Soviet Union might be somewhat higher than the rate of growth in the United States.

New.—An examination of the various factors of production (growth of labor input, agriculture, housing, etc.) in the United States and in the Soviet Union today gives strong grounds for expecting that the absolute gap in the size of the 2 economies will widen over the next 2 decades, although the rate of growth

145

in the Soviet Union might be somewhat higher than the rate of growth in the United States. But comparisons of overall growth have limited applicability and meaning when the structures of the two countries are so different. A review of individual sectors indicates that the Soviet industrial threat, particularly in areas closely related to military strength, is much more serious than any overall comparison indicates; in contrast, agriculture, many service activities, and consumer well-being in the Soviet Union are not improving in relation to the United States as fast as the average growth of the Soviet economy.

(The two conclusions are consistent, but the new report is more specific in analysis of the significance of the trends.)

IV. *Old.*—Economically, Western Europe has been growing somewhat more slowly since 1938 than has the Soviet Union, although its growth has been more rapid than that of the captive countries. If the rate of growth of Western Europe is not to fall even farther behind that of the Soviet Union it is necessary that certain "bottlenecks" be eliminated.
New.—Not within the scope of the new study.

(Western Europe, as a whole, however, has made good progress economically since the time of the previous study.)

V. *Old.*—A major reason for the slow economic progress of the captive countries of Eastern Europe has been the tremendous drain of their resources by the Soviet Union. As in the Soviet Union, the weakest sector has been agriculture.
New.—Not within the scope of the new study.

(Eastern Europe, however, since the time of the previous study, has experienced the revolt in Hungary, a shift of power in Poland, and other changes in the relations between the Soviet Union and the captive states in attempts to obviate further troubles.)

VI. *Old.*—Per capita personal consumption in the United States is more than 40 percent higher than it was before the war, while in independent Europe it has risen, on the average, by 11 percent. In contrast, per capita personal consumption in the Soviet Union and Poland is barely above the prewar level; in other captive countries, especially East Germany, it is still below that level. Thus, differences in living standards between the East and the West have widened over the past 15 years.
New.—Per capita personal consumption in the United States is half again as high as it was in 1928. In contrast, per capita consumption in the Soviet Union has been held so low by the emphasis on industrialization, by collectivization of agriculture, and by war, that it may be no higher today than it was in 1928; more precise comparison is not possible in the face of statistical limitations. In the period 1950 to 1955, United States personal consumption levels have continued to rise, although not as fast as in the Soviet case where the necessity to recover from the abysmally low levels of the war and early postwar periods was acute. Overall, Soviet levels of living can be judged in United States terms to be about one-seventh those of the United States, or in Soviet terms, about one-fourth those of the United States.

(Any differences in the two conclusions are occasioned by changes of time and geographical coverage.)

VII. *Old.*—Prior to the war Eastern Europe was more dependent, tradewise, upon Western Europe, than Western Europe was dependent upon it. Since the war, trade between these two regions has contracted greatly.
New.—Not within the scope of the new study.

(There has been some tendency, however, for trade between these two regions to revive.)

VIII. *Old.*—Careful consideration should be given, on the one hand, to the restraints on East-West trade that are important for direct military reasons and, on the other, to the desirability of cultivating friendship with the people in Communist countries via trade in nonstrategic goods. The line of demarcation between goods in each of these categories and other goods should be drawn as clearly as possible. At one extreme is the possibility of cutting off all trade between the free world and the Communist bloc. At the other, is the possibility of encouraging the importation of needed raw materials from Communist countries in exchange for consumer, as opposed to producer, goods.
New.—Not within the scope of the new study.

(In general, however, the trend has been in the direction of fewer restrictions on trade since the previous study was written.)

IX. *Old.*—The West has tremendous economic power whereas the Soviet bloc, through propaganda and unfulfillable promises, has been hiding its lesser economic strength. It is in the interest of the United States that these facts be made known throughout the world, particularly in underdeveloped areas.

New.—The United States has tremendous economic power, and though the Soviet Union is now the second greatest single economic power, it lags and will continue to lag for the indefinite future behind the United States. It is in the interest of the United States that the facts of continued United States economic growth be made known throughout the world, with an equally clear identification of the high costs and continuing difficulties associated with the Soviet growth. While confident of our abilities to hold our overall lead in total output, consumer well-being, and technological progress, we must recognize that these gains and leadership will be held only by continued attention to emerging conditions, by proper foresight in adjusting trends in production, resource availability, and trained manpower, and by the preservation of those institutions and attitudes which have created our advantage over other economic systems.

(The conclusions are consistent. The new report places more stress on the continuous exercise of all our abilities to safeguard our expected leadership. Our continued expected lead depends upon exercise of all our abilities to keep it so.)

X. *Old.*—The Communist bloc will continue intense efforts to increase its output, especially heavy industry, with little regard for human costs. In view of this fact, appreciation of the substantial successes of the United States and independent Europe, acting in close cooperation, in achieving both industrial expansion and better living is essential. Such cooperation, continued in the future, can serve as a basic weapon in the East-West struggle.

New.—The Soviet Union will continue intense efforts to increase its output, especially heavy industry, with less regard for human costs than is common to the West. In view of this fact, the United States must make full use of its resources within the framework of its free institutions to serve as an example to the rest of the world and to maintain its commanding lead in output in the full range of goods required for a strong and balanced economy.

(The conclusions are consistent, aside from the difference in the scope of the two studies. International cooperation in the free world is still important, although not studied in this new review. (See reports of the Subcommittee on Foreign Economic Policy.) The former Communist bloc policies of little regard for human costs have proved sufficiently disastrous since the previous report was prepared that some concessions in living conditions have been forced in both the captive countries and the Soviet Union itself.)

XI. *Old.*—It is important that the Western countries intensify their efforts in the field of education. The more immediate need is to train adequate numbers of scientists, engineers, and technicians. In the longer run, it is essential to keep raising the level of general education.

New.—It is important that the United States intensify its efforts in the field of education. The more immediate need is to train adequate numbers of scientists, engineers, and technicians. In the longer run, it is essential to keep raising the level of general education.

(The two reports are consistent, aside from their coverage of this problem. Much more detailed information is available on this topic than was true at the time of the previous study, and if anything, the needs can be more forcefully and specifically stated today.)

XII. *Old.*—Superiority in economic strength and economic growth are desirable ends in themselves, but they do not assure political and military security. In fact, an economy that is already largely mobilized for war can operate with great effectiveness, and for some time, against a considerably stronger economy that is not so mobilized.

New.—Superiority in economic strength and economic growth are desirable ends in themselves, but they do not assure political and military security. In fact, inadequate attention to foreign affairs can allow disastrous political defeats for the strongest nation, paving the way to a most unfavorable military situation. Also, a smaller economy mobilized for war and equipped with the means to deliver attack with unconventional weapons in quantity can destroy a larger economy less well prepared, even though the attacker may have his home base destroyed as well. Plans for defense cannot be based on the presumption of time to mount a traditional mobilization of the economy after hostilities have begun. Defense must rest upon three major elements: (1) Forces in being to meet a range of eventualities to discourage the resort to war by aggressive forces; (2) a growing and flexible economy able to keep up with the technological race which tomorrow could upset the present balance of terror; (3) adequate attention to the political, moral, and economic forces which can turn away the need for war and preserve a growing prosperity for mankind.

(This conclusion goes beyond the detailed study contained in these pages to draw on other work conducted by the Subcommittee on Foreign Economic Policy during 1956. It is not inconsistent with the conclusion of the previous study, but reflects a shift in emphasis from any possible implication that a major war would follow the pattern of World Wars I and II which allowed the United States gradually to marshal its greater economic strength to turn the tide in warfare. Such strength is important, but now mostly for its ability to maintain the correct balance of active forces and to have freedom of choice in pursuing other economic and political policies in the world.)

APPENDIX B

A CROSS COMPARISON OF SELECTED SUMMARY DATA FROM THE PREVIOUS REPORT AND THE PRESENT REPORT

The previous study by the Legislative Reference Service carried summary tables contrasting the economies of the United States, Western Europe, the Soviet Union, and captive Europe. Because of changes in scope and treatment, and additional statistical information, not all categories of information in that report and this current effort can be cross compared. However, some linkage can be provided, and headings appearing in the previous report are repeated here, showing both the previously reported information and the current figures which correspond, with brief explanations of any significant shifts.

Item and years	United States	U. S. S. R.
Population change:		
1938–52 (old)	20 percent	9 percent.
1926–55 Soviet and 1930–55 United States (new).	34 percent	33 percent.
1950–55 (new)	9 percent	9 percent.
(The 2 sets of figures are not inconsistent, for the former comparison was of the World War II period, while the newer comparisons mask the effects of the war.)		
Population size:		
1953 (old)	161 million	212 million.
1955 (new)	165 million	198 million.
(This represents the significant change in estimate of the Soviet population in the light of information not available at the time of the earlier report.)		
Labor force size:		
1939 or 1940 (old)	56 million	95 million.
1953 (old)	67 million	108 million.
1926 Soviet and 1930 United States (new).	50 million	83 million.
1955 (new)	69 million	108 million.
Agricultural production:		
1940–52 (old)	50 percent	10 percent.
1928–55 (new)	49 percent	Not available.
Arable land:		
1953 (old)	177 million hectares	225 million hectares.
1954 (new)	186 million hectares	220 million hectares.
Agricultural Labor:		
1953 (old)	14 percent of total	50 percent of total.
1955 (new)	11 percent of total	48 percent of total.
Tractors in use:		
1953 (old)	4 million	0.4 million.
1955 (new)	4.8 million	0.8 million.
(This represents both further Soviet progress in production and particularly the availability of better data.)		
Steel production:		
1949 (old)	71 million tons	Not available.
1953 (old)	102 million tons	38 million tons.
1955 (new)	106 million tons	45 million tons.
Coal production:		
1953 (old)	437 million tons (North America).	Not available.
1955 (new)	450 million tons	310 (392) million tons.
Petroleum production:		
1953 (old)	323 million tons	52 million tons.
1955 (new)	335 million tons	71 million tons.
Electricity generation:		
1953 (old)	513 billion kilowatt-hours	133 billion kilowatt-hours.
1955 (new)	625 billion kilowatt-hours	170 billion kilowatt-hours.
Rail freight volume:		
1953 (old)	605 billion ton-miles	538 billion ton-miles.
1955 (new)	613 billion ton-miles	647 billion ton-miles.
Motor-vehicle production:		
1953 (old)	7.3 million	0.5 million.
1955 (new)	9.1 million	0.4 million.

Item and years	United States	U. S. S. R.
GNP growth:		
1938–53 (old)	120 percent (5 percent per annum)	62 percent (3 percent).
1948–53 (old)	27 percent (5 percent per annum)	43 percent (7 percent).
1928–55 per annum average (new)	3 percent (?)	4 percent (?).
1950–55 per annum average (new)	4 percent (?)	7 percent (?).

(The apparent differences in rates are not inconsistent. The previous report in its first comparison tends to reflect the differential effects of World War II, while the newer study takes a longer span of years for comparison. The text of the new study deliberately refrains from drawing up such a table of comparison for this period on grounds of possible noncomparability of data, although the figures shown here are hazarded in the text. In both countries, the more recent postwar comparison shows slightly lower rates.)

Item and years	United States	U. S. S. R.
National accounts:		
1952–3 (old):		
Agriculture	7 percent	23 percent.
Industry	41 percent	46 percent.
Services	52 percent	31 percent.
1955 (new):		
Agriculture	6 percent	29 percent.
Industry	43 percent	41 percent.
Services	51 percent	30 percent.
National accounts:		
1952–3 (old):		
Consumption	63 percent	47 percent.
Government	20 percent	27 percent.
Gross investment	14 percent	15 percent.
1955 (new):		
Consumption	69 percent	57 percent.
Government	13 percent	16 percent.
Gross investment	19 percent	27 percent.

(The differences in this case represent primarily changes of definition, rather than any significant shift in the economies concerned. Both sets of figures were developed in consultation with the same specialists. The more recent figures represent both an attempt to achieve greater comparability with the Bergson-Heymann and Hoeffding figures whose derivation is available in printed form, and also to refine to greater accuracy the distributions in the light of later statistical information.)